The

Cabala

of

Pegasus

_____

THE

CABALA

OF

PEGASUS

Giordano Bruno

TRANSLATED AND ANNOTATED BY
Sidney L. Sondergard and Madison U. Sowell

Yale University Press
New Haven & London

Set in Minion Roman type by Keystone Typesetting, Inc., Orwigsburg, Pennsylvania.
Printed in the United States of America.

Library of Congress Cataloging-in-Publication Data
Bruno, Giordano, 1548–1600.
    [Cabala del cavallo pegaseo. English]
    The cabala of pegasus / Giordano Bruno ; translated and
annotated by Sidney L. Sondergard and Madison U. Sowell.
        p.   cm.
Includes bibliographical references and index.
    ISBN 0-300-09217-2 (alk. paper)
1. Mental efficiency—History—16th century. 2. Donkeys—Miscellanea.
I. Sondergard, Sidney L. II. Sowell, Madison U., 1952– III. Title.
B783 .A4 E5 2002
195—dc21
2002005870

A catalogue record for this book is available from the British Library.

The paper in this book meets the guidelines for permanence and durability
of the Committee on Production Guidelines for Book Longevity of the
Council on Library Resources.

10   9   8   7   6   5   4   3   2   1

Contents

Acknowledgments

Giordano Bruno (1548–1600) stands judged and acknowledged today as a seminal thinker and an intriguing character in the evolution
from Renaissance to modern world. Scholars variously identify him
as Galileo's precursor, modern science's first martyr, Hermetic
magus, and kabbalist mystic. Such wide-ranging interpretations of
this philosopher underscore the complexity of his enigmatic persona and arcane thought; they also invite translations of his writings
for the burgeoning body of nonspecialists captivated by his itinerant
lifestyle, provocative work, and fiery demise. This translation, therefore, is intended both for general (albeit sophisticated and informed) readers and for cultural historians of the early modern
period, inasmuch as Bruno scholars and Italianists will continue to
read and cite the text in the original.

Following the examples of previous Bruno translators, we have
inserted paragraph divisions into lengthy speeches and have sub-
divided some interminable periodic constructions into discrete sentences. We have tried to resist idiomatizing Bruno's Italian, and this
has been aided by the many unambiguously wry phrasings of the
original text that would render such an attempt superfluous at any
rate. Textual insertions meant to clarify intended subjects or objects,
or to make a phrase more grammatically intelligible in English, have
been placed within brackets.

This text provides the first full English-language translation of Bruno's *Cabala del cavallo pegaseo* and is well complemented by the recent English translation of Nuccio Ordine's *La cabala dell'asino: Asinità e conoscenza in Giordano Bruno* (Napoli: Liguori, 1987) by Henryk Baranski in collaboration with Arielle Saiber, *Giordano Bruno and the Philosophy of the Ass* (New Haven and London: Yale University Press, 1996), as well as by Karen de León-Jones's *Giordano Bruno and the Kabbalah: Prophets, Magicians and Rabbis* (New Haven and London: Yale University Press, 1997). Any critical work on the life and writings of Giordano Bruno must depend heavily on the foundation editions and studies of Giovanni Gentile, Vincenzo Spampanato, and Frances A. Yates, and the influence of Gentile's learned edition of the Nolan's *dialoghi* is ubiquitous in this translation's commentaries, as anyone familiar with his work will immediately note. The source text for the following translation of Bruno's *Cabala del cavallo pegaseo*, then, is Giovanni Aquilecchia's 1958 revised edition of Gentile's *Giordano Bruno: Dialoghi italiani*.

For inspiration and for practical suggestions, Sid wishes to cite Jackson I. Cope, the *pedante* who sent him to read Bruno, and to whom he returned with grave reservations about the Nolan's emotional stability. He has retained those reservations, as well as a permanent gratitude and respect for the man who invited him to play the best game in town.

Other colleagues, including Thomas L. Berger, David Frederick, Richard S. Ide, Moshe Lazar, and Dorothy Limouze, have also offered advice and insights that have helped to shape this volume. What remains of the truly asinine, rather than the divinely foolish, must be credited to the translators rather than to them. We also wish to thank the director and staff of the Huntington Library for their generous assistance and their invaluable resources.

Sid thanks his most patient and discerning reader—his wife, Ramona Ralston, a scholar and a gentlewoman.

Madison expresses gratitude to his Harvard mentor Dante Della Terza, who first initiated him into the intricate tapestry and exalted rhetoric of early modern Italian thought; to two former research assistants, Brian O. Call (now at Yale) and Joseph Porter, who sought answers to seemingly unanswerable questions; and to his wife, Debra, who doubles as his favorite dance historian, and daughters, MariLouise and Laura, for their unflagging support and loving devotion.

Finally, we thank Linda Hunter Adams of the Brigham Young University Humanities Publications Center for aid in proofreading and Gretchen Rings and Laura Jones Dooley of Yale University Press for their assistance in producing this volume.

Bruno's Design for the *Cabala*

Authority and the Power of Words

To study Giordano Bruno is to consider a life of discord and paradox, dedicated to the forging of an ecumenical philosophy in which divergent perspectives and apparently self-negating claims might be reconciled into a transcendent vision of human aspiration. Before introducing his portraits of Oxford dons as impotent sophists in *La cena de le Ceneri* [*The Ash Wednesday Supper,* or *The Dinner of Ashes*] (1584), Bruno designates himself a member of a select group of philosophers "ne la medicina esperti, ne la contemplazione giudiziosi, ne la divinazione singolari, ne la magia miracolosi, ne le superstizioni providi, ne le leggi osservanti, ne la moralità irreprensibili, ne la teologia divini, in tutti effetti eroici" [in medicine expert, in contemplation judicious, in divination without equal, in magic miraculous, in superstitions provident, in laws observant, in morals irreproachable, in theology divine, in all effects, heroic] (44).[1]

Such self-aggrandizement, though typical of its author's attempts to generate authority, did little publicly to dispel the impression that he was "unsuccessful in human relations, devoid of social tact or worldly wisdom, unpractical to an almost insane degree" (Singer 1950, 3). Because of the intensity of Bruno's emotional and intellectual vendetta against academicians, however, warnings like those of the interlocutor Maricondo in *De gli eroici furori* [*On the Heroic Frenzies*] (1585) proved far more influential than his extravagant self-praise: "Veggiamo bene che mai la pedantaria è stata piú in exaltazione per governare il mondo, che a' tempi nostri; la quale fa tanti camini de vere specie intelligibili ed oggetti de l'unica veritade infallibile, quanti possano essere individui pedanti" [We clearly see that pedantry has never been more glorified for controlling the world than in our own times, which creates as many roads to the true intelligible species and the qualities of the one infallible truth as there are individual pedants] (1116).

A potent emotional force does much to aid the cultural dissemination of a particular idea, as the extreme example of martyrdom demonstrates; yet it can also form an insulating barrier that resists analytical scrutiny. The individual disputants offering interpretations and options at the Council of Pandemonium in Book Two of *Paradise Lost*, for example, do not address the problem of free will because acknowledgment of its jeopardy or loss would signify the hopelessness of their situation. Bruno's writing, particularly in the philosophical dialogues published in London (1584–1585), displays both the fervor and the frustration of an individual trying to make arguments designed to effect change on a culture-wide—even universal—basis. Scholars have argued that the emotional impact of overt condemnations of authority figures, particularly those associated with institutionalized learning, in late Elizabethan culture may have helped to ensure their survival in a wide range of antihumanist texts.[2] Giordano Bruno contributed the icon of the "menacing pedant" to other English cultural subversions via such vernacular dialogues as the *Cabala del cavallo pegaseo* (London [though stamped "Parigi"], 1585); yet his attacks on intellectuals and academia are ultimately idiosyncratic, and analysis of the man behind them must address the surprising potency of the emotion he transfers to this icon. To forgo analysis of the complex of semantic causalities shaping any cultural belief is to take a teleological view of cultural coherence, where form subsumes content, where ideas rather than their derivations matter most. This has always been a danger with discussions of Bruno's life and works, and even a scholar as conscientiously thorough as Dame Frances A. Yates warns that no single analytical perspective "may ever serve to catch or to identify this extraordinary man" (1966, 307). Hence assessment of the contributions made by Bruno's *Cabala* to antihumanist[3] sentiments in sixteenth- and seventeenth-century England should be pursued from perspectives both ideological and causal.

The locus of his "menacing pedant" icon is Oxford University; though the few specific references to Bruno's presence there exist outside the university's records,[4] documentation of his presence and participation in debates there circa June 1583 has been exhaustively discussed by modern scholars.[5] Two of these references provide assessments of Bruno's emotional behavior during this period as well as clear indices to his previous history. His memory treatise *Ars reminiscendi* (London, 1583), which contains the *Explicatio triginta sigillorum* [*The Interpretation of the Thirty Seals*] and *Sigillus sigillorum* [*The Seal of Seals*], includes in some editions (see Boulting 1914, 82n2) the hyperbolic epistle *Ad excellentissimum Oxoniensis academiae Procancellarium, clarrisimos doctores atque celeberrimos magistros* [*To the Excellent Vice-Chancellor of Oxford University, Its Most Illustrious Doctors and Renowned Teachers*]. In this purported introduction, the author employs the energetic language and imagery that also characterize his six Italian dialogues published in London (1584–1585); at the same time, he exhibits anxieties that may have been precipitated (as he later says) by abrasive or doctrinaire attitudes he encountered at the university, or conversely may simply be reoccurrences of conflict patterns experienced before he arrived in England. Bruno describes himself as magis laboratae theologiae doctor, purioris et innocuae sapientiae professor, in praecipuis Europae academiis notus, probatus et honorifice exceptus philosophus, nullibi praeterquam apud barbaros et ignobiles peregrinus . . . praesumtuosae et recalcitrantis ignorantiae domitor . . . qui non magis Italum quam Britannum, marem quam feminam . . . togatum quam armatum . . . quem stultitiae propagatores et hypocritumculi destestantur, quem probi et studiosi diligunt, et cui nobiliora plaudunt ingenia. (2.2.76–77)

[doctor of a more difficult theology, professor of a pure and quite blameless wisdom, distinguished in the preeminent academies of Europe, a philosopher approved and honorably accepted, a foreigner nowhere except among the barbarous and ignoble . . . conqueror of the presumptuous and recalcitrant ignorant . . . who [prefers] the Italian no more than the British, male than female . . . someone in a toga than someone in armor . . . whom the propagators of foolishness and the hypocrites detest, whom the good and studious esteem highly, and whose mind the more noble applaud.]

It is tempting to read these descriptive images as no more than playful self-aggrandizement. But in the First Dialogue of the *Cabala*, Bruno's persona Saulino likens the overweening pride of pedants to that of the Genesis 11:1–9 account of "gli superbi e presumptuosi sapienti del mondo, quali ebbero fiducia nel proprio ingegno, e con temeraria e gonfia presunzione hanno avuto ardire d'alzarsi alla scienza de secreti divini e que' penetrali della deitade, non altrimente che coloro ch'edificâro la torre di Babelle, son stati confusi e messi in dispersione, avendosi essi medesimi serrato il passo . . . alla sapienza divina e visione della veritade eterna" [the proud and presumptuous sages of the world, who had confidence in their own individual genius and with reckless and swollen presumption had the daring to raise themselves to the knowledge of divine secrets and the innermost parts of deity—no different from those who built the Tower of Babel—have been confused and scattered, themselves having shut the passage . . . to the divine wisdom and vision of the eternal truth]. This implicitly argues that what is needed is the appropriate kind of direction toward unity from the appropriate kind of leader, placing Bruno again in the (to him, apparently, comfortable) role of messiah.

DOCTOR OF A MORE DIFFICULT THEOLOGY

The identification of Bruno with fierce self-assertion and individualism is a historical commonplace, as Rollo May demonstrates when describing prototypes of modern social ideologies: "One is Giordano Bruno (later to be burned at the stake by the Inquisition) whose idea of Creation as concentric circles with the self at center gave the original philosophical orientation for modernism" (1967, 58). It may be a surprise to readers, then, to discover that Bruno's hyperbole at times resembles bravado masking a fundamental insecurity, as in passages such as this response to an ignorant public in *De l'infinito universo e mondi* [*On the Infinite Universe and Worlds*] (1584): "Eccone, dunque, fuor d'invidia; eccone liberi da vana ansia e stolta cura di bramar lontano quel tanto bene che possedemo vicino e gionto. Eccone piú liberi dal maggior timore che loro caschino sopra di noi, che messi in speranza che noi caschiamo sopra di loro" (360) [Behold us, then, distanced from envy; behold us freed from the vain anxiety and foolish care of coveting from afar that significant good which we possess nearby and adjoining us. Behold us freed from the prevalent fear that they overwhelm us, even more than from the hope that we overwhelm them]. It could hardly be otherwise; Bruno was an intellectual fugitive for fifteen years before his 1591 arrest in Venice. A fustian rhetoric may have been as essential to his survival as his timely departures from one European cultural center after another, often narrowly ahead of the Holy Office's pursuit.

Sometime between the ages of fifteen and seventeen, Filippo Bruno of Nola was admitted as a probationer to the brotherhood of St. Dominic at Naples by its prior, Ambrogio Pasqua. To signal his covenant there, Filippo was renamed after Jordan of Saxony, who had succeeded founder Domingo de Guzman in 1221 as master of the order. Giordano took his vows in 1566, was ordained a priest in 1572, and sang his first Mass at San Bartolomeo in Campagna, electing thereafter to become one of the Preaching Friars of his mendicant order (P. Michel 1973, 13). Although Dominican intellectual beliefs were sympathetic with Aristotelian and Scholastic philosophy, particularly as expounded by their own brethren Albertus Magnus and Thomas Aquinas, Bruno opposed what he perceived to be the static determinism of his order's ideology. In later years he preached an eclectic synthesis of Monadism, Copernicanism, Neoplatonism, Hermeticism, and elements of various occult philosophies.[6] His hermetic aspirations for humanity to seek (re)union with the Creator found consonance with the Neoplatonist passages of Augustine's *Soliloquies,* which are expressed as the individual's "task, when whole and perfect, it is to bear upward away from these shadows to that higher Light, which it befits not to disclose itself to those shut up in this cave" (1910, 41–42).

The Dominicans could not allow Fra Giordano the syncretist independence of his views: the "Hounds of the Lord" (derived from the pun *Domini canes Evangelium latrantes per totum orbem,* "The Dominicans / Hounds-of-the-Lord announce / bark the good news throughout the entire globe") had traditionally served the dictates of the Inquisition and referred to their founder after his death as the *persecutor haereticorum;* here we are reminded that the authors of the witch-smashing *Malleus maleficarum,* Jacobus Sprenger and Heinrich Kramer, were German Dominicans. Warned of charges related to his sympathy with the Arian heresy (itself a spiritual severance of Son from Father) and his consultations of heretical texts (including those by humanists such as Erasmus), the Nolan[7] fled San Domenico in 1576, approximately eleven years after entering the monastery, to become his own father, to give birth to a more difficult theology than that professed by the Dominicans.[8]

DISTINGUISHED IN THE PREEMINENT
ACADEMIES OF EUROPE

With more anger than self-parody, Bruno designates himself "Academico di nulla academia" [Academician of no academy] on the title page of his comedy *Il candelaio* [*The Chandler* or *The Light-Bearer*] (Paris, 1582) and includes as his motto "In tristitia hilaris, in hilaritate tristis" [In sadness happy, in happiness sad]. This introduction at once confirms his apparent desire to occupy an academic post—demonstrated by his previous and subsequent pursuit of lectureships at various universities—and his self-evaluation as an intellect superior to those directing the European academies. If his self-description is interpreted as a rationale, then his motto must function as metarationale, its paradox a semantic resonance of the psychic conflict implicit in rejection, in viewing himself as a displaced academician of no academy.

Before joining the Dominicans in June 1565, Bruno benefited from public and private study in Naples, attending lectures delivered by Vincenzo Colle at the Studium Generale and receiving tutelage from Teofilo de Vairano at the Augustinian monastery (Singer 1950, 10). The young Dominican's erudition and impressive memory techniques (see Yates 1966, 199–319) earned him an audience with Dominican Pope Pius V in approximately 1571; refinements of his Lullist mnemonic systems published between 1582 and 1588 assured his general reputation throughout European academia. In spite of his accomplishments as scholar and theorist, however, the stubborn, volatile philosopher regularly alienated his students and institutional patrons. At Genoese Noli, in 1576, Bruno attempted to instruct both adults and children, but his "impatience and his highly involved symbolic and allusive mode of expression must have made him a superlatively bad instructor of children, and it is no wonder that his pedagogic career was brief" (Singer 1950, 13). Undaunted, Bruno denoted his desire for recognition as an intellectual by boldly signing himself "Philippus Brunus Nolanus, sacrae theologiae professor, 20 May 1579" (Boulting 1914, 42) upon arrival at the Academy of Geneva.

The *Ad excellentissimum* introduction also depicts Bruno as a scholar-warrior, "conqueror of the presumptuous and recalcitrant ignorant," and an incident during his stay at Geneva begins to codify his configuration of the "menacing pedant" icon, specifically suggesting why he attacks his targets in the London dialogues so vehemently and why he focuses his pedant portraits primarily on university doctors. On 6 August 1579, Bruno and printer Jean Bergeon were arrested; persuaded by Bruno's philosophical rationale and forceful personality, Bergeon had published "certaines responses et invectives contre M.r de le Faye [Pastor Antoine de la Faye, respected professor of philosophy], cottans 20 erreurs d'iceluy en une de ses leçons" (Spampanato 1933, 33). On 13 August, Bruno was invited to appear and "to acknowledge his transgression in that he had erred in doctrine and called the pastors of the Church of Geneva pedagogues" (Boulting 1914, 46). He refused. Participating in the intellectual forum of the university environment, Bruno had attacked one lecture of one professor—yet had been unexpectedly censured by a coalition vindictive enough to incarcerate him for his criticism. His release on 27 August was secured after his publicly "recognizing that he had made a great error" ("recognoissant en ce avoyr fait grande faulte" [Spampanato 1933, 36]); this additional humiliation undoubtedly fueled rather than diminished his intellectual pursuits, confirming for him that he simply had not yet found the Academy of his destiny.

At Toulouse from late 1579 to 1581, Bruno quickly took a doctorate of theology degree and lectured on Johannes de Sacrobosco's *Sphere* after students at the university chose him by election to occupy a vacant position in philosophy. Further demonstrating respect for his scholarship, a collection of his lectures on Aristotle's *De anima*, no longer extant, was published during his stay there. Though seemingly an ideal situation for him, general resentment expressed toward the controversial relaxation of religious restrictions on new faculty's participation in the sacrament may have contributed to Bruno's decision to leave Toulouse for Paris. Upon arriving, he displayed once again the conflicting impulses to protect his theories from unworthy intellects but also to seek general acclaim for them. At the heart of both motivations is Bruno's sensationalist epistemology. His earliest extant Paris publication, *De umbris idearum* [*On the Shadows of Ideas*] (1582), dedicated to Henri III, was couched in overtly kabbalistic figures and terminology to prevent popular access to, and dissemination of, his mnemonics system; at the same time, he was offering to lecture on the thirty divine attributes of Thomistic theology and was invited to share his memory techniques with the king. Henri III was a loyal supporter of occult philosophies, but other idiosyncrasies may have stimulated his interest in Bruno, including his indiscriminate superstition or his homosexuality. Expectations for the Nolan's art were high, and whether he "lent himself willingly to any imposture in his exposition of mnemonics, cannot be asserted. But it is certain that the public were led to expect from his method more than it could give" (Symonds 1887, 139). Soon his welcome in Paris was also exhausted,[9] and the philosopher dubiously distinguished in the preeminent academies of Europe followed the French ambassador, Michel de Castelnau, marquis de

Mauvissière, to England. Bruno must have expected an intellectual hero's welcome awaiting him there—when in fact his presence stirred up great controversy due to avid though theoretically inaccurate[10] pro-Copernican views (which he would reiterate in what he describes as a rhetorical victory over the Oxford doctors Torquato and Nundinio in *La cena*) and his reluctance to balance Aristotelian notions of essence and cause with Christian accommodation of them: "Speaking of the soul, he taught that nothing in the universe is lost, everything is in a state of transformation; therefore body, spirit and matter, are equally eternal. The body may dissolve, but becomes transformed; the soul transmigrates, and, drawing around itself atom to atom, it reconstructs for itself a new body. The spirit which animates and moves all things is One" (Boulting 1914, 39). Scorning the differences in intellectual atmosphere between medieval and Elizabethan Oxford, Bruno defensively insulated himself from criticism, rationalizing, for example, in the *Ad excellentissimum* that he and his ideas were considered foreign "nowhere except among the barbarous and ignoble."

NO MORE MALE THAN FEMALE, SOMEONE IN A TOGA THAN SOMEONE IN ARMOR

Though there can be little doubt that Bruno's negative social experiences exacerbated his eccentric behavior and responses, he worked as an author to erase the causal relationships between his personal experience and his textual revelations. Even within the document that so clearly communicates it, the shallowly repressed anger of the *Ad excellentissimum* is couched in pseudo-equanimity by a series of rhetorically balanced clauses (for example, the Nolan is someone "who [prefers] the Italian no more than the British") that pretend to deny the very antitheses they clearly represent. Two of these clauses (declaring that the author no more respects "male than female" or "someone in a toga than someone in armor") further reflect the complex social and psychological dynamics that produced personal conflict for Bruno.

The nomadic structure of Bruno's life was antithetical to formulating emotional relationships of any duration; nevertheless, he "made no secret of the admiration which the beauty of women excited in his nature" (Symonds 1887, 132). This proves difficult to reconcile with Sophia's positive anticipation in the *Spaccio della bestia trionfante* [*Expulsion of the Triumphant Beast*] (London 1585) of a return to the golden age's *legge naturale,* or natural law,

> per la quale è lecito a ciascun maschio di aver tante moglie quante ne può nutrire et impregnare; perché è cosa superflua ed ingiusta, ed a fatto contrario alla regola naturale, che in una già impregnata e gravida donna, o in altri soggetti peggiori, come altre illegitime procacciate,—che per tema di vituperio provocano l'aborso,—vegna ad esser sparso quell'omifico seme che potrebbe suscitar eroi e colmar le vacue sedie de l'empireo. (Gentile 1958, 583)

> [by which it is permissible for each male to have as many wives as he can feed and impregnate; because it is a superfluous and unjust thing and entirely contrary to natural law that upon an already impregnated and gravid woman, or upon other worse subjects, such as others illegitimately procured, who for fear of disgrace induce abortions, there should be spilt that man-producing semen, which could give rise to heroes and fill the empty seats of the empyrean. (Imerti 1964, 96)]

The exaggerated valuation of male procreative prerogative is complemented here with a profound devaluation of women, who are meaningful only as receptacles for the propagation of "heroes"—like the persecuted philosopher himself. Bruno is simultaneously attracted to and repulsed by the contemplation of women; and additionally verifying his virtually systemic rejection of Dominican values, discussion of celibacy as a response to female stimuli is noticeably absent. The female characters of the *Candelaio*[11] represent little resolution of Bruno's ambivalence toward women: "A strain of masochism accompanies man's hedonism" in relationships with women, and the comments of female characters like Carubina on the subject of love ultimately "record the perversion of something initially attractive" (Barr 1971, 361). Although it might be tempting to speculate about the impact of maternal love (or lack thereof) on Bruno's childhood gender role formulation, all that is known for sure about Fraulissa Savolina is the *fralezza*, frailty, of her name. In testimony before the Venetian Inquisitors, he identified her simply as "mia madre Fraulissa Savolina" [my mother Fraulissa Savolina] who "è morta" [is dead] (Spampanato 1933, 79).

The "someone in a toga than someone in armor" clause would seem at first glance contradictory, as the soldier, a conventional sign of anti-intellectualism, is balanced rhetorically with his opposite, clad in the university toga—though Bruno's documented misadventures in academia help to reconcile the author's assertion that there is no antithesis between them. It also suggests the degree of his militant anger at those who opposed his intellectual agenda, displayed for example in *La cena,* the first of his London dialogues, with a verse "To the Malcontent" warning, "Since you have confronted me with injustice, / I shall stretch and pull your skin all over; / And should my body too fall to the ground, / Your shame will be recorded in hard diamond" (Jaki 1975, 42). Brandishing the invective typical of his subsequent dialogue attacks on pedants, Bruno concludes the *Ad excellentissimum* epistle with a curse on the "diluvii asinorum stercora malis aureis" [floods of evil golden manure from asses] who have infiltrated the university environment until "nunc cuilibet stulto et asino liceat in nostras positiones hic vel alibi" [now any fool and ass is allowed into our positions here and elsewhere] (2.2.78). This oxymoronic "golden manure" alludes to the Ciceronian ornamentation of the Oxford rhetoricians (see Yates 1982, 137), gilding their stubborn resistance to his ideas. Intrusion upon his objectives ("*our* positions") forced the philosopher into a warrior posture, so he appropriated its archetypally male authority in order to battle the childish, irreverent professors. As with his mother Fraulissa, virtually nothing is known about Bruno's own father, Giovanni, except his profession: "Uomo d'arme"—soldier. Whether externally or internally imposed, the oppositions of male versus female and man-of-action versus man-of-contemplation fueled Bruno's intellectual foment and torment.

WHOSE MIND THE NOBLE APPLAUD

On 10 June 1583, following a visit with Queen Elizabeth and her court that had begun in April, the Polish palatine Albertus Alasco, accompanied by Sir Philip Sidney at the request of the university's chancellor, the earl of Leicester, arrived at Christ Church, Oxford. During his stay through 13 June, dramatic performances and fireworks displays were arranged for the palatine's entertainment in the evenings, while tours and disputations were conducted each day.[12] Although there is no specific record among Oxford historical accounts that Bruno participated in the Alasco disputations, two outside sources document such an occasion. George Abbot's *The Reasons VVhich Doctovr Hill Hath Brovght* reports, "When that Italian Didapper, who intituled himselfe *Philotheus Iordanus Brunus Nolanus, magis elaborata Theologia Doctor, &c* with a name longer then his body, had in the traine of *Alasco* the Polish Duke, seene our Vniversity in the year 1583, his hart was on fire, to make himselfe by some worthy exploite, to become famous in that celebrious place"(1604, 4ᵛ). Abbot documents the zeal, if not the particulars and the ultimate result, of Bruno's participation in the debates. To the detriment of the Nolan's reputation, however, Abbot also reports two occasions on which the doctor of theology was allegedly caught plagiarizing from Marsilio Ficino's *De vita coelitus comparanda.* Thus Bruno's passion to be recognized by Oxford—that is, by medieval Oxford, haven of freethinkers such as Roger Bacon—for his pioneering spirit and syncretic approach to knowledge was manifested during his tenure at the university even in irrational and irresponsible responses. The philosopher's own description of the debate in *La cena de le Ceneri* awards him a significant victory:

> E se non il credete, andate in Oxonia, e fatevi raccontar le cose intravenute al Nolano, quando publicamente disputò con que' dottori in teologia in presenza del prencipe Alasco polacco ed altri della nobiltà inglese. Fatevi dire come si sapea rispondere a gli argomenti; come restò per quindeci sillogismi quindeci volte qual pulcino entro la stoppa quel povero dottor. (Gentile 1958, 133)

> [And if you don't believe it, go to Oxford and make them recount to you the things that happened to the Nolan when he publicly disputed with some doctors of theology in the presence of the Polish prince Alasco and others of the English nobility. Make them tell you how he knew to respond to their arguments; how for fifteen syllogisms fifteen times that poor doctor stayed without knowing which way to turn.]

In the bombastic emotion of this account, fact merges with fantasy, fustian becomes *persuasio.* Bruno interprets his performance as heroically inspired and enacted, his victory as complete. Nevertheless, he feels compelled to continue his scathing satirical attacks on university doctors as authority figures, employing them to reinforce his self-esteem. Reflected consciously or unconsciously in the hyperbole, neologisms, and abstractions of his own works, he most frequently targets the elaborate, Latinate grammar of the schoolmen as the quintessence of their design to overawe and dominate the unlearned.[13] Given previous patterns of frustration, including the Dominican rejection of his attempts to develop a syncretic philosophy, that predisposed him to react defensively, we can readily see why

Bruno responded so strongly to the disappointments—which may have varied from public embarrassments to simple lack of acclaim—associated with the Oxford experience. We can also see why he includes, as a separate agenda, his "anti-pedant" campaign in the works composed after he returned to London.

Bruno's attack was empowered by a genuine zeal, and the emotional intensity of his anger is displayed in his depictions of pedants not merely as wrongheaded but as cruel and vindictive. His goal of subversion is not disguised in the least; either he is seizing the martyr's image to strengthen his own self-conception (and to evoke the sympathy of readers), or his "extraordinary vanity" has remained largely undiminished by "his disappointment over being so little appreciated" (Pellegrini 1941–1942, 310). Writing to Gian Vincenzo Pinelli about Bruno in a letter dated 6 June 1586, Jacopo Corbinelli declares it "Basta che in Inghilterra ha lasciato scismi grandissimi in quelle scuole" [Sufficient that he has left huge schisms in those schools in England] (Yates 1983, 117).[14] The anti-Aristotelianism and affirmation of Cabalism of the *Cabala del cavallo pegaseo* are reflective of its author's vendetta against the Oxford university doctors specifically, and against all pedagogues generally.[15]

The Wisdom of Asininity

Even within the corpus of writings by an author as eccentric as Bruno, the *Cabala del cavallo pegaseo* must be considered an unusual piece of literature. Interpretive difficulties for readers and translators begin with the work's title—literally, "the cabala of the Pegasean horse," though textual elaboration reveals in time that by this "Pegasean horse" Bruno means in fact the ass, icon of "saintly asininity,"[16] a secular variation on the simple Christian faith designated "learned ignorance" in Nicholas of Cusa's *De docte ignorantia:* "The greatest and profoundest mysteries of God, though hidden from the wise, may be revealed to little ones and humble folk living in the world by their faith in Jesus" (1962, 88). The asininity that Bruno singles out for praise in the *Cabala*—and that he encourages his readership to affirm (by accepting his doctrines)—is a simple, unquestioning attitude that facilitates, rather than precludes or impedes, faith. The text is also "Pegasean" in that the interlocutor Onorio, who appears in the work's second dialogue and retains the ability to recall his many previous incarnations, which include an ass and Aristotle—the two being intimately related, suggests Bruno—was once reincarnated *as* Pegasus. The text is itself a "Pegasean" messenger, celebrating and authorizing its creator, winging its way into the hands of the reader. Even the *assonanza* of the title (*cabala* / *cavallo*) is a punning reference to the arcane significance of the ass to Bruno's personal agenda of intellectual freedom.

There are structural symmetries within the *Cabala* that can be enjoyed purely as literary games, though they also serve the practical function of pointing the reader to central authorial concerns.[17] To evoke consideration of the relation between authority and wisdom, the author praises the dialogue's dedicatee, the nonexistent Bishop Don Sapatino of Casamarciano, for being able by virtue of knowledge and title "entrar per tutto, perché non è cosa che vi tegna rinchiuso" [to penetrate the whole, because there is nothing that can restrict you] (837); conversely, the learned Ass of the dialogue appended to the *Cabala* proper, "L'Asino Cillenico del Nolano" [The Nolan's Cillenican Ass], is denied access to the Pythagorean Academy until Mercury himself arrives to deliver the gods' will that the Ass "possi entrar ed abitar per tutto, senza ch'alcuno ti possa tener porta o dar qualsivoglia sorte d'oltraggio o impedimento" [may enter and reside anywhere, without anyone able to bar the door to you or to give any sort of insult or impediment] (923). Employing passive voice in the dedicatory epistle that fails to disguise the source of his anguish at personal rebuffs, Bruno demands that a man's

intellect be recognized as his credentials: "Se è dottor sottile, irrefragabile ed illuminato, con qual conscienza non vorrete che lo stime
e tegna per degno consegliero?" [If he is a shrewd, resolutely superior, and enlightened doctor, with what conscience will you refuse to
esteem him a worthy counselor?] (843).

Similarly, when the validity of the Ass's argument for being accepted into the Pythagorean Academy is ignorantly denied, he cries,
"Credete ch'io abbia fatto questo per altro fine che per accusarvi e
rendervi inexcusabili avanti a Giove?" [Do you believe that I've done
this for any other purpose than accusing and rendering you unpardonable before Jove?] (921). Bruno also intersperses three sonnets
through the *Cabala,* and typical of his ass wordplay throughout, all
three are in the style of the *sonetto caudato / codato,* or "tailed"
sonnet.[18] Onorio's asininity is Pythagorean in literally every sense,
even when this leads to amusing contradictions. The reader learns in
the Second Dialogue that Onorio was an ass in a former incarnation,
making him pejoratively Pythagorean thanks to the vicissitudes of
the philosopher's doctrine of metempsychosis. Far more positively,
however, Bruno's sense of a mathematically formulaic method of approaching the deity (for example, in *De magia mathematica* [1590]:
"Ascendit animal per animum ad sensus, per sensus in mixta, per
mixta in elementa, per elementa in caelos, per hos in daemones
seu angelos, per istos in Deum seu in divinas operationes" [3:493])
matches S. K. Heninger's description of the Pythagorean secret society open to men and women, which "held out to its members the
hope of divine perfection" through a program of mathematics instruction, followed by "a study of physics and the investigation of
primary principles, and finally promised knowledge of the deity"
(1974, 22).[19] Onorio, even etymologically, is the perfect meeting
place for these divergent Pythagorean directions. Although *onos* is
Greek for "ass," Giovanni Gentile adds that Bruno may be employing *rio* to signify "wicked" ass, or *rio* may simply function as a

"suffisso derivativo" (1958, 882n1). The name proves wonderfully encompassing in its ambiguity, inasmuch as Onorio has been previously incarnated as Pegasus; he has also been the asinine (that is, inflexibly stubborn) philosopher Aristotle, who professed ideologies and doctrines that Onorio eventually confesses never to have understood.

The second dialogue of the *Cabala* is a mélange of diverse ontologies, idiosyncratic condemnations of philosophical tenets, and gnostic assertions about physics and physical reality. With typical Brunist syncretism, Pythagorean metempsychosis combines with the monadist conviction that "di medesima materia corporale si fanno tutti gli corpi, e di medesima sustanza spirituale sono tutti gli spiriti" [all bodies are made from the same corporeal matter, and all spirits from the same spiritual substance] (890) to produce Onorio's conclusion that "l'execuzione della giustizia divina" [the execution of divine justice] prescribes "cotal modo di resuscitazione . . . secondo gli affetti ed atti ch'hanno exercitati in un altro corpo" [precisely such a revivification, according to the emotions and actions they have exercised in another body] (891). Bruno's anti-Aristotelianism, prominently adopted after his disastrous intellectual debut at Oxford University, the very *fons Aristotelis*, is evident in Onorio's remarks about the egregiously uninformed opinions on physics and metaphysics he disseminated while incarnated as Aristotle. His condemnatory remarks culminate in the pronouncement, "Son fatto quello per cui la scienza naturale e divina è stinta nel bassissimo della ruota" [I am the tool by which natural and divine knowledge is stuck on the lowest point of the wheel] (893–894).[20] Bruno joins his voice to popular attacks on Skepticism and Pyrrhonism that accused their proponents of the puerile dismissal of others' epistemological theories, and of espousing doubt about the security (Skeptics) or even possibility (Pyrrhonians) of knowledge, angrily charging that "per non pregiudicar alla lor vana presunzione confessando l'imbecilità del proprio ingegno, grossezza di senso e privazion d'intelletto" [by not risking their vain presumption, confessing the imbecility of their own mind, their coarseness of sense and privation of intellect], they finally "donano la colpa alla natura, alle cose che mal si rapresentano, e non principalmente alla mala apprensione de gli dogmatici" [lay the blame on nature, for the evil things they represent, and not principally on the bad understanding of the Dogmatics] (905).[21]

As Augusto Guzzo and Romano Amerio observe in their edition of Bruno's vernacular *dialoghi*, the text appended to the dialogue proper, "The Nolan's Cillenican Ass," is "una satira dell'ordine dottorale" [a satire of the doctoral order] (1956, 541n1). A talking Ass applies for admission to the Pythagorean Academy, and although the school's representative acknowledges the miraculous capabilities of this prospective student and the Ass is properly deferential in making his application, he is ultimately denied entrance on the basis of his appearance. This amplifies earlier physiognomic theorizing by Onorio that animals are inferior to humans solely by virtue of the fact that "non hanno tal complessione che possa esser capace di tale ingegno; perché l'universale intelligenza . . . per la grossezza o lubricità della material complessione non può imprimere tal forza di sentimento in cotali spiriti" [they don't have a constitution ample enough for such genius, because the universal intelligence . . . due to the bulk or lewdness of their material constitution, cannot inculcate so much power of understanding into such spirits] (887). Unlike his *pedanti* characters, university-trained intellectuals who approach thinking and discourse syntactically (as grammar-school pedagogues) rather than epistemologically, Bruno portrays himself and his philosophy as absolutely unbiased by any specific ideology or methodology. Although this ensures that a work like the *Cabala* will prove exciting and innovative in its theses, it also means that there are certain textual intricacies that remain virtually inscrutable to the reader. But it would not be a truly Brunist Kabbalah if this were not so.

The Kabbalah as Model and Metaphor for the *Cabala*

The Brunist persona Saulino lectures on the Sefirot early in the first dialogue of the *Cabala*, detailing the dimensions, the intelligences, the spheres, the spirits (*motori anime*), and the "quattro terribili principi" (866) that introduce a kabbalistic system derived primarily from Cornelius Agrippa's *De occulta philosophia* (Yates 1964, 137–141, 259–261; Santonastaso 1973, 500; cf. de León-Jones 1997, 31–36).[22] Bruno is obviously attracted by Agrippa's attempts, like those of Giovanni Pico della Mirandola and Ficino, "to establish the unifying core of the revelations given by God and to use it to recover the full understanding of man's [godlike] nature" (McKnight 1989, 75) as established in the *Corpus Hermeticum*. This is because the ten physical emanations of God (the infinite creative force that Bruno refers to as *ensofico*, derived from the Hebraic *'en-sof* or *Ain Sof*), the Sefirot, represent the "*Adam kadmon*, or archetypal man" and "form the highest of four worlds, the world of emanation, *aziluth*. From this world evolve successively the world of creation, *beriah*, the world of formation, *yetrizah*, and the world of making, *asiyah*" (Blau 1944, 12; see also Scholem 1987, 130; and Sheinkin 1986, 191). Bruno's commitment to achieving enlightenment through the reconciling of opposing forces and ideologies, through making the impossible possible, recognizes in the Sefirot a guide and a possible means to those ends. Alfonso Ingegno, in *La sommersa nave della religione: Studio sulla polemica anticristiana del Bruno*, notes that the Nolan's attraction to Jewish mysticism parallels his shift away from the Christian perspective of the church militant (1985, 25), enabling him to focus on a synthesis of ideologies that emphasizes the individual's godlike potential.

Saulino's explanation that certain Talmudists teach that "l'asino è simbolo della sapienza nelli divini Sefirot, perché a colui che vuoi, penetrare entro gli secreti ed occolti ricetti di quella, sia necessariamente de mistiero d'esser sobrio e paziente, avendo mustaccio, testa e schena d'asino" [the ass is symbolic of the wisdom in the divine Sefirot, because whoever wishes to penetrate its secret and occult quarters must be necessarily sober and patient by profession, having the whiskers, head, and back of an ass] makes explicit his manipulation of kabbalistic tradition's erudite decoding of holy texts. The archetype of scholarly patience represented by the kabbalist who reviews every meaningful permutation of a text promotes Bruno's program throughout his Italian dialogues of trying to examine ideology, philosophy, and even natural phenomena from new perspectives. In addition, his veneration of Jewish methodology also allows him to reassert the importance of syncretism and cultural tolerance while attacking the scholarly perspective of the universities, which suggested all knowledge and wisdom of significance in the ancient world to have been derived from the Greeks, Persians, and Romans:

> Cossí perseveri nel tuo pensiero ad aver l'asino ed asinità per cosa ludibriosa; quale, qualunque sia stata appresso Persi, Greci e Latini, non fu però cosa vile appresso gli Egizii ed Ebrei. Là onde è falsità ed impostura questa tra l'altre, cioè che quel culto asinino e divino abbia avuto origine dalla forza e violenza, e non piú tosto ordinato dalla raggione, e tolto principio dalla elezione.

> [So you persevere in your thinking about treating the ass and asininity as something for mockery; though whatever the state may have been for the Persians, Greeks, and Latins, it wasn't necessarily something vile for the Egyptians and Hebrews. There where there is falsehood and deceit, among the others,

that divine asinine cult had its origin via force and violence, and was not rather ordered by reasons and based on the principle of choice.]

The formal connection of kabbalistic lore to the literature of the ass is also made explicit through interlocutor Sebasto's accusation that the Hebrews stole the mysteries of the Sefirot and the ass from the Egyptians,[23] and Bruno's exercise of arcane Hebraic wisdom in the *Cabala* is revealed shortly thereafter to be more metaphorical than technical. After outlining three varieties of asinine ignorance, Saulino concludes that "come tre rami, si riducono ad un stipe, nel quale da l'archetipo influisce l'asinità, e che è fermo e piantato su le radici delli diece sephiroth" [like three branches, they converge at a single trunk—in which asininity influences from the archetype and which is resolute and planted upon the roots of the ten Sephiroth] (876). This grafting of Nicolas of Cusa's learned ignorance with the Kabbalah's second of the Sefira, Chokmah (Bruno's *Hocma*), which connotes wisdom (*sapienza*) in the tradition, is a necessary product of Bruno's argument that new insights can be derived only from the merging of wisdom and foolishness, knowledge and ignorance. To achieve this, individuals must resolve the paradox (by employing a kabbalistic reading of the *Cabala*) of arriving "a quella vilissima bassezza, per cui fiano capaci de piú magnifica exaltazione" [at that most vile baseness by which they are made capable of more magnificent exaltation] (879).

At the same time, Bruno does not explicate a detailed methodology for applying the facets of the Kabbalah and its tradition of intellectual scrutiny to the pursuit of knowledge. Saulino quickly moves from discussing the symbolic resonance of the ten Sefirot to consideration of the symbolic significance of the twelve tribes of Israel and to the twelve signs of the zodiac. Consistent with the theme of learned ignorance, then, Bruno's attraction to Jewish mysticism for the purpose of the *Cabala del cavallo pegaseo*'s discussions

of enlightened asininity may have much more to do with his ultimate philosophical objectives than with any personal belief in the
value of kabbalism. While he derived much if not most of his specific
kabbalistic system from Cornelius Agrippa, it is important to recall
that Agrippa himself expresses deep skepticism about it in chapter 47
of *On the Vanitie and Vncertaintie of Artes and Sciences:* "this Iewishe
Cabala is nothing else but a certaine most pestilent superstition,
wherewith at theire will they doo gather, deuide, and transpose the
woordes, names, and letters dispersed in the Scripture," to "vnbinde
the members of the truthe" in order to construct "communications,
inductions, and parables" (1984, 138). If the polysophist Bruno di-
verges from his usual close association with Agrippan methodology
and philosophy in this instance, the rationale is more likely to be
found in his aim to provoke reconsideration of conventional assumptions and to instigate change than in a personal shift in metaphysical belief.

NOTES

1. All citations of Bruno's Italian works are from either Giovanni Gentile's
edition *Giordano Bruno: Dialoghi italiani* (1958) or Isa Guerrini Angrisani's
edition *Candelaio* (1976) and are followed in parentheses by page references. All
citations of Bruno's Latin works are from F. Tocco and H. Vitelli's edition *Opere
Latine Conscripta* and are followed in parentheses by references to the volume,
part (where relevant), and page number(s): for example, (2.2.76–77). All translations are ours unless otherwise noted.

2. On the conceptual structure of the resistance to humanism, see Jonathan Dollimore (1984, 249–253); cf. Hiram Haydn's notion of the "Counter-
Renaissance." For Bruno's contributions to antihumanism, specifically his rejection of conventional humanist pedagogy and assumptions, particularly through
the *Cabala,* see Ordine (1986, 203–221), Puglisi (1983, 17–22), and Sondergard
(1994, 282n40).

3. The insinuation of such condemnations into Elizabethan literature,
and particularly into the drama, has been discussed at length in two Bruno
studies: Hilary Gatti, *The Renaissance Drama of Knowledge* (1989), and Sidney L.
Sondergard, "Bruno's Dialogue War on Pedantry: An Elizabethan Dramatic
Motif" (1986).

4. In George Abbot ([1604, F4v–F5]; also cited in McNulty [1960, 302–303]); in N. W.'s preface to *The Worthy Tract of Paulus Iovius* (Daniel 1896, 4:7); in correspondence between Thomas Hariot to Sir William Lower (cited in Badaloni [1955, 300–301]; Singer [1950, 67–68]); and in Gabriel Harvey marginalia (cited in Moore Smith [1913, 156]; Yates [1964, 207n2]).

5. Giovanni Aquilecchia (1963, 3–15) discusses the Harvey marginalia; Boulting (1914, 81–88); Elton (1902, 1–36); Imerti (1964, 7–9); Limentani (1933, 317–354) demonstrates the profound difference between the Oxford Bruno expected and the institution he actually encountered; McIntyre (1903, 21–26); McNulty (1960, 300–305); Pellegrini (1941–1942, 303–316) challenges the assumption that Bruno was invited by Oxford to dispute; Traister (1984, 15–16); Weiner (1980, 1–13) speculates on the antagonism that Bruno's Francophile attitudes probably generated; Yates (1964, 205–234) and (1982, 134–152, 175–178). The most recent reconsiderations of documents relevant to the Oxford visit are those of Ernan McMullen (1986, 85–95) and John Bossy (1991, 22–27).

6. Bruno reminds the pedant Prudenzio in *La cena de le ceneri* of the many "sciences" predating Aristotelianism: "Prima che fusse questa filosofia conforme al vostro cervello, fu quella degli caldei, egizii, maghi, orfici, pitagorici ed altri di prima memoria, conforme al nostro capo; da' quali prima si ribbelorno questi insensati e vani logici e matematici, nemici non tano de la antiquità, quanto alieni da la verità" (41) [Prior to this philosophy that suits your brain, there was that of the Chaldeans, Egyptians, Magi, Orphics, Pythagoreans and others of early memory, that suits our head—from which these insane, vain logicians and mathematicians rebel, not so much enemies of antiquity, as of the truth]. For analysis of Bruno's magical theology, see Couliano (1987, 87–106, 157–162); Howe (1976, 39–85); Thorndike (1941, 5:573, 6:426–428); and Yates (1964).

7. Though a tacit acknowledgment of his past, this title was frequently employed by Bruno to designate his identity as philosopher and became a favorite "dramatis persona" (Maiorino 1977, 317). Whether to shield his family from persecution or simply to deny its existence, Bruno apparently never returned to Nola.

8. A description of the potency of this magical theology is given to the interlocutor Tansillo (i.e., the poet Luigi Tansillo, a friend of Bruno's father, whose verse the philosopher occasionally quotes and whose style he imitates) in *De gli eroici furori:* "Piú possono far gli maghi per mezzo della fede, che gli medici per via de la verità: e ne gli piú gravi morbi piú vegnono giovati gl'infermi con credere quel tanto che quelli dicono, che con intendere quel tanto che questi facciono" (1035) [The magi can do more by means of their faith than the physicians by way of their truth; and in the most grave maladies the infirm come to benefit more from believing what the former are saying than by understanding what the latter are doing].

9. Bruno refused an ordinary professorship offered him at the University of Paris "because in order to hold it he would have had to attend mass," though Henri III subsequently awarded him "an extraordinary professorship" without this obligation (Whittaker 1884, 237). Thorndike reports, "At Paris on May 28–29, 1586, he was said to have orated publicly against the errors of Aristotle, to have challenged anyone to answer, and then to have cried even louder that the victory was won. But when a young lawyer answered him and dared Bruno in turn to reply, he remained silent. The students present, however, would not let him leave until he had promised to answer him on the morrow, but he failed to appear" (1941, 6:423–424). John Bossy speculates that Henri III may have sent Bruno to London because it is "likely that he had found Bruno's presence in Paris embarrassing and invited him to go to England until the embarrassment had blown over" (1991, 14).

10. Bruno's frequent appeals to verification via empirical data explain, for example, the presence of the myriad diagrams and charts found throughout his Latin and vernacular works. However, his interpretation of such data or structures is as often metaphorical (and wildly inaccurate) as literal. See Jaki (1975, 106–109, 119–123, 163–167) and his comment that Figure 9 marks "A pathetic conclusion to a pathetic book" (1975, 166n69) for examples of the discrepancies between Bruno's explanations of his diagrams and the physical laws that render them untenable. For speculation on the reasons behind Bruno's "frequently shocking mathematical reasoning" (Westman 1977, 34), see Westman (1977, 34–41).

11. The comedy is dedicated to the deceased Lady Morgana B., and her function parallels Sophia's in the *Spaccio*: existing on an idealized, transcendent plane, the woman is in position to act as advocate to the gods for the philosopher and his ideas. Authorial ambivalence exists even here, however, inasmuch as Bruno is addressing a *dead* woman, and Sophia / Wisdom serves as the mouthpiece for antifeminist attitudes expressed in the *Spaccio*. Yet Bruno's ironies are not limited to the feminine gender: Prudenzio, the ridiculous pedant of *La cena*, is called "more prudent than prudence itself, for you are prudence *masculini generis* [of male gender]" (Jaki 1975, 53). In response to apparent misogyny in the *Eroici furori*, see Sondergard (1986, 106–107).

12. See Binns (in Gager 1981, 7, 9); à Wood (1786, n.p.); and Yates (1964, 206–208, 210). Following his highly publicized, lavishly celebrated sojourn at Oxford, Alasco was invited to the relative seclusion of John Dee's Mortlake estate, as is reported in Dr. Dee's dialogue *A True & Faithful Relation* (1659, 4, 30, 33). Bossy believes that Bruno may have been among the company that visited Dee on 15 June (1991, 23).

13. See McIntyre (1903, 25) and Yates (1982, 134–142). In the *Cabala*, Bruno's interlocutor Coribante, a pedagogue, obfuscates his responses with regular infusions of pedantic Latin. In general, such characters infuriate, rather than

impress, other interlocutors with their frequently macaronic Latin because it is employed to make unnecessary, obtuse (and occasionally inaccurate) references. See Ciliberto (1978, 151–179; 1986, 24–59); Puglisi (1983, 17–22).

14. Compare the letter from Alberico Gentilis to John Hotmann that—without specifically mentioning Bruno—describes having heard "from the greatest of men assertions strange, absurd and false, as of a stony heaven, the sun bipedal, that the moon doth contain many cities as well as mountains, that the Earth doth move, the other elements are motionless and a thousand such things" (Singer 1950, 43).

15. This is best demonstrated by tracing the development of the "menacing pedant" icon in the London dialogues and by noting how their emotional structures may have assisted these portraits' dissemination through Elizabethan literary culture. See Appendix B, "Antipedantry in Bruno's London Dialogues."

16. See Gentile (1958, 835n1). Considerable interest has been expressed in recent criticism concerning the centrality of the literature and lore of the ass to Bruno's work generally and to the *Cabala* in particular. The foundation texts for such study are Vincenzo Spampanato, *Giordano Bruno e la letteratura dell'asino* (1904), and Nuccio Ordine, *La cabala dell'asino: Asinità e conoscenza in Giordano Bruno,* translated as *Giordano Bruno and the Philosophy of the Ass* (1987). See also Ciliberto, "Asini e pedanti: Ricerche su Giordano Bruno" (1984); Ordine, "Giordano Bruno et l'âne: Une satire philosophique a double face" (1986); Santonastaso, "Il cavallo pegasèo di Bruno" (1973), and chapters 7–9 of de León-Jones's *Giordano Bruno and the Kabbalah* (1997, 109–136).

17. The discovery of any one of these symmetries encourages the reader to continue investigating the "kabbalistic" structure of the dialogue. But Brunist metaphysics actively resists final resolution, and the reader learns that rather than being able to find and control the textual "thread that unravels the text and prevents it from achieving closure, thus constantly opening it up to the play of interpretations" (Sedley 1984, 14), the deconstructionist thread is in fact held by the author, looped back into the fabric of the text, making the *Cabala* in the postmodernist sense a distinctly self-referential, self-reflexive reading experience. Perhaps the best example of this is contained in the third dialogue of the *Cabala,* where Saulino reveals that *The Cabala of Pegasus* has yet to be written—though he plans to force it out of his fellow interlocutors when next they meet.

18. J. S. Smart explains that following the conventional fourteen lines, "the poem is continued by the *tail,* which is composed of a half-line and a couplet. There may be one tail, or two, or three, or as many as the poet cares to add in the development of his theme. . . . Unlike the regular sonnet, which is usually reserved for serious and elevated subjects, the *Sonetto Caudato* is used in verses of a humorous and satirical kind" (1966, 112). Each of the *sonetti caudati / codati* in the *Cabala* employs a single half-line and couplet tail. Thomas C. Chubb's assessment of the tails in Aretino's sonnets being "full of venom" like the tails of

scorpions (Aretino 1967, 7) applies equally well to Bruno's *Cabala* sonnets praising asininity.

19. Concerning what Bruno would take to be the "pedantic" imposition of
rules upon probationary students in the Pythagorean academy—which he ridicules in "The Nolan's Cillenican Ass"—see Heninger (1974, 23–26).

20. Charles B. Schmidt acknowledges the significant contribution of Bruno
to a critical tradition that included Copernicus, Petrus Ramus, and Francesco
Patrizi, among others, and that guaranteed "that Aristotelianism failed to revive
itself as a viable general philosophy" (1983, 8). As an additional context for the
discussion of Bruno's Oxford fiasco below, it is telling that Schmidt notes that
"the writings of Bruno were certainly not systematic enough for teaching pur-
poses" (1983, 44) themselves to be entertained as viable alternatives to what the
philosopher considered the university's rigid Aristotelianism.

21. Bruno's tone is all vitriol here, aimed at discrediting rather than engaging these philosophical positions. Montaigne answered such attacks in the
mid-1570s by arguing in the *Apologie de Raimond Sebond* that Skepticism is
neither nihilistic nor intellectually static (1969, 3:227).

22. For a concise summary of Bruno's use of technical Kabbalah in the first
dialogue, Karen de León-Jones's chart of Bruno's Jewish Cosmology in the
Cabala (1997, 45) details the author's Italianization, and translation, of the
names of the ten Sefira, and the symmetry with which he assigns intelligences,
angelic orders, heavenly *sfere,* and angels that correspond to them. De León-
Jones directly challenges Yates's assertion that Bruno merely adopted the form
of Kabbalah in the *Cabala,* asserting that it is "exactly what its title claims to be:
a work of Kaballah" (1997, 17).

23. Although this sounds like anti-Semitism to modern readers, Bruno is
simply repeating a traditional view reflected in sources such as Tacitus, *Histories,* 5:4 (1931, 179) and Flavius Josephus, *Ad Apionem* [*Against Apion*] (1871,
885).

Bruno's *Cabala* and
Italian Dialogue Form

Writing in Italy in 1585, the same year in which the *Cabala del cavallo pegaseo* appeared in London, Torquato Tasso philosophized on the art of the dialogue in a short but elegant treatise, *Discorso dell'arte del dialogo*. In this discourse the Ferrarese court poet and dialogist highlighted what he regarded to be the essential role of imitation and verisimilitude in composing dialogues, and he specifically sanctioned the Platonic tradition:

> We have said that dialogues are imitations of discussions and that dialectical dialogues imitate disputations. It follows that those who are involved in discussing and disputing will reveal both their opinions and their character, and these—opinions and character—are the other essential parts of the dialogue. The writer of a dialogue must be an imitator no less than the poet; he occupies a middle ground between poet and dialectician. No one performs this imitation or expresses the art of the dialogue better than Plato.[1]

Tasso learned his mimetic approach to the art of the dialogue from at least two of his teachers at the University of Padua: Carlo Sigonio, who wrote *De dialogo liber* (1562), and Sperone Speroni, who composed an *Apologia dei dialoghi* (not published until the year after Tasso's death). A Counter Reformation poet who seems to have suffered from a mental illness akin to delusional paranoia, Tasso apparently saw in the dialogue an instrument that allowed him a certain degree of intellectual freedom in the age of the Inquisition—the right to express somewhat heterodox opinions within a climate of orthodoxy or repression.[2] By openly postulating that dialogues by their very nature must imitate life, including real discussion and realistic characters of diverse opinions, Tasso was subtly striving to create a rationale for multiple voices. Apparently he hoped to find protection among those voices, none of which could definitively be ascribed to the author.

In theory, the obliqueness or ambiguity innate in the dialogue's form does offer protection. A variety of characters present contrasting points of view. The interlocutors disagree with each other and argue openly the pros and cons of their various positions. Ideally, the debate has the effect of inviting readers to participate in the argument and to take sides. In practice, as Bruno discovered, dialogues do not mask perfectly. The author's viewpoint is often ascribed, whether rightly or wrongly, to the most sympathetic character or to the most rhetorically persuasive interlocutor. The result is that any protection of the authorial voice may prove to be transitory, even fatally fleeting. In fact, the manner of Bruno's death was calculated to silence his *voice* once and for all, literally and symbolically. His tongue was pulled forward and encased in a wooden vise *(una morsa di legno);* only after this official act of silencing was he removed from prison and paraded into Rome's Campo di Fiori, where he was stripped naked, tied to a stake, and burned alive. His books were also placed on the Index and burned in a futile attempt to erase any written record of his supposedly heretical views.

Tasso, as we have noted, articulated his dialogue theory in the exact year in which Bruno published the *Cabala.* Although the author of *Gerusalemme liberata* composed numerous dialogues (twenty-five between 1578 and his death in 1595) and treated many topics, he followed a dialogue tradition mirrored only in small part by the Nolan. Bruno followed the general structure of the classically inspired dialogue, which presents two or more interlocutors debating one or more topics, but the nature of those who speak in the *Cabala* (including a talking ass and a mythological deity) and what they discourse on diverge widely from the Tassian model and praxis.

To understand better the similarities and differences between these sixteenth-century contemporaries, we must first acknowledge that both Tasso and Bruno, in fashioning their Italian dialogues, drew on philosophical and literary traditions that had long, rich, and complex histories even before the genre arrived in Italy. Although Platonism and Platonic forms dominated Renaissance Italy, other dialogue traditions existed and had roots in Greek soil.

It is widely known that, as a means of philosophical expression, the dialogue germinated in Greece in the fifth century B.C.E. with Socrates. He introduced dialectic, a new method of approaching knowledge, and philosophized by means of question and answer. Nevertheless, he left no written record. In the next century, however, the writings of Plato, Xenophon, and Aristotle developed, expanded, and refined the art of the written dialogue. But even Plato's dialogues, undoubtedly the most famous of antiquity, evolved over time. The earliest are highly Socratic (for example, the *Apology* and the *Gorgias*). In his middle years he produced the great discursive dialogues (the *Republic, Phaedo, Symposium, Phaedrus, Timaeus,* and *Philebus*), which in general treat the panoramic relationship of the soul, the state, and the cosmos. His late dialogues (*Theaetetus,* the *Parmenides,* and the *Sophist*) primarily focus on technical philosophical issues.[3]

Xenophon exerted great influence on the dialogue form through his own *Symposium,* which helped popularize the setting of the dialogue as a convivial meeting for drink, music, and intellectual engagement.[4] The dialogues of Aristotle, on the other hand, are extant only in fragments, and their style is surmised chiefly through the Roman orator Cicero, who claimed to imitate them.[5] The typical Aristotelian dialogue apparently focused on a single rhetorician or logician, such as Socrates, who controlled and dominated the discussion. Cicero's *Tusculanae disputationes,* following that model, are chiefly in the mouth of one speaker.[6]

Following Rome's conquest of Greece, Greek philosophy entered the mainstream of Roman thought, eventually flooding it. In the first century B.C.E. Cicero imitated what he esteemed to be the Aristotelian style but also revealed indebtedness to Socrates, who (like the Roman orator) investigated and privileged ethical issues. Cicero perfected the Latin dialogue as philosophical treatise in such works as *De re publica* and the aforementioned *Tusculan Disputations,* "dialogues, not of the dramatic type with which we are familiar in [early] Plato, but of a later kind where there is much less of question and answer and much more of continuous exposition."[7] This Ciceronian tradition continued on Italian soil until the late fourth century, when St. Augustine converted from classical philosophy to Christian faith, rejected the pagan emphasis on rhetoric, and embraced scriptural exegesis as the primary basis for education. For almost a millennium, from the time of Augustine's conversion in Milan to the rise of Italy's fifteenth-century humanists, the classical dialogue tradition was largely replaced by philosophical soliloquies, religious catechisms, and Scholastic dialectics.[8]

The father of humanism, Francesco Petrarca (or Petrarch), initiated the dialogue's revival in fourteenth-century Italy with his autobiographical *Secretum* (written in the 1340s). A Petrarchan equivalent to Augustine's *Confessions,* the *Secret* consists of a colloquy between Petrarch's worldly persona and the religious Augustine. The candid interchange between the heterodox poet and the orthodox Church Father inspired several fifteenth-century humanists to consider the dialogue a worthy form for their own philosophizing and questioning of authority. Because Petrarch championed Cicero as the model for Latin prose, and because Cicero's dialogues often treated themes dear to the hearts of Florentine civic humanists, it was only natural that the Italian quattrocento emphasized the Ciceronian form of the dialogue: balanced, reflective, and elegant explorations of both sides of a question. Dialogues were no longer to be catechistic (that is, Augustinian-inspired) repetitions of the party line; rather, they were to examine the pros and cons of every argument.

Bruno, in his drive to explore multiple facets of philosophical issues, can be considered to that small degree Ciceronian. But the irreverent and comical spirit, not to mention the paradoxical content, of Bruno's dialogues is decidedly another thing. After all, Cicero purported to imitate Aristotle, and anything smacking of Aristotelianism provoked biliousness or was anathema to the ex-Dominican friar. To understand the spirit of Bruno's *Cabala* in particular, we must return to the Greek dialogue's history and to the example of the satirist Lucian (c. 125–after 180 C.E.), the author of *Dialogues of the Gods* and *Dialogues of the Dead*.

As David Marsh has succinctly argued, in addition to the Ciceronian tradition that dominated the Latin humanistic writings of fifteenth-century Italy, three subsidiary traditions coexisted. He labels these "the Platonic" (in the style of the Socratic question-and-answer dialogues of Plato, in which the author does not usually appear), "the symposiac" (in the mode of learned banquet discussions or postprandial debates of Xenophon and other Greek and Latin writers), and "the Lucianic" (after the pattern of Lucian's comic, satiric, or allegorical dialogues).[9] Marsh traces these subsidiary forms through the Latin dialogues of fifteenth-century Italy, situating Lorenzo Valla largely, though by no means exclusively, in the Platonic tradition; Francesco Filelfo's *Convivia mediolanensia* and some aspects of Giovanni Pontano's later dialogues, such as the *Actius* and *Aegidius,* in the symposiac; and Leon Battista Alberti's *Intercoenales* and *Momus* in the Lucianic. Nonetheless, neo-Ciceronian dialogues abound in the fifteenth century, including a number written by Leonardo Bruni (*Dialogi ad Petrum Paulum Histrum*) and Poggio Bracciolini (*De avaritia*) as well as by Valla (*De vero falsoque bono*) and Alberti (*Libri della famiglia*).

In other words, the "form" of a dialogue (how many speakers, the type of interlocutors, and the dramatic or narrative form of their speeches) may belong to one style while the "content" (a focus on secular problems or, by contrast, on questions of religion or ecclesiastical authority) may relate more to another tradition. And Bruno, ever one to confront authority and promote innovation, seems to specialize in this type of conflation. Not unlike the Neapolitan Pontano, who in the second half of the quattrocento synthesized Greek and Latin dialogue traditions in such works as the mythologically charged *Charon,* Bruno mixes and juxtaposes traditions with comparable abandon more than a century later.

Meanwhile, the mainstream of vernacular dialogue tradition that lies between Pontano, who died in 1503, and Bruno, who was burned alive in 1600, remained imbued with Neoplatonism. We see this in Pietro Bembo's *Gli Asolani* (1505), which exalts Platonic love and exerts an enormous influence on subsequent Renaissance treatises on the love of women.[10] We find Neoplatonic notions throughout Baldesar Castiglione's *Il libro del cortegiano* (1528), which discusses the ideal or perfect courtier and discourses on the spiritual kiss.[11] Finally, to return to the poet with whom we started, we discover Neoplatonism in the various dialogues of Tasso that deal with such topics as love, friendship, beauty, virtue, and art. Just as Bruno's hybrid Italian fails to heed Bembo's injunction that good Italian prose be modeled on Boccaccio's Tuscan dialect, so Bruno's Italian dialogues—brimming with satire and poking fun at pedantry in all its forms—refuse to adhere to the norms of Neoplatonizing tradition.

The Italian dialogue tradition, however, does not stop with

Bruno's death but stretches in its recognizably classical outline from Tommaso Campanella and Galileo Galilei through Giuseppe Parini's eighteenth-century "Dialogo della nobiltà" to at least the *Operette morali* of Giacomo Leopardi.[12] A pertinent question to conclude this introduction to our translation of the *Cabala,* therefore, is this: What effect, if any, did the Nolan's dialogues have on the subsequent Italian tradition? Even more specifically, because we can surmise that a key element that drew both Tasso and Bruno to this genre—its ambiguity—also attracted their contemporaries Campanella and Galileo, do we see any evidence of direct Brunist influence in their dialogues?

In 1594 the Dominican Campanella was accused of sodomy, arrested for heresy in Padua, tortured, recaptured after attempting to escape, and turned over to the Inquisition in Rome.[13] There he was incarcerated in the same prisons of the Holy See in which Bruno was confined and awaiting execution. Ironically, it appears that neither of these persecuted magician-philosophers was aware of the other's presence.[14] Though of different generations (Campanella was born twenty years after Bruno) and widely different temperaments (Bruno being rigid and caustic and Campanella pliable and cordial), both were born into poor families in southern Italy and proved to be highly precocious children. Both witnessed firsthand the oppressiveness of the Habsburg-Spanish tyrannical rule in the Kingdom of Naples. Both chose to affiliate with the Dominican order and yet rebelled against Dominican attempts to reconcile Catholic theology and Aristotelianism. Both also elected to write seminal works in Italian and in dialogue form.[15]

Though Campanella does cite Bruno (sometimes positively and sometimes negatively) in various writings dealing with astronomical concerns, the younger Dominican does not cite the older author in his political dialogue, *La città del sole* (1602). Rather, this dialogue portrays highly personal and utopian thoughts of a perfect and harmonious community, a theocratic republic in dramatic contrast to Italy's Machiavellian states and principalities.[16] The interlocutors are only two in number, a Hospitaler Knight and a Genoese sea captain, but the knight merely asks polite and simple questions while the Genoese discourses in a genteel fashion and at length about the City of the Sun. There is little indication of any Lucianic inspiration; indeed, the question-and-answer format is unimaginatively Platonic.

Brunist echoes that are readily recognizable are few and far between; they ostensibly consist in isolated notions rather than in overall tone or structural parallels. For example, the Genoese captain makes quite clear that the people in the City of the Sun are enemies of Aristotle, whom they call (in typically Brunist fashion) a pedant: "Son nemici d'Aristotile, l'appellano pedante."[17] While granting "the extremely different literary form" of the *Città* and Bruno's *Spaccio* dialogue, Frances Yates nevertheless hypothesizes that deeper parallels exist between these two authors when one recognizes "that the City of the Sun represents something like the magical and Ficinian reform of religion and morals of which Bruno foresaw the imminent return through Copernicanism as a portent, a sign in the sun."[18] In essence, Yates finds Bruno's influence on Campanella to be one of parallel Hermetic missions. Whether one accepts that view or not, their dialogue forms remain worlds apart.

In the case of Galileo, we are dealing with an experienced master of the dialogue who was definitely influenced by Bruno's astronomical theories. In fact, two of Galileo's greatest works are dialogues, *Dialogo sopra i due massimi sistemi del mondo* (1632) and *Dialoghi delle nuove scienze* (1638). After the edict of 1616 in which the Congregation of the Index condemned the ideas of Copernicus, including that of heliocentrism, Galileo cautiously selected the dialogue form to advance his Copernican theories. Furthermore, for both works he selected to defend the Copernican system two interlocutors who were contemporary supporters but deceased at the time of the composition of the dialogues: G. F. Sagredo (died 1621) and Filippo Salviati (died 1614). The defender of the Ptolemaic system, on the other hand, cannot be identified as a historical person; he is called simply "Simplicio" (Simpleton).

Although Bruno's "philosophy of the Ass" allows for the possibility of a Wise Fool, Galileo's Simplicio, the embodiment of Aristotelian pedantry, utterly fails to qualify. And although Galileo's contempt for idolaters of Aristotle (though not necessarily for Aristotle himself) obviously reflects Bruno's disdain, Galileo omits any citation of or tribute to the Nolan.[19] Jack Lindsay has speculated as to the probable reason for this glaring omission: "Presumably Galileo, fighting a hard enough battle with the Church, did not want to make things worse by admitting any link with a heretic burnt at the stake."[20] In fact, the spirit of the wooden vise that silenced Bruno's tongue prevailed for centuries after the vise itself had been reduced to ashes.

As for Brunist influence in Italian society prior to the explosion of interest in him in the twentieth century, Lindsay observes the following: "In the 19th century, in Italy and Germany, Bruno became a legendary figure symbolising the struggle for emancipation. The climax came after the liberation of Italy, when on June 9th 1889 some 30,000 people assembled to honour his monument unveiled on the Field of Flowers."[21] In brief, Bruno's influence in the seventeenth century cannot be measured in terms of citations to his work or imitations of his dialogue form. Such citations were simply too risky in the long shadow of the Counter Reformation. Giovanni Gentile notes that only in the eighteenth century did the Nolan begin to attract the major attention of scholars, "che nel Bruno videro un precursore di Spinoza e di Leibniz" [who saw in Bruno a precursor of Spinoza and Leibniz].[22] Then, in the era of the Risorgimento, Italian fascination with Bruno came out into the full light of day.[23] It expressed itself, however, not in imitation of his idiosyncratic language or syncretistic dialogue forms but in admiration for the larger message of his liberating philosophy and signifying death.

NOTES

1. Torquato Tasso, *Tasso's Dialogues: A Selection, with the "Discourse on the Art of the Dialogue"* (1982, 33).

2. See Carnes Lord (1979, 22–45). Lord makes the following cogent claim: "The dialogue is an ideal vehicle for the discussion of ideas for which an author may want to avoid taking complete responsibility. Tasso freely avails himself of the opportunities afforded by the dialogue form to discuss, whether thematically or incidentally, a variety of topics that bear on contemporary political and religious controversies" (23).

3. For further reading on the Platonic dialogue tradition, see Charles H. Kahn, *Plato and the Socratic Dialogue: The Philosophical Use of a Literary Form* (1996), and Michael C. Stokes, *Plato's Socratic Conversations: Drama and Dialectic in Three Dialogues* (1986).

4. The idea of the intellectual banquet becomes quite popular in Italian letters because of the early and notable example of Dante's *Convivio,* an intellectual treatise in which the poems constitute the victuals and the commentary the bread of a spiritual feast. Bruno's *La cena de le Ceneri* (1584) participates nominally in this same tradition, though in a highly playful and paradoxical manner. The epistle that introduces the dialogue stresses, first of all, what kind of dinner it is (e.g., "non un convito . . . di Platone" [not a banquet of Plato]), and then presents a pairing of opposites for what it is (e.g., "un convito sì grande, sì picciolo; . . . sì sacrilego, sì religioso; sì allegro, sì colerico" [a banquet both large and small; sacrilegious and religious; happy and irascible]). It is, after all, a "dinner of ashes."

5. See Cicero, *The Letters to His Friends,* I.9.23: "scripsi igitur Aristoteleo more, quemadmodum quidem volui, tres libros in disputatione ac dialogo *De Oratore*" [I have written, I say, on the model of Aristotle—at least that is how I wanted to do it—three books in the form of a discussion and dialogue, entitled *The Orator*].

6. For this initial discussion of the dialogue in Greek and Latin letters, we are indebted to Rudolf Hirzel, *Der Dialog: Ein literar-historischer Versuch* (1895), and David Marsh, *The Quattrocento Dialogue: Classical Tradition and Humanist Innovation* (1980).

7. J. E. King in Cicero, *Tusculan Disputations* (xi).

8. For a fuller discussion, see Marsh (1980, 3–4 and passim).

9. See Marsh (1980, 5–10).

10. For an extensive discussion of love treatises in the sixteenth century and their relationship to Bruno's dialogues known as the *Eroici furori*, see John Charles Nelson, *Renaissance Theory of Love: The Context of Giordano Bruno's "Eroici furori"* (1958, especially 67–162). Nelson also details the intellectual connection of the *Eroici furori* to Dante's *Convivio* as well as to "philosophically minded predecessors in the genre of love treatises, from Marsilio Ficino and Leone Ebreo to Flaminio Nobili and Francesco de' Vieri, [all of whom] show a great respect for Aristotle" (240). Bruno's antagonism to Aristotle always stands out in sharp contrast to those who attempted to reconcile Platonic and Aristotelian thought.

11. Castiglione traces his literary and philosophical ancestors in his prefatory remarks to the *Courtier,* stating that if he has erred in the manner in which he has gone about fashioning the perfect courtier, he is "content to have erred with Plato, Xenophon, and Marcus Tullius [Cicero]." See Baldesar Castiglione, *The Book of the Courtier* (1959, 7).

12. Parini's "Dialogo della nobiltà" is between the dead spirits of a Noble and a Poet and exemplifies the author's early period. A didactic dialogue, it ridicules the pomp and vanity of those nobles who rely on their titles for respect while engaging in actions that are ignoble. The moral point is that true nobility is not acquired by birth but by living a virtuous and high-minded life. Leopardi's *Operette morali,* which the author called "poesia in prosa" (poetry in prose), are melancholic and acerbic meditations on the purpose of life. Though these imaginative dialogues include mythological figures and personification allegories of a wide variety, collectively they present a highly pessimistic view of life. In 1850 the Roman curia placed the *Operette morali* on the Index, where they joined Bruno's works.

13. The classic treatment of Bruno and Campanella is found in chapter XX, "Giordano Bruno and Tommaso Campanella," of Frances A. Yates, *Giordano Bruno and the Hermetic Tradition* (1964).

14. For a comparison of the similarities and profound differences between Bruno and Campanella, see Luigi Firpo's introduction to *Scritti scelti di Giordano Bruno e di Tommaso Campanella* (1965, 9–25). Firpo notes, for the record, "vissero insieme due anni e non pare che s'avvedessero l'un dell'altro" [they lived together (in the sense that they were in the same prison) for two years and it does not seem that they were aware of each other].

15. For recent biographies of Bruno, see Bertrand Levergeois, *Giordano Bruno* (1995), and Saverio Ricci, *Giordano Bruno nell'Europa del cinquecento* (2000).

16. Campanella traveled to Calabria in 1598 and organized a short-lived revolution against the Spanish government during that year and the next. Captured and confined to a Neapolitan prison in late 1599, Campanella fashioned his ideal City of the Sun while imprisoned and probably began writing his dialogue in 1602, two years after Bruno's execution.

17. Tommaso Campanella, *La città del sole e altri scritti* (1991, 93).

18. Yates (1964, 372–373).

19. Dorothea Waley Singer develops this point much more fully in *Giordano Bruno: His Life and Thought* (1950, 188–191), reviewing Kepler's purported reproach of Galileo for failing to cite his debt to Bruno.

20. Jack Lindsay in *Cause, Principle and Unity: Five Dialogues by Giordano Bruno* (1962, 41). In the brief section devoted to Bruno's influence (41–44), Lindsay also notes that it was nevertheless via Kepler and Galileo that Bruno's cosmological ideas found their way into the mainstream of scientific thought.

21. Lindsay (1962, 43).

22. Giovanni Gentile in *Giordano Bruno: Dialoghi italiani* (1958, xxxvii).

23. Again, see Singer (1950, 192–201) for a rapid review of Bruno's influence during the Romantic period. She notes that "his Italian bibliographer enumerates in the nineteenth century alone no less than 634 publications in which Bruno figures" (200).

The Cabala of Pegasus
With the Addition
of Mercury's Ass

Described by the Nolan
Dedicated to the
Bishop of Casamarciano

Paris,
On the Premises of
Antonio Baio,
Year 1585

Dedicatory Epistle on the Following Cabala
To the Most Reverend Signor Don Sapatino,
Abbot Successor of St. Quentin
and Bishop of Casamarciano.[1]

Most Reverend Father in Christ,

Just as befalls a potter who has arrived at the end of his workday (the end being imposed not so much by the fading daylight as by the scarcity and depletion of his remaining supplies), who—holding in hand a piece of glass, or wood, or wax, or other material insufficient for making a vase—hesitates for a while, uncertain and unable to conclude, wondering what he can do with it, not wishing to throw it away unprofitably, and desiring in spite of everything that it serve some purpose, so that finally he finds it predestined to form a third handle, the lip of a vessel, a flask's stopper, a lining, a plaster, or a plug that repairs, fills, or covers up some split, hole or crack: similarly it happened to me, after having given dispatch not to all my thoughts, but only to a certain sheaf of writings, that finally, having nothing else to send, more by chance than by design, I cast my eyes upon a tattered manuscript I had previously scorned and had used as a wrapper for those other writings, and I discovered that it contained in part what you are about to see presented to you.[2]

---

1. Casamarciano is a fictional bishopric, though Giovanni Gentile notes that from 1576 Sabatino Savolino was a cleric of the parish of Santa Prima and became chaplain to another church in 1586 (1958, 835n1; see also Guzzo and Amerio 1956, 541n1). Bruno implies that Don Sapatino will have a difficult time of it as the successor to "St. Quintino," for St. Quentin or Quintinus, a martyr who died in 287, was a Roman missionary to Gaul who "was so successful around Amiens" (Delaney and Tobin 1961, 968) that he suffered imprisonment and torture, and eventually was beheaded at Augusta Veromanduorum, on the Somme, now called St. Quentin. "Casamarciano," literally the house of St. Mark, recalls another Roman martyr who was beheaded.

2. This passage describing the once-discarded *fascio de scritture*, a sheaf or bundle of writings, may be read variously as a rhetorical ploy to disarm the

At first I thought of giving this present to a knight, who, having set his eyes on it, said that he had not studied sufficiently to be able to understand its mysteries, and thus could take no pleasure in it. Then I offered it to one of these *ministri verbi Dei* [preachers of the word of God], and he said that he was a lover of the literal sense and took no delight from such expositions like those of Origen,[3] which

reader, as autobiography, or as literary convention. Bruno's pervasive theme in the *Cabala* of learned asininity, of the simultaneous acknowledgments that wisdom is elusive yet may best be achieved through inspired insight rather than devoted study and meditation (see the "Sonnet in Praise of the Ass"), is aided by his introduction here, which treats the dialogue not as a revelatory text so much as an entertaining and instructive novelty. John Bossy, however, chooses to read the passage as a literal reflection of Bruno's method of composing the dialogue: "After Christmas [1584] he dug out his abortive theological dialogue, the *Cabala del cavallo Pegaseo* (we can see him shuffling the papers on his table and finding what he had written of it used as a cover for the *Spaccio*)" (1991, 109). Perhaps the more likely reading is that Bruno is employing, if not actually parodying, the convention of an author reclaiming writings previously rejected. The *Vita nuova* of Dante (composed between 1290 and 1292) is itself a work revisited in the manner of Bruno's coming back to the manuscript of the *Cabala,* for he writes in its opening section, "In my Book of Memory, in the early part where there is little to be read, there comes a chapter with the rubric: *Incipit vita nuova* [The new life begins]. It is my intention to copy into this little book the words I find written under that heading—if not all of them, at least the essence of their meaning" (1973, 3). The author claims to have abandoned his previous treatment of the subject of Beatrice after experiencing "a miraculous vision in which I saw things that made me resolve to say no more about this blessèd one until I would be capable of writing about her in a nobler way" (1973, 86). Petrarch, who of his enthusiasm for letter-writing declares, "It's curious; I feel like writing, and I don't know what to write or to whom. It's a grim sort of pleasure, but paper, pen, and ink and midnight vigils make me happier than sleep or rest" (1966, 118), developed his own literary genre (of "Familiar Letters") after discovering the sole surviving manuscript of Cicero's *Letters to Atticus* in 1345; taking his own letters, he "collected and edited them, discarding some, revising others, possibly even creating some anew" (Morris Bishop in Petrarch 1966, v).

3. Though very few of his writings have survived, Origen (c. 185–c. 254) was possibly the early church's most prolific author: Epiphanius estimated his collective output to number six thousand pieces, and portions of his works have been preserved in various forms by other early commentators such as Rufinus,

are embraced by scholars and other enemies of their persuasion. I placed it in front of a gentlewoman, and she said it was not to her liking by not being lengthy enough for the subject matter of both a horse and an ass. I presented it to another lady; although she did enjoy it when she gave it a taste, she said that she wished to "reflect on it" for a few days. I tried to offer it to a lay sister; she told me, "I do not welcome it if it speaks of other than the rosary, the virtue of the blessed beads, and the *agnus dei*."[4]

I stuck it under the nose of a pedant; sneering, he told me that he rejected all extraneous study and subject matter except for a few annotations, glosses, and interpretations of Virgil, Terence, and Marcus Tullius.[5] I heard from a versifier who didn't want it if it wasn't a collection of *ottave rime* or sonnets. Some said that the best tractates had been dedicated to individuals who were no better than

---

Photius, and Eusebius. His belief in the preexistence of the soul and his practice of a cryptic exegesis, at times highly metaphorical and "kabbalistic" in the liberal sense employed throughout *Cabala del cavallo pegaseo,* must have had strong appeal for Bruno (see Frances A. Yates, *Giordano Bruno and the Hermetic Tradition* [1964, 68]).

4. The ordering of these elements (i.e., the rosary, beads, and *agnus dei*) cumulatively signifies the lay sister's superstition rather than her pious devotion, inasmuch as for Bruno the *agnus dei*—"a medal of consecrated wax bearing the stamped image of the Lamb of God" (Zingarelli 1984, 47: "Medaglia di cera consacrata portante impressa l'immagine dell'Agnello di Dio")—is a talisman rather than a religious icon. John Florio's *A Worlde of Wordes* (1598) lists "Agnus dei, *a little lambe with a crosse painted for Christ, figured by Saint Iohn Baptist*" (11). His 1611 revision, *Qveen Anna's New World of Words,* includes two idiomatic usages: "*Guardare in agnus dei,* that is to looke backe, because the *agnus dei* in Saint Iohn Baptist doth so. It is also taken for to looke or be harmlesse and innocent" (15). Cf. *Il Candelaio,* 5.24, where Ascanio describes the talents of venerable wise-woman Angela, citing her as the source for relics and artifacts from the *agnus dei* to the oily, fatty marrow grease rendered from the bones of St. "Piantorio," a name Angrisani glosses as "chiaramente oscena" (322).

5. The point here, of course, is not that the pedant prefers Roman authors Virgil, Terence, and (Marcus Tullius) Cicero, staples of any Renaissance pedagogue. Rather, his preference is significantly for "annotazione, scolia ed interpretazione" of these authors, not for the authors' own primary texts.

they themselves. Others for different reasons seemed disposed to owe me little or no thanks had I dedicated it to them; and not unreasonably, for, to tell the truth, every tractate and commentary must be paid for, distributed, and placed before someone of suitable profession or rank.

Standing then with my eyes fixed on the matter of this encyclopedic material, I was reminded of your encyclopedic mind, which seems to embrace everything, though less for fecundity and richness than for a certain singular excellence does it seem to possess the whole and more than the whole. Certainly no one could be more expressly able than you to comprehend the whole, because you exist outside of the whole; you are able to penetrate the whole, because there is nothing that can restrict you; you are able to possess the whole, because you possess nothing.[6] (I doubt whether I shall explain myself any better in describing your ineffable intellect.) I don't know if you are theologian, philosopher, or cabalist—but I know for sure that you are all of these: if not by essence, by participation; if not in act, in capacity; if not from nearby, from afar. At any rate, I believe that you are as proficient in one area as in the other. And therefore, here you have it—cabala, theology and philosophy; I mean, a cabala of theological philosophy, a philosophy of kabbalistic theology, a theology of philosophical cabala.[7] Concerning these

6. That is, due to monastic vow. The Dominicans (Bruno's order) became mendicants (like the Franciscans) upon their founder's advice, adopting a corporate vow of poverty: that is, that the order would own no property (except the monastic buildings) and would survive solely on charity and begging. Additionally, they eschewed meat and observed midnight office, silence, and frequent mortification as part of their order's ascetic disciplines.

7. These permutations seem to reflect Bruno's layman understanding of kabbalistic techniques such as *gematria* (meaningful manipulation of "the fact that . . . the letters of the alphabet also represented numbers" [Blau 1944, 8]), *notarikon* (an acrostic system wherein "initial or final letters of the words of a phrase might be joined to form a word which was then given occult significance" [Blau 1944, 8]), and *themurah* (a combination "of the letter substitutions

three items, I don't know whether you possess them as a whole, as a part, or as nothing; but this I know for certain, that you possess the whole of nothing in part, part of the whole in nothing, nothing of the part in the whole.

Now, to come to us, you'll ask me, "What is this you send me? What is this book's subject? Of what thing have you deemed me worthy?" And I answer that I bring you the gift of an Ass: I present you the Ass that will do honor to you, will increase your rank, will place you in the book of eternity.[8] It doesn't cost you anything to acquire it from me and have it for your own; it won't cost you anything to maintain it, because it doesn't eat, doesn't drink, doesn't dirty the house. It will be yours eternally, and will last longer than your miter, purple robe, cope, mule, and life—as, without much discussion, you and others may perceive. I have no doubt here, my most reverend monsignor, that the gift of the ass will not be unrewarding to your prudence and piety: I do not say this by reason derived from the custom of presenting great masters not only with a gem, a diamond, a ruby, a pearl, a perfect horse, an excellent vase, but also with an ape, a parrot, a monkey,[9] an ass. And this ass, then, is necessary, exceptional, doctrinal, and not of the ordinary—! The

---

of the code and the anagrammatic interchange of the resultant letters" [Blau 1944, 9]).

8. As explained in Chapter 102, "A Digression in praise of the Asse," of Cornelius Agrippa of Nettesheim, *Of the Vanities and Vncertaintie of Artes and Sciences* (James Sanford's 1569 translation of *De incertitudine et vanitate scientiarum et artium*), clearly a profound influence on Bruno's discussion of asininity and ass lore throughout the *Cabala* (1974, 382–385).

9. For *gattomamone:* John Florio's *A Worlde of Wordes* (1598) defines "gatto maimone" as *"a great munkie"* (144), while his revised edition, *Qveen Anna's New World of Words* (1611), glosses the term *"a great Cat-munkie"* (204). Zingarelli defines *gattomammone* as "Mostro immaginario delle fiabe spesso evocato per spaventare i bambini" [An imaginary monster of fairy tales frequently evoked to frighten children] (1984, 795) and notes its etymological derivation from *scimmia,* monkey, and *gatto,* cat ("per le movenze" [due to its movements]). Cf. the German *meerkatze,* or "long-tailed monkey."

ass of India is precious, and a papal gift in Rome; the ass of Otranto
is an imperial gift in Constantinople; the ass of Sardinia is a royal gift
in Naples.[10] And the kabbalistic ass, which is ideal and therefore
celestial—do you wish it to be less precious in whatever part of the
world by whatever personage of rank, when through certain benign

10. These asinine gifts can be read, respectively, as insults to Pope Gregory
XIII in Rome, to the sultan in Constantinople, and to the presence of the
Inquisition and Spanish Catholicism in Naples.
   A "papal gift in Rome": This could be an example of condemnation by
contrast with the posthumous praise for Pope Pius V (see p. 11 and note 15),
implying disapproval of current Pope Gregory XIII (1572–1585); and/or con-
tinuing his efforts at courting his English "hosts" (as in his dialogue dedications
to Sir Philip Sidney), Bruno could be alluding to Gregory's support of the
unsuccessful attempts at invading England from Ireland (1578 and 1579) and his
subsequent approval of attempts to assassinate Queen Elizabeth.
   The "ass of Otranto . . . imperial gift in Constantinople": The *Candelaio*, 1.5,
refers to the "Mud Ass of Otranto, Dunce of Avella" ("asino di Terra d'Otranto,
menchione d'Avella"), and Angrisani says of this popular insult "The mud asses
of Otranto were famous: the inhabitants of Avella, a village close to Nola . . .
were mocked for their lack of sophistication" ("Gli asini di terra d'Otranto
erano famosi: gli abitanti di Avella, villaggio presso Nola . . . erano derisi per la
loro semplicità" [1976, 156]). Bruno may be alluding to the *de casibus* decline of
the Ottoman Empire under Murad III, sultan from 1574 to 1595, an "ostentatious
and puerile prince" of "changing humours" whose accession "had inaugurated
an age of pomp and splendour" (Braudel 1973, 1150, 1174, 1199). Though the
relevance of the observation to Bruno's allusion is difficult to establish, an emis-
sary named Aurelio de Santa Cruz traveled from Constantinople to Otranto and
then to Naples in 1578 on behalf of Spanish ambassador to Turkey, Don Marín
de Acuña (Braudel 1973, 1151).
   The "ass of Sardinia . . . royal gift in Naples": Following the capture of the
Kingdom of Naples in 1503 by Ferdinand the Catholic, Spanish viceroys governed the Neapolitans throughout the sixteenth century; it was under the vice-
roy Pedro de Toledo (1484–1553) that the Inquisition was introduced in 1547. To
understand Bruno's linkage of Sardinia and Naples, note Zingarelli's suggestion
that the Latin root, *sardus,* may be an "allusion to the unwholesome air of
Sardinia" [allusione all'aria malsana della Sardegna], explaining it was "An-
ciently, the place outside a port where carrion and offal from slaughter were
piled up" [Anticamente, luogo fiori porta ove si ammucchiano le carogne e i
rifiuti della macellazione] and more popularly the "Division of a slaughter-
house employed for the destruction of contaminated or spoiled meat" [Reparto

and lofty promises we know that one finds the terrestrial even in heaven? I am certain, then, that it will be accepted by you with the same spirit with which it is given you by me.

Take it if you please, oh father, for a bird—because it's winged and the most amiable and merry that one may keep in a cage. Take it, if you wish, for a wild beast—because it's unique, rare and exotic on one hand, and there is nothing finer that you could keep fast in a den or cave. Treat it, if you please, like a servant—because it's obsequious, courteous, and servile, and it's the best companion you can have at home. See that it doesn't bolt from your hand, because it's the best steed that you can pasture; or, to be more specific, that you can feed right in its own stable. Better yet, it can be for you an intimate comrade and an entertainment in your bedroom. Handle it like a gem and a precious thing, because you cannot have a more excellent treasure in your vault. Handle it like something sacred and gaze on it like something of great importance, because you cannot have a better book, better icon, and better mirror in your study.[11]

---

del macello adibito alla distruzione delle carni infette o avariate] (1984, 1692). In the *Spaccio*, Mercury warns Sophia that "mad and fierce Discord has threatened to kindle in this Parthenopaean Realm [i.e., Naples]" due to "Great Avarice, who continues working with the pretext of wanting to preserve religion" (195–196). Imerti identifies this as Don Pedro de Toledo's institution of the Inquisition into the Kingdom of Naples, "causing the uprising of May 17th of that year, which continued for two months. For this act of defiance the Neapolitans were fined 100,000 ducats by the Spaniards" (302n16). The Spanish reprisal was motivated more by desire for profit than punishment of heresy; hence Bruno's conjunction of Naples with the linguistically pejorative Sardinia.

11. Isa Angrisani glosses a similar usage in the dedicatory section of the *Candelaio*, explaining *cabinetto* as deriving "dal francese 'cabinet': stanza riservata ed intima" [from the French 'cabinet': a private, interior room] (1976, 118).

In this passage (beginning "Take it if you please, oh father, for a bird") Bruno employs the word *uccello* to signify "bird" literally, and the "*Membro virile*" (Zingarelli 1984, 2076) figuratively, creating sexual connotations for "the best companion you can have at home"; "See that it doesn't bolt from your

Finally, if despite all these reasons you cannot stomach it, you will be able to give it to someone else—who can't possibly be ungrateful to you. If you consider it something silly, give it to some good knight, so he can place it in the care of his pages—deeming it something precious to be kept among his apes and monkeys. If you regard it as something of the common herd, give it to a peasant who will shelter it between his horse and ox. If you consider it something wild, hand it over to some Actaeon who will let it wander with mountain goats and deer.[12] If it seems to you a small pet, bestow it on some damsel who can hold it in lieu of a marten and puppy.[13] If finally it seems to have something of a mathematical air about it, give it to a cosmographer so that it may be skimming and skipping between the arctic and antarctic poles of one of these armillary spheres—to which it will be able, with not much effort, to give the same perpetual motion that the infused quicksilver was able to bestow on the sphere of Archimedes, to produce a

---

hand . . . you can feed it right in its [own] stable"; "it can be for you an intimate comrade and an entertainment in your bedroom"; and so forth. This is psychologically appropriate for the *Cabala del cavallo pegaseo*, as Richard Caldwell writes: "Flying and horses both symbolized victorious male sexuality in Greek culture, and there are other indications of Pegasos' role as magic phallus for Bellerophon: he is called by Hesiod . . . the carrier of Zeus' thunderbolt, and both Pegasos and Bellerophon are said to have Poseidon as father . . . which would make horse and rider half-brothers" (1989, 191n10).

12. The myth of Actaeon, the unfortunate hunter who offends the goddess Artemis / Diana and at her direction is devoured by his own hounds, is a favorite of Bruno, appearing in his vernacular works in such places as the *Candelaio* (Angrisani 1976, 129: used derisively here to mark the comeuppance of Bonifacio), the *Spaccio* (Imerti 1964, 262), and throughout the *Eroici furori* (e.g., the myth as Neoplatonist metaphor: Memmo 1964, 123–127, 138–139; see also 123n2). For a discussion of Actaeon's vision of the goddess as a metaphor for the individual's pursuit of intellectual transcendence, see De Léon-Jones (1997, 73–82ff).

13. Cf. Bruno's attack on fashion-conscious noblewomen (e.g., those who prefer "a she-puppy, a marten," and the like to their own children) in the third dialogue of the *Spaccio* (Imerti 1964, 244–245).

more efficacious model of the macrocosmos, from whose intrinsic soul hangs the concord and harmony of both linear and circular motion.[14]

But if you are wise, as I esteem you, and you consider with mature judgment, you will keep it for yourself, not thinking that I have presented to you something less worthy than what I have been able to present to Pope Pius V (to whom I have consecrated *l'Arca di Noè*), to King Henri III of France (whom I immortalize in *De umbris idearum*), to the king's legate in England (to whom I have granted *l'Explicatio triginta sigillorum*), and to the knight Sidney (to whom I have dedicated *la Bestia trionfante*).[15] For here you have not only the triumphant beast alive, but also the thirty seals opened, holiness perfected, the shadow explicated and the ark steered, where the ass (who does not envy the longevity of the wheels of time, the universe's vastness, the bliss of the angelic intelligences, the sun's light, or Jove's canopy) is moderator, announcer, comforter, unsealer, and president.

14. This passage effectively demonstrates the syncretism that distinguishes Bruno so remarkably from his contemporaries: it alludes to the world soul of Plato's *Timaeus*; it boldly proposes a *coincidentia oppositorum* inconceivable to the father of hydrostatics, Archimedes; and it is all predicated upon the speaker's access to a magic or philosophy Lynn Thorndike characterizes as "natural and true, based on the occult natures and virtues of things, an intimate part of philosophy, free from all superstition and pure from the artifices and malefices of demons. It divides into physics, mathematics and *praestigia*" (note that with his application of the term "cosmographer" who can "infuse" mercury and water, Bruno incorporates elements of all three) (1958, 7:282).

15. Singer lists *De arca No[è]* as a lost work by Bruno, most likely a "symbolic exposition of moral philosophy" (1950, 204) akin to *Cabala del cavallo pegaseo* and dated no later than 1572. The other three works, also by Bruno, are extant: *De umbris idearum, implicantibus artem quaerendi, inveniendi, iudicandi, ordinandi et applicandi* (Paris, 1582); *Explicatio triginta sigillorum ad omnium scientarum et artium inventionem dispositionem et memoriam* (London, 1583; dedicated to Henri III's ambassador to Queen Elizabeth, Michele de Castelnau); and *Spaccio de la bestia trionfante* (London [though imprinted "Stampato in Parigi"], 1584).

He is *not* an ass from the stable or the herd, but from among those able to appear anywhere, to go anywhere, enter anywhere, preside over everything, communicate, understand, advise, define, and do everything. Considering that I see him hoe, water, and irrigate, why don't you want me to call him a gardener? If he ploughs, plants, and sows, doesn't that make him a farmer? How can he not be a builder, who is laborer, master, and architect? Who restrains me from calling him an artist if he is so imaginative, industrious, and restorative? If he is such an exquisite reasoner, lecturer, and apologist, aren't you pleased that I call him a scholar? Being such an excellent shaper of morals, institutor of doctrines, and reformer of religions, who will resist calling him an academic and esteeming him archimandrite[16] of the written word? Mustn't he who is choral, capitular, and accustomed to dormitory life be a monk? If he is by vow poor, chaste, and obedient, will you censure me if I call him a monk? Will you impede me from calling him conclavistic, since he can be graduated, is eligible, and can be made a prelate through active and passive voice?[17] If he is a shrewd, resolutely superior, and enlightened doctor, with what conscience will you refuse to esteem him a worthy counselor? Will you hold my tongue, that I may not publicly call him a domestic householder, since in that head is planted all political and economic morality? Will the power of canonical authority forbid me from considering him a pillar of the church if he demonstrates a pious, devoted, and chaste manner to me? If I take him to be so lofty, blessed, and triumphant, will heaven and the

16. Devious wordplay from Bruno, given the context of the ass throughout the dialogue: archimandrite, designating an abbot in the Eastern Church, derives from the ecclesiastical Greek *arkhi-* "enclosure, stable" + *mandra* "monastery." For additional linguistic punning on these roots, see Onions (1966, 48).

17. Bruno makes it linguistically possible to "be made a prelate through active and passive voice" when he joins the term "prelatibile" to the series "graduabile, eligibile" (843).

whole world be able to stop me from calling him divine, Olympian, celestial? In conclusion (to no longer crack your head and mine), it seems to me that he is that World Soul itself, all in all, and everything in every part.

Now you see, therefore, the great importance of this venerable subject, about which we make the present discourse and dialogues, concerning which, if you happen to see a large head either without much neck or with a little tail, don't be discouraged, don't be offended, don't be astonished. One finds many species of animals in nature that have no other limbs than the head, or that seem to be entirely head, since that part is so large and the others imperceptible; for all that, they lack nothing to be most perfect in their own genus. And if this reasoning doesn't satisfy you, you must further consider that this little work contains a description, a picture—and that in portraits it is generally enough to have represented the head by itself without the rest. I acknowledge that excellent artifice occasionally is shown in forming only a hand, a foot, a leg, an eye, an elegant ear, half a face that sticks from behind a tree or the corner of a window;[18]

18. The image of limbs / organs created in isolation from the body here seems to combine aspects of two popular topoi in sixteenth-century European art. Recalling Bruno's potter, who is looking for forms to bring to life within his leftover supplies at the beginning of the *Cabala*, H. W. Janson cites the opening of Leon Battista Alberti's *De statua* as an illustration of the aesthetic behind the "image made by chance" topos: Artists "would at times observe in tree trunks, clumps of earth, or other objects of this sort certain outlines (*lineamenta*) which through some slight changes could be made to resemble a natural shape. They thereupon took thought and tried, by adding or taking away here and there, to render the resemblance complete" (Janson 1974, 55). On Arcimboldo's "Imperial Heads" as examples of both the isolated limb as artistic image and the "image made by chance," see Kaufmann (1978, 87–92). The other more widely circulated topos suggested here is the gryllus / grillus, a grotesque composite of human and animal imagery, or merely the connection of dissimilar human limbs (Wright 1968, 152–156, 254–262; Kaufmann 1984, 194–198).

or it's like a carving on the bulge of a bowl[19] that has for a base a goose's foot, or an eagle's, or some other animal's; it is not condemned or despised for that, but rather is more accepted and approved for its craftsmanship. Thus I am persuaded, I am even certain, that you will accept this gift as something quite perfect—since it comes offered to you with most perfect love. *Vale.*

Sonnet in Praise of the Ass

    Oh holy asininity, holy ignorance,
2   Holy foolishness, and pious devotion,
    Which alone can make souls so good
4   That human genius and study cannot advance it;
    One does not reach by wearisome vigilance
6   Of art (of whatever kind), or invention,
    Nor by the contemplation of philosophers
8   To the heavens where you build your home.[20]
    What's the point, oh curious ones, to study,
10   To wish to know what nature does,
    If the stars are but earth, fire, and sea?

19. Bruno's word, *tazza,* here indicates a popular footed bowl, an elaborately decorated table vessel featuring fantastic or grotesque forms and carved out of rock crystal, semiprecious stones, horn, and the like.

20. Including a possible reference to the projected *Cabala del cavallo pegaseo,* Sophia reports Jove's ruling upon the asinine presence in the heavens as part of the first dialogue of the *Spaccio:*

> Concerning the upright majesty of those two Asses, who sparkle in the space of Cancer, I do not dare to speak, because to these, especially belongs the Kingdom of Heaven, by right and by reason, as on other occasions, with many most efficacious arguments, I propose to show you. For of so great a matter I do not dare to talk, as it were, in passing.
> But for this alone I grieve and greatly lament: that these divine animals have been given such niggardly treatment. They are not made to feel that they are in their own home, but, in the asylum of that retrograde aquatic animal. They have been rewarded with the pittance of no more than two stars, one star being given to the one, and one to the other, the two stars together being no larger than one of the fourth magnitude. (Imerti 1964, 109)

12   Holy asininity does not care for that,
      But wants to remain, hands joined, and on bended knees,
14   Waiting for its reward from God.[21]
      Nothing lasts,
16   Except the fruit of eternal rest,
      Which God grants after the funeral.

21. The *ventura*, a reward but also a quest, ultimately derived from the Latin *venire* and literally suggesting "le cose che verranno" [the things that will come] (Zingarelli 1984, 2129), is the adventure, task, or plan revealed to or bestowed upon a knight by God. Bound to God by oaths of obedience taken during the knighting ceremony (Barber 1974, 47–48), the knight was required to fulfill God's holy plan for him by successfully carrying out his *ventura*. Bound by the *consecratio ensis* [benediction of the sword], the knight swore to use his weapon as "a defense and protection of churches, widows and orphans, for all servants of God against the rage of the heathen, and that it may bring fear and horror to its enemies" (Bumke 1982, 89). The sardonic tone of Bruno's mockery of the *ventura* may perhaps be the result of two different spheres of influence. In the first, the notion of the chivalric quest (which in "Sonnet in Praise of the Ass" favors the ignorant innocent over the scholar) loses its romantic charm when viewed through the cynical eyeglass of history as a pretext for wholesale slaughter. The Crusades was the archetype of the *ventura* with a holy purpose and an unholy execution (Gibbon 1932, 426–427).

The second sphere derives from the Roland / Orlando mythos, with its origin in the 778 c.e. massacre at the pass of Roncesvalles, when Charlemagne's nephew Roland was left in the ill-fated rearguard. Italian storytellers inheriting the French legends began to elaborate on them rather irreverently, as even Charlemagne becomes "a figure of fun, a weak, injudicious, quick-tempered monarch always convinced of his rectitude" (Waldman in Ariosto 1983, xii). By the time Luigi Pulci wrote his *Morgante* (1482), "every foible of every Christian knight, every Saracen warrior was well known," and Guido Waldman explains that the poet's educated Tuscan wit convinced him to write his chivalric epic "in a plebeian style, injecting a rich vein of farce into his narrative" (Ariosto 1983, xii). At the beginning of each canto of the *Morgante*, Pulci "echoed the traditional prayer of the *cantastorie* [jongleurs, minstrels]," evoking thereby "the familiar scene of the motley crowd surrounding the professional storyteller on the streets of Florence" (Durling 1965, 99). Giuseppe Fatini writes that the characters of the poem "traggono vita dalle varie correnti del tempo, unificate dallo spirito comico dell'autore che le domina" [draw life from the various currents of the time, unified by the comic spirit of the author who controls them] (Pulci 1948, 15). For a review of Pulci's indebtedness to the *cantastorie* tradition, see Sowell (1982, 65–74).

Matteo Maria Boiardo, a vassal of the ducal house of Este in Ferrara, wrote

Declamation to the Studious, Devoted, and Pious Reader

Alas, my listener: who without ardent sighs, wanton tears and tragic complaints, but with affection, with the eyes, and with reason is unable to call to mind my genius, to raise the voice, and to declare my arguments? How fallacious is the perception, turbid the thought, and impaired the judgment that with the art of a corrupt, wicked, and biased judgment does not see, does not consider, does not define according to the duty of nature the truth of reason and the right of justice regarding the pure goodness, royal sincerity, and magnificent majesty of saintly ignorance, learned sheepishness, and divine asininity! Alas! to what great wrong to some is this celestial excellence so vehemently detested among living men; against which some make themselves censurers with flaring nostrils, others make biting remarks with bared fangs, yet others make themselves mockers with ludicrous laughter. While on all sides they despise, ridicule, and vilify something, you do not hear them say anything other than, "That fellow is an ass," "This action is asinine," "This is an asininity"—notwithstanding such words actually befit more mature dis-

Orlando innamorato (1495) to evoke the court rather than the marketplace of Pulci's Morgante (Durling 1965, 92). And in his rifacimento of Orlando innamorato, Francesco Berni's censorship of "possibly blasphemous or at least disrespectful" references made by the author (Woodhouse 1982, 158; see 158–164) indicates that like Pulci, Boiardo was not entirely averse to taking liberties with the fundamentals of chivalric knighthood. Such liberties are exercised even more freely in Orlando furioso (1516), published while Ludovico Ariosto was in the service of the duke of Este. Ariosto "reveals his awareness of the gap between chivalric ideals and actual behavior in his frequent address to his readers, and in the ironic asides that sometimes underscore the difference between the way his characters behave and the way they would behave if they were real people caught up in similar situations, and sometimes suggest instead that the 'gran bontà de' cavallieri antiqui' (1.22.1) is as illusory in the world of the poem as it had become in sixteenth-century Italy" (Hart 1989, 40). Bruno's apparent scorn of the ventura, then, is as likely an Italian literary heritage as it is an authorial perception of contemporary knighthood.

courses, more steadfast resolutions, and more thoroughly considered judgments.

Alas! why with grief in my heart, sorrow of spirit, and burdened soul is this impaired, foolish, and profane multitude presented before my eyes that so falsely thinks, so mordantly speaks, so recklessly writes in order to produce villainous discourses in so many monuments that go through the press, booksellers and all, beyond their expressed mockery, contempt and reproach (*The Golden Ass, The Praise of the Ass, The Encomium of the Ass*);[22] where one thinks of nothing but to diminish the glorious asininity with ironic maxims, in sport, amusement, and scorn? Now who on earth will not think that I am doing the same? Who will be able to restrain the tongues so that they do not put me in the same predicament, as one who chases after the footprints of those who ridicule this subject? Who will be able to contain them so they won't believe, affirm, and confirm that I do not intend truly and seriously to praise the ass and asininity, but rather am arranging to add oil to that lamp already lit by others?

However, oh my arrogant and reckless judges, oh slothful and scoundrel slanderers, oh gloomy and impassioned detractors: halt your step, turn your eyes, take a look. Observe, probe, and consider whether the bare concepts, the expressed maxims, and the syllogistic discourses that I set forth on behalf of this sacred, unpolluted, and saintly animal are pure, true, and demonstrative—or are really feigned, impossible, and mere appearances. If you see them, in effect, built upon the bases of the strongest foundation, if they are beautiful, if they are good, don't avoid them, flee them, or

22. That is, Lucius Apuleius's romance *The Golden Ass*, Machiavelli's laudatory poem by the same name (an edition of his *L'asino d'oro* was published in England by John Wolfe, 1588, with the imprint "Roma" [Raab 1964, 52]), and the *Encomium asini* of Cornelius Agrippa of Nettesheim. Gentile notes the possible influence of two other cinquecento compositions praising the ass: A. F. Doni, *Il valore degli asini de l'inasinito accademico Pellegrino*, and Teofilo Folengo, *Chaos del Triperuno* (1958, 847).

reject them. Rather accept them, follow them, embrace them—and be not further bound to customary belief, conquered by the arrogance of thought, and guided by vain speech, if otherwise the light of intellect shows you, the voice of harmonious doctrine intones, the act of experience confirms.

The ideal kabbalistic ass, which is proposed in the corpus of sacred letters—just what do you believe it is? What do you imagine Pegasus to be, that has been treated as a figure in poetic pieces?[23] Do you believe the Cillenican ass worthy of being placed *in croceis* in the most honored academies imaginable? Leaving thought of the second and third questions to the side for now and going to the matter of the first (equally Platonic and theological), I want you to recognize that testimony is not wanting from divine and humane letters— dictated by sacred and profane doctors—that speak with the shadow of science and the light of faith. It will be known, I say, to him who is only moderately skilled in these doctrines that I do not lie, when it happens that I declare the ideal ass to be a supernaturally productive, formative, and perfective principle of the asinine species. Even though it can be seen in the ample bosom of nature to be distinct from the other species, and in secondary minds is perceived through a different conceptualization than that by which other forms are known; nevertheless (which is all-important) in the First Mind it is the same as the Idea of the human species, as the species of the earth, moon, and sun, the same as the species of intelligences of the demons, of the gods, of the worlds, or of the universe. In fact, it is that very species from which not only asses, but also humans, stars, worlds, and mundane creatures all are derived: that, I say, in which

23. For a list of these poetic fragments, see Lemprière (1984, 492)—though it omits "Olympia 13" from Pindar's *Olympian Odes,* describing Bellerophon's employment of "the serpent Gorgon child, / Pegasos" and noting that for the steed's bold service to the young hero, "to Pegasos were given on Olympos / the lordly mangers of Zeus" (1947, 39–40).

there is no difference of form and subject, of thing and thing, but is most simple and one.

You must see, then, whence derives the motive that the saint of saints without any reproach now is called not only lion, unicorn, rhinoceros, wind, tempest, eagle, pelican—but also inhuman, the disgrace of mankind, plebeian scum, sheep, lamb, worm, image of guilt, even to the point of being called sin and worse.[24] Contemplate the principle behind the reason that the Christians and Jews do not take offense, but rather congratulate each other in proud victory, when through the metaphorical allusions of sacred scripture they are represented by asinine titles and definitions, are called asses, are explained as asses: so that wherever that blessed animal is discussed—through morality of the letter, allegory of sense, anagogy of purpose—one understands the just man, the saintly man, the man of God.

However, when the redemption and transmutation of man are mentioned in Exodus, they are accompanied by mention of the ass. "You will exchange the first-born of the ass," it says, "with the lamb; you will redeem the first-born of man with a ransom."[25] When in the

24. God / Christ is depicted in powerful, natural terms with references to the lion (e.g., Hosea 5:14), unicorn (Numbers 23:22), rhinoceros (e.g., praised in Edward Topsell's *The History of Four-Footed Beasts* [1607] for strength that could "cast up a bull into the air with his horn as if he had been a tennis ball" [1981, 158]), wind (John 3:8), tempest (Job 27:20), eagle (Deuteronomy 32:11–12), and pelican—though the latter's proverbial altruism, construed as a facet of the notion of Jesus as the Ass of God (e.g., as God's beast of burden, Romans 8:3) and of Christian believers as similarly asinine, anticipates the pejorative list in the second half of this sentence. The lamb's presence in this latter sequence (and its typically positive New Testament significations, e.g., John 1:29; Revelation 5:6) points to the revelation so crucial to Bruno in 1 Corinthians 1:18–29. The lamb of God, Christ, though archetypally foolish in sacrificing himself for mankind, possesses a wisdom that transcends human understanding of cause and effect and that codes the sacrifice of any believer on behalf of the faith as similarly divine foolishness. This is Bruno's sense of the "asininity" praised in the *Cabala,* further reinforcement for his messianic self-image and characterization as martyr for intellectual freedom.
25. Exodus 13:13.

same book the law limits a man's desire to his own wife or servant, you see the ox and the ass placed in the same passage:[26] as if it is of no less consequence to resolve the matter of appetitive sin in the one case than in the other. Therefore when Deborah and Barak, son of Abinoam, sang in the Book of Judges, saying "Hear, O kings, give ear, O princes, who ride on white asses and sit in judgment,"[27] the saintly rabbis interpret this as "O governors of the earth, who are superior to the liberal populace and with the sacred scourge govern them, chastising the wicked, rewarding the good and justly disposing of matters."[28]

Whenever the Pentateuch commands that you must straighten and redirect the wandering ass and ox of your neighbor back to their path, the learned doctors interpret this morally—when our neighbor in God, who is inside us and throughout us, happens to deviate from the way of justice, he must be corrected and cautioned by us. When the head of the synagogue reproved the Lord, who was healing on the sabbath, He replied that no good man ever resists coming to extricate the ass or ox from the well into which it has fallen.[29] The holy writers intend that the ass represents the simple man; the ox, the natural man; the well, mortal sin. That which removes the ass from the well is divine grace and its minister, who redeems his beloved ones from the abyss. Behold, then, how the redeemed, worthy, desirable, well-managed, chastened, advised, corrected, liberated, and, finally, predestined populace is signified by the ass and is called ass. And that the asses are those by whom divine benediction and grace showers over human beings, in such a way that woe befalls those who lose their ass, certainly can be seen in the importance of the curse that rains down

26. Exodus 20:17.

27. Judges 5:1, 3, 10.

28. *The Geneva Bible* glosses Judges 5:10, "Speake ye that ride on . . ." with "Ye gouerners." Cf. the apocryphal Wisdom of Solomon 12:22.

29. Luke 13:14–15, 14:5.

in Deuteronomy, when God threatens, "Thine ass shall be taken away violently, and will not be returned to you."[30]

Cursed be the kingdom, unfortunate the republic, desolate the city and home from whence the ass is banished, removed, and driven away! Woe to the senses, conscience, and soul where there is no participation in asininity! And it is even a commonplace adage *ab asino excidere* [to fall off the ass][31] that signifies being destroyed, undone, lost. Origenes Adamantius, respected among the orthodox and sacred doctors, determined that the fruit of the seventy-two disciples' preaching[32] is signified by the seventy-two thousand asses that the Israelite nation won against the Moabites: it is understood that each of the seventy-two won a thousand (that is, a perfect number) predestined souls, dragging them away from the hands of Moab (that is, freeing them from the tyranny of Satan).[33] Hence it is that the

30. A malediction aimed at those who disobey the Ten Commandments: Deuteronomy 28:31.

31. Further underscoring Bruno's point about the abundant idiomatic presence of asininity, Florio's *Qveen Anna's New World of Words* includes entries such as: "Asineggiare, *to play the Asse*. / Asinelli, *two starres called the little Asses*. / Asinire, nisco, nito, *to become an Asse* [cf. Bruno's use of the infinitive *inasinire*, to make an ass of one's self]. / Asinocidio, *murthering of Asses*" (1611, 42).

32. This draws upon Christ's commission of the seventy disciples described in Luke 10:1, while recalling Gervasio's condemnation of the pedant Poliinnio in the third dialogue of Bruno's *De la causa, principio e uno* (259–260):

> GERV. Most learned sir, Poliinnio, I'd like to inform you that if you had all the tongues, which our preachers declare are seventy-two—
> POL. *Cum dimidia.*
> GERV. —it still would not only fail to follow that you are capable of judging philosophers, but also it would show that you couldn't help being the biggest blundering creature that exists in human form. (Lindsay 1962, 98)

33. Bruno's figure is off by eleven thousand in reckoning the total number of asses halved for tribute according to God's commands to Moses as support for the tabernacle-keeping Levites (Numbers 31:30–47). As for the origin of his reference to the seventy-two disciples, see the arcane logic of Origen, *Homily XXVII on Numbers*, section 11 (Greer 1979, 260).

more devout and saintly men, lovers and executors of the ancient and new law, have been—absolutely and by particular privilege—called asses. And if you don't believe me, go study what is written in that Gospel: "Release the ass and the colt, and bring them to me."[34]

Go contemplate the discourses that the Hebrew, Greek, and Latin theologians make about that passage which is written in the book of Numbers: *Aperuit, Dominus os asinae, et locula est* [God opened the mouth of the ass, and it spoke].[35] *And notice how they reconcile many other passages in the sacred letters where the provident God is often introduced to open the mouth of diverse holy and prophetic individuals, like the one who says "Oh oh oh, Lord, I don't know how to speak."*[36] *And there where it says "The Lord opened his mouth."*[37] *Besides, many times it is recorded,* Ego ero in ore tuo [I will be on your lips];[38] many times, He is beseeched, "Lord, open my mouth, and my mouth will praise you."[39] Moreover, in the New Testament, "The mute speak, the poor preach."[40]

All of this is figured by the fact that the Lord opened the mouth of the ass, and it spoke. By the authority of this—by the mouth, voice and words—secular science (puffed up, proud, and foolhardy) is tamed, conquered, and trampled; and every highness that dares to lift up its head toward heaven is razed to the foundation, because God has chosen the weak things to confound the strong ones of the

34. Matthew 21:1–2. Cf. Mark 11:1–2 and Luke 19:29–30, which omit the reference to the ass and focus solely on the colt.

35. On God doing precisely this to Balaam's ass, see Numbers 22:28–30.

36. Cf. Jeremiah 1:6.

37. Ezekiel 3:27.

38. Exodus 4:10–12.

39. Psalm 51:15: "Open thou my lippes, "Lord, and my mouth shal shewe forthe thy praise."

40. Gentile (1958, 851) and Guzzo and Amerio (1956, 545) cite Luke 7:22, though the mute are not mentioned in this scripture's list of the blind, lame, leprous, deaf, dead, and poor.

world. Foolish things have risen in reputation, considering that that which could not be restored by knowledge has been repaired by saintly foolishness and ignorance: still, the wisdom of the wise is censured and the prudence of the prudent is rejected. The world's foolish have been those who have shaped the religion, the ceremonies, the law, the faith, the measure of life. The biggest asses in the world (which are those who, void of all other reason and doctrine, and emptied of every civil spirit and custom, putrefy in perpetual pedantry) are those who by the grace of heaven reform the foolhardy and corrupted faith, heal the wounds of the ulcerated religion, and—removing the abuses of superstitions—restitch the splits in its garment; they are not those who move with impious curiosity or have otherwise gone hounding the mysteries of nature, calculating the vicissitudes of the stars.

See if they are or have ever been concerned about the secret causes of things; if they excuse any squandering of kingdoms, waste of the people, conflagrations, bloodshed, violence, and destruction, whether they mind that the whole world perishes due to these things—provided that their pauperish soul is saved, provided that they make their home in heaven, provided that they store up their treasures in that blessed homeland, caring nothing about the fame and glory of this frail and uncertain life, in favor of that other which is certain and eternal. These are conditions signified by the allegory of ancient scholars (to whom the divine spirit has not wished to fail to reveal anything, toward the end of making them accountable) in that pithy fable of the gods who battled the rebel giants, sons of the earth and bold predators of heaven, who with the voice of the asses were confused, frightened, terrified, conquered, and dominated.[41]

41. Eliotropio in *De la causa* declares "the mounts of Silenus [the asses] will bray on behalf of the hard-pressed gods to put panic into the giants more stupid than themselves" (Lindsay 1962, 58). The myth is repeated in Bruno's *De imaginum, signorum et idearum compositione* (1591), though he reconfigures the "gi-

The same is sufficiently expressed where, raising the veil from the consecrated image, the eyes gaze at the anagogical meaning of that divine Samson, who with the asinine jawbone took the life of a thousand Philistines[42]—because the holy commentators say that in the jawbone of the ass (that is, of the preachers of the law and the ministers of the synagogue) and in the jawbone of the colt of the asses (that is, of the preachers of the new law and ministers of the church militant) they are *delevit eos* [destroyed on that account] (that is, deleted, that thousand done away with, that complete number, all of them), as it is written, "The thousand fall on your one side, and the ten thousand on your other"; and the place is called *Ramath-lechi,* "exaltation of the jawbone." From this, thanks to preaching's harvest, not only does the ruin of adversaries and loathsome powers follow, but also the salvation of the resurrected: for from the same jawbone (that is, by virtue of that same preaching) those waters have gone forth and come together that proclaim the divine wisdom, disseminate celestial grace, and make the people who drink capable of life eternal.

Therefore, O strong, victorious, triumphant jawbone of a dead ass, O heavenly, gracious, saintly jawbone of a deceased colt: now mustn't there be some sanctity, grace, and holiness, strength, victory, and triumph of the whole, entire, and living ass—ass, colt, and mother—if the glory and exaltation of this bone (and sacrosanct relic) is so great?[43] I turn to you, O beloved listeners; to you, yes you, I

---

gantes, id est huius mundi principes et sapientes (qui contra deos rebellarant)" (2.3.238). Gentile cites a parallel passage in Pseudo-Eratosthenes (1958, 852).

42. Judges 15:15–17. *The Geneva Bible* glosses the site name, Ramath-Lèhi, as "*the lifting vp of the iawe*" (1969, 116).

43. Cf. Sophia's observation in the *Spaccio:* "Now if a piece, a relic, of a dead beast, is in so much repute, what must you think of a live and whole beast that has horns planted upon it only because of the eternal kindness of Nature?" (Imerti 1964, 246); and *De imaginum, signorum et idearum compositione* wonders that if Samson, wielding the "Mandibula longa" of a dead ass "potuit

turn myself, O literate friends of my writing and listeners of my voice—and I tell you, warn you, exhort you, implore you to be true to your natures. Protect me from your malevolence, make up your mind to side with what is good for you; distance yourselves from the fatal pride of the heart, retreat into the simplicity of the spirit, be humble of thought, renounce reason, extinguish the consuming light of the intellect which inflames you, burns you, and consumes you; flee those degrees of knowledge that necessarily increase your woes. Renounce each sense, make yourselves captive to the holy faith, become that blessed ass, reduce yourselves to that glorious colt for which alone the Redeemer of the world said to His ministers, "Go to that city that is before you"[44]—that is, go by means of the universal, sensible, and corporeal world, which as a simulacrum is opposed to and placed above the intelligible and incorporeal world. "You will find the ass and the colt tied up"; you will meet the Jewish and Gentile people, subdued and tyrannized by the bondage of Belial.[45]

Furthermore, He says, "Untie them," take them out of captivity through the preaching of the Gospel and effusion of the baptismal water, and "lead them to Me," that they serve Me, that they be Mine—so that by bearing the weight of My body, that is, of My holy institu-

---

occidisse mille Philistaeos (quid putas, dicebam, facere potuisset cum integro, vero et vivo asino?)" (2.3.238).

44. See opening line of "A Very Pious Sonnet Concerning the Signification of the Ass and the Colt," below.

45. This seems a creative way for Bruno to equate his positive characterization of asininity with his previous exhortation to readers "to be true to your natures." To restrain asininity—figured here in the ass and its colt—is to capitulate to Belial, construed in the Old Testament not as a distinct individual but as "wicked men" in Deuteronomy 13:13; Judges 19:22, 20:13; and 1 Samuel 2:12, 10:27. Jeffrey Burton Russell comments that the "term *belial* is often simply a common noun signifying people who act reprehensibly" (1977, 188n17), or perversely—i.e., against their natures—as in Deuteronomy 13:14 ("abominacioun"), Proverbs 19:29 ("scorners . . . fools"), and Nahum 1:11 ("euil . . . wicked counselour").

tion and laws on their backs, and being guided by the bridle of My divine councils, they may be made worthy and capable of entering with Me into triumphant Jerusalem, into the celestial city. Here you see those who are the redeemed, who are the called, who are the predestined, who are the saved: the ass, the ass's foal, the simple, the impoverished of argument, the little children,[46] they who have spoken like children—those, those who enter into the kingdom of heaven—those who through contempt of the world and its facades trample on its garments, have banished from themselves every care of the body, of the flesh wrapped around this soul, if they have placed it beneath their feet, have discarded it upon the earth, to make the ass and its dear foal pass more gloriously and triumphantly.

Pray, pray to God, O dear friends, if you are not yet asses that he make you become asses. Wish only for this, for without a doubt the grace will be granted you most easily: because no matter how naturally you exist as asses and your mutual discipline is none other than asininity, you must pay attention and consider carefully whether you are asses according to God (I mean, if you are among those unfortunates who remain tied up outside the entrance while the fortunate others walk right in). Remember, O ye faithful, that our first parents at one time were pleasing to God and were in His grace, His safekeeping, content in the earthly paradise, in which they were asses, that is, simple and ignorant of good and evil, when they could be tempted by the mere desire to know good and evil and consequently were unable to know anything of it, when they could believe a lie told them by the serpent, when they gave themselves to understand even this: that although God had said that they would die, it might be the contrary. In such a state they were grateful; they were acceptable, free from every pain, care and trouble. Remember as well that God loved the Hebrew race when it was afflicted, enslaved, degraded, oppressed,

46. Mark 10:13–16.

ignorant, heavy-laden, a coffin-bearer, a beast of burden, lacking nothing but the tail to be a simple ass under the dominion of Egypt: then it was called by God His nation, His people, His chosen progeny. It was called depraved, villainous, reprobate, adulterous when it was under the disciplines, dignitaries, grandeurs, and likenesses of the other nations and kingdoms honored by the world.

There is no one who does not praise the golden age when humans were asses, didn't know how to work the earth, didn't know how to dominate each other or to understand more than one another. They had caves and caverns for homes; they offered their backs for each other as do the beasts; there were not so many covers, blinds, and dressings for lust and gluttony. Everything was held in common; the repast was apples, chestnuts, acorns in the form that they are produced by mother nature.[47] There is no one who does not know equally that, not only in the human species but in every genus of the animals, the mother loves the youngest child more, caresses him more, keeps him more happy and idle (without care and fatigue), embraces, kisses, squeezes, guards him, as one who does not know evil from good, has some qualities of a lamb, of a mere beast, and is an ass, who consequently does not know to speak and is unable to converse much. And as he goes about increasing his wisdom and prudence, always, little by little, he stops appreciating the love, the diligence, the pious affection that he has received from his parents.

There is no enemy who does not pity, embrace, and show favor to that age, to that individual who is not yet manly, is not devilish, is not a man, is not masculine, is not yet shrewd, not yet bearded, not yet well grounded, not yet mature.[48] However, when one wishes to move the Lord his God to pity and commiseration, said the prophet,

47. Cf. Erasmus, *Encomium Moriae* (1989, 33). See Bruno's praise of golden age innocence also in the *Spaccio* (Gentile 1958, 729–730; Imerti 1964, 202–203).
48. Erasmus's *Folly* praises the innocent ignorance of childhood in just this manner (1989, 13–14).

Ah ah ah, Domine, quia nescio loqui; where, with such braying and judgment, he shows himself to be an ass. And in another place says: *quia puer sum.*[49] But when one longs for the remission of sin, frequently the case is presented in the divine scales by saying *Quia stulte egimus, stulte egerunt, quia nesciunt quid faciant, ignoramus, non intellexerunt* [Because we have acted foolishly, they have acted foolishly, because they don't know what they should do, we don't know, nor do they understand (this)].[50] When one wishes to entreat greater favor of Him, and to obtain greater faith, grace, and authority among men, it is said in one place that the apostles were thought to be inebriated;[51] in another place that they didn't know what they had said, because it wasn't they who spoke;[52] and one of the more excellent ones, in order to demonstrate how simple he was, said that he was transported to the third heaven, heard unspeakable mysteries, and didn't know whether he was dead or alive, whether he was in his body or out of it.[53] Another said that he saw the heavens open,[54] and many other matters to which the blessed of God adhere, to whom is revealed what is arcane to human wisdom and is exquisite asininity to the eyes of rational discourse: for these insanities—asininities and bestialities—are considered wisdoms, heroic acts, and intelligences by our God. Those whom He calls His chicks, His flock, His sheep, His brood, His fools, His foals, His ass . . . are those who believe in Him, love Him, follow Him.

There just isn't, I say, a better mirror placed before human eyes than asininity and the ass—which most explicitly according to all the

---

49. Jeremiah 1:6.

50. See 2 Chronicles 16:9; Proverbs 14:24, 15:2, 14; and 1 Corinthians 14:38.

51. See the defense in Peter's sermon, delivered with the other disciples at his side, Acts 2:15.

52. Following one of Jesus' addresses to his disciples, Luke 18:34.

53. See Paul's report of this man in 2 Corinthians 12:2–5.

54. Cf. John's vision of the New Heaven and Earth in Revelation 21:1–27, 22:1–5.

numbers shows what one must be who, toiling in the vineyard of the Lord, must await the compensation of his daily wages, his taste of the beatific supper, the rest that follows the course of this transitory life. There is no better or similar compliance that leads, guides, and conducts us to the eternal salvation more actively than can this true wisdom approved by the divine voice; as, on the other hand, there is nothing that more efficaciously drops one to the inner and infernal abyss than philosophical and rational contemplations that spring from the senses, flourish in the discursive faculty and ripen in the human intellect. Force yourselves, force yourselves, therefore, to be asses, O you who are humans. And you who are already asses, study, procure, devote yourselves to proceeding continually from good to better, in order that you arrive at that finish, at that dignity which not by wisdom and works (although grand), but by faith is acquired, and not by ignorance and misdeeds (although enormous), but by incredulity (as they say, according to the Apostle)[55] is lost. If thus you prepare yourselves, if such you will be—and thus will govern— yourselves, you will find yourselves written in the Book of Life, you will receive mercy amid this battling, and you will obtain glory in that triumphant congregation in which God lives and reigns forever and ever. Amen!

A Very Pious Sonnet Concerning the Signification of the Ass and Colt

—Go to the city that before you stands,
2   Where you'll find the ass with her son:
    Untie their reins and taking them with you,
4   Lead them to me, my holy servants.
    If anyone, to oppose these many mysteries,

55. That is, incredulity like that of King Agrippa when his prisoner Paul challenges him (Acts 26:8).

6   Against you will make the slightest whisper,
      You will respond with raised brow:
8   That the great Lord wishes to make them triumphant.—[56]
      Thus speaks the holy scripture
10   To point out the salvation of the believers
      By the Redeemer of human nature.
12   The faithful of Judah and of every nation
      With lives equally simple and pure
14   Can ascend to those eminent seats.
      Devoted and patient
16   Come to make of the colt with its mother
      Stablemates to the angelic hosts.

First Dialogue

Interlocutors: Sebasto, Saulino, Coribante[57]

SEBASTO: The worst is that they'll say you put forth metaphors, tell stories, reason in parable, weave riddles, jumble similitudes, treat mysteries, chew tropologies.

SAULINO: But I tell it exactly as it is; and such as it is, I place it before their eyes.

56. Matthew 21:1–3.
57. Gentile identifies Saulino (i.e., Savolino) as "Nome del casato materno del Bruno, molto comune nei quattro censimenti nolani del sec. XVI. . . . Tra tanta gente, per la mancanza di qualsiasi indicazione, è impossibile riconoscere l'interlocutore dello *Spaccio* e della *Cabala*" [Bruno's maternal surname, quite common in the Nolan censuses of the sixteenth century. . . . Among so many people, due to the lack of any information, it is impossible to identify the interlocutor of the *Spaccio* and the *Cabala*] (1958, 571n1). The possibility that Andrea Savolino may have served as the model for this character (1958, 571n1) makes Saulino, for Gentile, the dialogue's "solo interlocutore reale" [lone real interlocutor] (1958, 861n1). Guzzo and Amerio concur with this identification, adding that "*Sebasto* rappresenta la santa asinità . . . *Coribante* un pedante di pedanteria pazza" [Sebasto represents the holy asininity . . . and Coribante a pedant of insane pedantry] (1956, 551n2).

CORIBANTE: *Id est, sine fuco, plane, candide* [That is, without obscurity (stain), simply, distinctly]; but I wish it were thus, as you say, indeed.

SAULINO: Hence it should be pleasing to the gods that you make yourself other than a fool for your gesticulation, toga, beard, and eyebrow: as, regarding the mind, *candide, plane et sine fuco* you show to us the concept of your pedantry.

CORIBANTE: *Hactenus haec* [That's it]? Such that Wisdom should lead you from place to place, seat by seat?

SAULINO: Yes.

SEBASTO: Do you want to say something concerning the arrangement of these seats?

SAULINO: Not right now, unless you are ready to allow me the opportunity to clarify for you more points concerning them by challenging and rousing up my memory, which lacks the power of suggesting even a third of the notable propositions worthy of consideration.

SEBASTO: To be truthful, I'm still dangling so much from the desire to know what it is that the great father of the gods has caused to happen in those two great seats, the one Northern and the other Southern,[58] that a thousand years has seemed to me to pass

---

58. Jove's methodology in the *Spaccio* of replacing all of the vices occupying positions in the heavens with virtues—generally the vices' polar opposites—involves moving by consensus of the gods from constellation to constellation in each hemisphere of the cosmos. The question arises, for example, of what to do with Canis Minor:

> Gentle Venus then arose and asked the gods as a favor that he be allowed as a pastime for her and her maidens, to play upon their bosoms, during the time of their vacations, with that graceful movement of his person, with those big kisses, and with that gentle wagging of his tail.
>
> "That is well," said Jove, "but you must see, daughter, that I want greatly beloved Assentation and Adulation as well as perpetually hated Fanaticism and Scorn to depart with him, for in that place I want

before seeing the end of your thread, though it be curious, useful and worthy: for the more I have been spurred by the desire to understand your proposition, the more you have deferred to make it heard.

CORIBANTE: *Spes etenim dilata affligit animum, vel animam, ut melius dicam; haec enim mage significat naturam passibilem* [Hope deferred crushes the mind, or rather the heart, as I should say; for this better signifies (that part of our) nature which is capable of suffering].

SAULINO: Fine. Consequently, so you torment yourself no longer in waiting for the resolution: know that in the seat immediately adjoining the site where Ursa Minor was, and in which you know the Truth has been exalted; Ursa Major having been removed from it[59] (in the form that you have understood it) and by providence of the aforementioned counsel, Asininity has succeeded it there in the abstract; and there where you still see the river Eridanus in fantasy, it pleases them that you find Asininity in concrete, so that from all three celestial regions we are able to contemplate Asininity, which—where

---

Friendliness, Courteousness, Placability, Gratitude, Simple Respect, and Loving Service." (Imerti 1964, 263)

For an overview of the changes Jove makes specifically in the constellations / inhabitants of the Northern (*Boreale*) and Southern (*Australe*) portions of the heavens, see the dialogue's explanatory epistle (Imerti 1964, 79–88).

59. See the *Spaccio*'s explanatory epistle: "There, then, where the Bear was, by virtue of the place's being the most eminent part of the heaven, Truth is placed first, who is the highest and most worthy of all things, rather, the first, last, and middle" (Imerti 1964, 80). Momus proposes the manner of disposing of the Great Bear: "And he said, 'Let her go, because she is old, as a lady companion of that smaller and younger one; and see to it that she does not become her procuress; if this happens, may she be sentenced to serve some beggar, who, by exhibiting her and allowing her to be mounted by children and others similar, in order to cure quartan-ague and other minor diseases, might earn a living for himself and her' " (Imerti 1964, 121).

the shell of Cancer is—in two torches has been like a welcome in the path of the planets.[60]

CORIBANTE: *Procol, o procol este, profani!*[61] This is a sacrilege, a profanity, seeking to dissemble (since it is not possible that such things are factual) about the honored and eminent seat of Truth becoming the image of such an impure and vituperous species—the which has been taken by the sage Egyptians in their hieroglyphics as the very type of ignorance, as Horapollo[62] testifies: the Babylonian priests

60. As a glance at any star chart will reveal, the head of the constellation Andromeda does in fact join with the tail of the constellation Pegasus. The link between imagination and asininity is suggested at the end of Momus's oration to Jove in the *Spaccio* concerning the disposition of Eridanus: " 'it seems to me to be fitting (since the river Eridanus has the property of being at the same time suppositiously and personally in various parts) that we let it be wherever it will be imagined to be, named, called upon, and revered. All of this can be done with very little expense, without any interest, and, perhaps, not without good gain. But let it be in such a manner that he who will eat of its imagined, named, called upon, and revered fish will, for example, be as if he did not eat, that he who will drink similarly of its waters will be like him who has had nothing to drink, that he who will in like manner have the Eridanus on his mind will be like him whose brain is vacant and empty, that he who in the same manner will have the company of its Nereids and Nymphs will be not less alone than even he who is out of his mind' " (Imerti 1964, 258).

61. Following the Cumaean Sibyl's invocations to Hecate and her command that Aeneas perform a series of sacrifices, she warns of the goddess's approach (Virgil, *Aeneid*, 6.258–259): " 'Procul o, procul este, profani' Conclamat vates, 'totoque absistite luco' " [" 'Stand clear!' cried the Priestess, 'all of you who are unhallowed: stand clear! Be gone from the Grove' " (1956, 155)]. Coribante's (mis)appropriation of the passage signals his self-righteous pedantry and immediately undercuts his credibility.

62. Moving beyond traditional reverence to the ancient Greek and Egyptian religions, Horapollo the Younger, a fifth-century Alexandrian, "proved that he was a man of the future by writing (or so it may be assumed) the highly misleading treatise on hieroglyphs (*Hieroglyphica*) that has been preserved under his name, and by eventually apostatizing to Christianity" (Fowden 1986, 185). Alfonso Ingegno notes that the *Cabala del cavallo pegaseo* marks a parallel shift by Bruno away from the Christian perspective of the church militant (1985, 25) to a hermetic synthesis that emphasizes the individual's godlike potential. Ioan P.

used a human chest and neck, completed with an asinine head, to designate an unskilled and undisciplined man.

SEBASTO: It isn't necessary to turn to the time and place of the Egyptians if there isn't now, nor ever was, a generation which, according to the customary manner of speaking, doesn't confirm what Coribante says.

SAULINO: This is the reason I have postponed discussing these two seats until the conclusion—expecting that from conventional speech and belief you would have believed me a parable-teller, and with less faith and care you would have persevered to listen to my description of the reform of the other celestial seats, if first I hadn't rendered you capable of that truth with long-winded strings of propositions. Truly, these two seats merit by themselves at least as much consideration, as you see they have such rich subject matter. Have you never ever heard that insanity, ignorance, and asininity of this world are wisdom, doctrine, and divinity in the other?

SEBASTO: Thus is reported by the foremost and principal theologians; but never has been used an expression so broad as is yours.

SAULINO: That is because the precept has never been clarified and explicated thus, as I am explicating and clarifying it to you at present.

CORIBANTE: Speak now, then: we're waiting attentively to hear you.

SAULINO: So that you don't get mired down, when you hear ass, asininity, bestiality, ignorance, or folly named, I first wish to pro-

---

Couliano explains that the treatise *Hieroglyphica*, "attributed to Horapollon and 'translated' into Greek by an unknown writer named Philip, was an attraction in Florence. . . . The codex had been discovered by Cristoforo Buondelmonti on the island of Andros and taken to Florence. The Greek text was only published in 1505 [as *Jeroglifici,* by printer Aldo Manuzio (Gentile 1958, 863n3)], followed, in 1515, by a Latin translation, but Ficino's contemporaries were well acquainted with it, since Leon Battista Alberti had extracted from it some whimsical explanations of hieroglyphics in his *De architectura* (1452)" (1987, 37). Gentile (1958, 863–864n3) identifies the first Italian translation, by Pietro Vasolli of Fivizzano, as *Delli segni jeroglifici* (Vinegia: Giolito, 1547).

pose for your eyes some considerations, and to recall to your mind the position of the enlightened cabalists[63] who, with other illumination than that of Lynceus, with other eyes than those of Argus,[64] penetrated—not, I say, as far as the third heaven, but into the profound abyss of the otherworldly and infinite universe. By the contemplation of those ten Sefirot that we call in our language branches and types, they penetrated, saw, conceived *quantum fas est* homini *loqui.*[65]

There are the dimensions Kether, which by us is called Crown; Chokmah, Wisdom; Binah, Providence; Chesed, Mercy; Geburah, Fortitude; Tiphareth, Beauty; Netzach, Victory; Hod, Glory; Yesod, Foundation; Malkuth, Kingdom.[66] They say ten orders of intelligences correspond hence, of which the first is called by them *Chaioth ha qadesh,* the second Auphanim, the third Aralim, the fourth Chasmalim, the fifth Choachim, the sixth Malachim, the

63. See the introduction, "Bruno's Design for the *Cabala.*"

64. Apollodorus's *Biblioteca,* 3.10.3, records that Lynceus, son of Aphareus and Arene, "excelled in sharpness of sight, so that he could even see things under ground" (1921, 2:13).

Argus Panoptes (the All-Seeing), according to Apollodorus, 2.1.2, "had eyes in the whole of his body" (1921, 1:131). Hence, for Bruno to claim for "the enlightened cabalists" an (in)sight greater than the famous "illumination" of Lynceus and "eyes" of Argus, and subsequently to declare that they were in turn "overwhelmed" by their contemplation of the Sefirot, is to transform for his readers the decidedly occult but largely unfamiliar Jewish system of textual interpretation into a mystery of mythic proportions.

65. A variation on the latter portion (*ac loquentes quae fas non est*) of 2 Maccabees 12:14: "So thei that were within it, put suche trust in the strength of the walles, and in store of vitailes, that they were the slacker in their doings, reuiling them that were with Iudas, and reproching them: yea, they blasphemed & *spake suche wordes as were not lawful*" [our emphasis]. Bruno's "enlightened cabalists," who seek to explore "the profound abyss of the otherworldly and infinite universe," do so through magical formulae, or linguistic "contemplation of those ten Sefirot"—and from the perspective of orthodox Christian practice, this is blasphemous or unlawful.

66. See Gareth Knight's "Table IIb: The Sefirot" (1978, I:248–249); Karen de León-Jones (1997, 45).

seventh Elohim, the eighth Beni Elohim, the ninth Maleachim, the tenth Ashim; that we call the first Holy Animals or Seraphim, the second Formative Wheels or Cherubim, the third steadfast Angels or Thrones, the fourth Image Makers, the fifth Powers, the sixth Virtues, the seventh Principalities or gods, the eighth Archangels or sons of gods, the ninth Angels or Ambassadors, the tenth Separate Souls or Heroes.[67] Whence in the perceptible world they derive the ten spheres: (1) the first heaven, (2) the starry heaven, or eighth sphere or firmament, (3) the heaven of Saturn, (4) of Jove, (5) of Mars, (6) of the Sun, (7) of Venus, (8) of Mercury, (9) of the Moon, (10) of the sublunary Chaos divided into four elements.[68]

67. Corresponding, respectively in descending order, to the ten Sefirot are the following divisions of angels: (1) Chaioth ha Qadesh, Holy Living Creatures (Bruno places the Seraphim here); (2) Auphanim, Wheels (the Cherubim appear here in Bruno's scheme); (3) Aralim, Thrones; (4) Chasmalim, Shining Ones (called "Effigiatori" [Image Makers] by Bruno); (5) Seraphim, Fiery Serpents (Bruno lists the unidentifiable "Choachim" here); (6) Malachim, Kings (Bruno's "Virtues"); (7) Elohim, Gods; (8) Beni Elohim, Sons of God; (9) Cherubim, the Strong (replaced by Bruno with the unrecognizable "Maleachim"); (10) Ashim, Souls of Fire (Knight 1978, 248–249, following the list of Moses Maimonides in the *Mishne Torah*). Bruno's confusion results from an apparent conglomeration of the celestial hierarchies as configured by Pseudo-Dionysius (and repeated in Thomas Aquinas, *Summa theologica*), Moses Maimonides, John of Damascus (in the *De fide orthodoxa*), and Dante (see Davidson's charts, 1967, 336–337).

See Tillyard's description (derived ultimately from fifth-century writer Dionysius the Areopagite) of the Christian, triunal grouping for the ranks of angels: the highest, "contemplative" division includes Seraphs, Cherubs, and Thrones (or the Father); the "psychological state" of the second is "rather of an attitude than of an action" and includes Dominations, Virtues, and Powers (or the Son); the third, Principalities, Archangels, and Angels (or the Holy Spirit/ Ghost), "form the medium between the whole angelic hierarchy and man" (1943, 41). For a list of individual functions for each of the nine ranks, see Yates (1964, 119).

68. Individual authors configured the sefirot idiosyncratically; see the examples in Marsilio Ficino's *De Christiana religione* (in Yates 1964, 118) and Pico della Mirandola's *Heptaplus* (1977, 40–41; see also Yates's clarification of Pico's system, 1964, 100–101, 100n3).

Assisting these are ten driving forces, or ten innate spirits: the first Metatron or the prince of faces, the second Ratziel, the third Tzaphkiel, the fourth Tzadkiel, the fifth Khamael, the sixth Raphael, the seventh Haniel, the eighth Michael, the ninth Gabriel, the tenth Samael;[69] below these figures are four terrible princes: the first of

69. Metatron, the "Archangel of the Sefira" traditionally identified as the being "who gave the Qabalah to man" (Knight 1978, 1:71), is generally accepted as the "angel or envoy whom God sends before Israel according to Exodus 23:20" (Scholem 1987, 187). Known variously as "king of angels, prince of the divine face or presence, chancellor of Heaven, angel of the covenant, chief of the ministering angels" (Davidson 1967, 192), Metatron is traditionally considered the angelic transmutation of the patriarch Enoch, possibly because ancient Jewish texts report, "Enoch was invested not only with garments of glory and a huge size but also with all-comprehensive knowledge" (Idel 1988, 60). Metatron dwells in the seventh heaven with God and is recorded in the *Zohar* as being in size " 'equal to the breadth of the whole world' " (Davidson 1967, 192).

Ratziel, or Raziel, is the personification of Chokmah, or Wisdom, the legendary author of the *Sefer Raziel* [*The Book of the Angel Raziel*]—more likely penned by "Eleazer of Worms or Isaac the Blind, medieval writers" (Davidson 1967, 242)—which one midrash suggests may have served as the instructional manual for Noah as he built the ark (Davidson 1967, 242–243).

Tzaphkiel, meaning "contemplation of God" (Davidson 1967, 294), is the "Archangel of Binah" (Knight 1978, 95), aligned with the Aralim, or Thrones (Davidson 1967, 289; Knight 1978, 87).

Tzadkiel is the "angel of justice" and "the intelligence or angel of the planet Jupiter; also the protecting angel of Abraham" (Davidson 1967, 291). He is also associated with the Chasmalim (Knight 1978, 113), or Shining Ones.

Sometimes identified as the angel who wrestled the patriarch Jacob, Khamael (or Camael) appears in Druidic mythology as "the god of war. This bears out the frequent citation of Camael in occultism as the ruler of the planet Mars" (Davidson 1967, 80). Identified with the Seraphim, or Fiery Serpents, Khamael "is protector of the weak and wronged and also the Avenging Angel who pursues transgressors of human or cosmic law" (Knight 1978, 134).

Raphael's participation in Christian legend is well known, and he is associated with "at least 4 of the celestial orders: seraphim, cherubim, dominions (or dominations), powers" (Davidson 1967, 240), and malachim (Davidson 1967, 181; Knight 1978, 137).

Haniel ("glory or grace of God" or "he who sees God") is "chief of the order of principalities, virtues (tarshishim), and innocents" (Davidson 1967, 134). Haniel functions as a source of "not only the awareness of harmony and beauty

which rules in the fire and is called Behemoth by Job;[70] the second rules in the air and is named Beelzebub commonly and by the cabalists, that is, prince of flies, *id est* of the flying contagion;[71] the third rules in the water and is called Leviathan by Job;[72] the fourth is president over the earth, traversing and surrounding everything, and is called Satan by Job.[73] Now behold here, that—according to the kabbalistic revelation Chokmah, to which correspond the figures or wheels you call Cherubim, which have influence in the eighth

in the lower worlds but also a great wisdom of the inter-relationships of all things" (Knight 1978, 153).

In the "Treatise on the Left Emanation," Rabbi Isaac ben Jacob ha-Kohen describes the angel Michael as "the prince of lovingkindness" (Dan 1986, 181). He "ranks as the greatest of all angels, whether in Jewish, Christian, or Islamic writings, secular or religious" (Davidson 1967, 193). Jude 9 records Michael's defiance of Satan over the possession of Moses' body: "Yet Michael the Archangel, when he stroue against the deuil, and disputed about the bodie of Moses, durst not blame him with cursed speaking, but saith, The Lord rebuke thee."

Gabriel is the "prince of Strength" (Dan 1986, 180) according to Rabbi Isaac ben Jacob ha-Kohen and serves as "the angel of annunciation, resurrection, mercy, vengeance, death, revelation" (Davidson 1967, 117). The angel appears by name in Daniel 8:15–27 and Luke 1:26–38.

Samael seems conspicuously out of place in this list when the archangel usually listed to complement Malkuth is Metatron, serving thus as the first and last of the archangels (see Davidson 1967, 348). In rabbinic literature Samael "is chief of the Satans and the angel of death" (Davidson 1967, 255), although Moshe Idel may point to a psychological motive on Bruno's part in noting Abraham Abulafia's "understanding of the two angels Metatron and Samael as two drives or inclinations inherent in human nature" (1988, 149).

The methodologies Pico, Ficino, and Reuchlin employed to invoke the archangels were undoubtedly of considerable interest to Bruno; see Yates (1964, 94–110).

70. Job 40:10–19; Behemoth is described in verses 12–13.

71. Kings 1:2–6; Matthew 10:25, 12:24–28; Mark 3:22; Luke 11:15–20. On the etymologies of Beelzebub, see Gettings (1988, 52) and Russell (1977, 189n17, 229n6).

72. Job 40:20–28; Psalms 74:14, 104:26; Isaiah 27:1.

73. Job 1:6–12, 2:1–7.

sphere, where the virtue of the intelligence of Ratziel appears—the ass or asininity is the symbol of wisdom.[74]

CORIBANTE: *Parturient montes.*[75]

SAULINO: Certain Talmudists provide the moral reasoning behind such influence, lineage, scale, or dependence, saying that nevertheless the ass is symbolic of the wisdom in the divine Sefirot, because whoever wishes to penetrate its secret and occult quarters must be necessarily sober and patient by profession, having the whiskers, head, and back of the ass; he must have a humble, suppressed, lowly disposition, and the kind of perception that sees no difference between thistles and lettuce.

SEBASTO: I would sooner believe that the Hebrews appropriated these mysteries from the Egyptians—who, in order to cover up a certain ignominy of their own, wished to praise the ass and asininity to the skies.

CORIBANTE: *Declara* [Explain].

SEBASTO: Ochus, King of the Persians, being represented by the Egyptians his enemies by the image of the ass, and soon after conquering them and having made them captives, compelled them to worship the image of the ass and to sacrifice the ox previously so venerated by them, reproving them in that their ox Opin or Apin would be sacrificed to the ass.[76] These [Egyptians] then, in order to

---

74. Though a significant portion of Bruno's angelic system and the sources behind it appears in the *De magia mathematica* (3:498–499), Ratziel and explicit connection to ass/asininity are omitted from his configuration.

75. Line 139 of Horace's *De arte poetica:* "parturient montes, nascetur ridiculus mus" [Mountains will labor, to birth will come a laughter-rousing mouse] (1947, 462–463).

76. An examination of this oppression as described in Plutarch's *De Iside et Osiris* [*Isis and Osiris*] contextualizes Bruno's occasional—and clearly negative—signification of asininity as perverse, anti-intellectual obstinacy. The unreflective violence of Artaxerxes III, known as Ochus before becoming king (and who

do honor to that other vituperous [Persian] cult and then to cover up that blemish, have tried to invent reasons for the cult of the ass; so that that which was matter for scorn and jest came to be matter for reverence to them. And thus onward—in the matter of adoration, admiration, contemplation, honor, and glory—they have made it kabbalistic, archetypal, sephirotic, metaphysical, ideal, divine.

Besides, the ass being a creature of Saturn and the Moon, and the Hebrews by nature, ability and fortune being saturnine and lunatic (a people always cowardly, servile, mercenary, solitary, incommunicative, and unsociable with other peoples, whom they despise brutally and by whom, for every reason, they are properly scorned), now they found themselves in the captivity and service of Egypt, where they were destined to be companions to the asses, carrying loads and working at the mills. This was partly for being lepers,[77] partly because the Egyptians understood that in these unclean people reigned the saturnine and asinine impression, for the interaction that they had with this species. Some wished them driven out from their borders, leaving the idol of the golden ass in their hands—the which, among all the gods, appears most favorably to this people and consequently to all the others enemy and snare, like Saturn to all the other planets.[78]

---

ruled from 359 B.C.E. until his death by poisoning in 338), is described in section 11 (1969, 5:29, 31). The ass is transcoded negatively in section 31, where Plutarch notes that "since they hated Ochus most of all the Persian kings because he was a detested and abominable ruler, they nicknamed him 'the Ass'; and he remarked, 'But this Ass will feast upon your Bull,' and slaughtered Apis" (1969, 5:77). Aelian's *De natura animalium* [On the Characteristics of Animals], 10:28, also treats this episode within a brief dissertation on the lore of the ass (1958, 2:323, 325). For Aelian's excellent history of the Apis, see 11:10 (1958, 2:365–373).

77. In all likelihood, Sebasto's remarks are based on Apion's criticism of the Jews, to which Josephus (*Ad Apionem*) responded; see Hata (1987, 181).

78. Bruno's defense of Saturn despite its conventionally "evil" planetary influence is perhaps best explained by Ernst Cassirer: "every constellation contains within its circle a multiplicity of different, even of contradictory possibili-

Whence staying with their own worship, leaving aside other Egyptian festivities, they were celebrating their own Saturn, manifested in the idol of the ass and the sabbaths,[79] and their own Luna, in the new moon[80]—so that not only one, but perhaps all of the Sefirot may be asinine to Jewish cabalists.

SAULINO: You say many authentic things, many nearly authentic, others resembling the authentic—some contrary to authentic and confirmed histories. Hence you voice some true and good views, but you say nothing truly and well, despising and ridiculing this hallowed people from whom is derived all the light that has come down to the world today, and who promise to give it for so many centuries. So you persevere in your thinking about treating the ass and asininity as something for mockery; though whatever the state may have been for the Persians, Greeks, and Latins, it wasn't necessarily something vile for the Egyptians and Hebrews. There where there is falsehood and deceit, among the others, that divine asinine cult had its origin via force and violence, and was not rather ordered by reason and based on the principle of choice.

SEBASTO: *Verbi gratia,* force, violence, reason, and choice of Ochus.

SAULINO: I'm speaking of divine inspiration, natural goodness and human intelligence. But before we come to the completion of this argument, consider a moment whether these Hebrews and other participants and consorts of their sanctimoniousness have ever had or should have had or held the idea and influence of the asses in

---

ties of life, and it leaves the final choice among them open to the will. Saturn is not only the demon of inertia and of unfruitful, self-indulgent melancholy; he is also the genius of intellectual observation and meditation, of intelligence and contemplation. . . . Thus, Saturn becomes the foe of all those who lead vulgar lives; but the friend and protector of those who try to develop the deepest virtues that lie within him—those who surrender themselves with their whole souls to divine contemplation" (1963, 113).

79. See Tacitus, *Histories* 5:4 (1931, 181).

80. See Plutarch's *De Iside et Osiride,* section 43 (1969, 5:105).

contempt. See whether the patriarch Jacob, celebrating the nativity and lineage of his progeny—and also the forefathers of the twelve tribes—with the figure of the twelve beasts[81] dared to leave out the ass. You have not noted how he made Reuben a ram, Simon a bear, Levi a horse, Judah a lion, Zebulun a whale, Dan a serpent, Gad a fox, Asher a cow, Naphtali a stag, Joseph a sheep, Benjamin a wolf; so he made the sixth-born Issachar an ass, whispering in his ear as testament this fine news and mysterious prophecy: "Issachar, strong ass, who rests between the boundaries, has found good rest and fertile land, has submitted his robust shoulders to the burden, and they are destined for tributary service."[82]

These twelve sacred progeny correspond, from here below to the twelve high signs of the zodiac that are in the belt of the firmament, as the prophet Balaam saw and declared when from the eminent position of a hill he discerned them in twelve fixed and distinct encampments on the plain, saying "Blessed and consecrated people of Israel, you are stars, you are the twelve signs put in such beautiful order like many noble flocks. Thus promised your Jehovah that He would multiply the seed of your great father Abraham like the stars of heaven, that is, according to the reason of the twelve signs of the zodiac, which come to be signified by the twelve names of twelve beasts."[83] Here you see how that enlightened prophet, having to bless them on the earth, went before them mounted on an ass; by the voice of the ass he was instructed in the divine will, with the strength

81. Genesis 49:1–27 recounts Jacob's prophecies concerning his sons and makes explicit only a few of the identifications Bruno cites: Judah, lion (v. 9); Issachar, ass (v. 14); Dan, serpent (v. 17); Naphtali, hind (v. 21); and Benjamin, wolf (v. 27).
82. Genesis 49: 14–15.
83. Balaam's story is told in Numbers 22–24; despite Balak's insistence that Balaam curse the Israelites, the prophet can only bless them (Numbers 24:5, 8–9).

of the ass he came there to them, from above the ass he spreads his hands toward the tents and blessed that holy and consecrated people of God to make evident that the saturnine asses and other beasts that have influence from the Sefirot, from the ass archetype, by means of the natural and prophetic ass had to be participants in great blessings.

CORIBANTE: *Multa igitur asinorum genera* [Many indeed are the species of the ass]: golden, archetypal, protective, celestial, intelligible, angelic, animal, prophetic, human, bestial, amiable, ethical, civil, and frugal; *vel* [or perhaps] essential, subsistential, metaphysical, physical, hypostatical, knowledgeable, mathematical, logical and moral; *vel* supernal, intermediate and infernal; *vel* intelligible, sensible, and fantastic; *vel* ideal, natural and knowledgeable; *vel ante multa, in multis et post multa* [or perhaps before many, in many, and after many (more)].[84] Now follow, because *paulatim*, gradatim *atque pedentim* [little by little, step by step and foot by foot], you begin to understand me more clearly, loftily and profoundly.

SAULINO: Concerning ourselves, then, it must not seem strange to you that asininity is placed in a celestial seat among the distribution of the chairs that are in the supernal part of this corporeal world and universe, given that this world must be correspondent and recognizing in it an analogy to the superior world.

CORIBANTE: *Ita contiguus hic illi mundus, ut omnis eius virtus inde gubernetur* [This world touches so close on that (world) that each of its virtues is governed thence]—as the prince of the Peripatetics

---

84. Gentile remarks that this is analogous to *ante rem, in re*, and *post rem*, "come si disse da Alberto Magno e S. Tommaso l'universale in sé (o nella mente di Dio), l'universale realizzato negli individui, e l'universale pensato quindi dalla mente umana" [as stated by Albertus Magnus and Saint Thomas, the universal in itself (or in the mind of God), the universal realized in the individual, and the universal thought from the human mind] (1958, 871).

proclaimed further, in the beginning of the first of the *Meteorologica*[85] meditations.

SEBASTO: O what ampullas, O what fine-sounding words are yours, O learned and high-sounding Signor Coribante.

CORIBANTE: *Ut libet* [How pleasing this is].

SEBASTO: But permit him to proceed to the proposition, and don't interrupt!

CORIBANTE: *Proh* [Phooey]!

SAULINO: Nothing is closer and more kindred to the truth than knowledge—which must be distinguished, as it is distinct in itself, in two kinds: that is, the superior and the inferior. The former is above created truth and is that same uncreated truth, the first cause; such that by it true things are true, and all that which is, is truly such as it is.[86] The latter, inferior truth which neither makes things true nor is itself true, but inclines toward, is produced, shaped, and informed by true things, and reflects them not in truth, but in quality and likeness: because in our mind, where is the knowledge of gold, one does not really find gold, but only its quality and likeness.

Therefore, there is one sort of truth which is the cause of things, and one finds it above all things; another sort one finds in things and is part of things; and another third and final sort, which exists after

---

85. Coribante takes his cue from "al mondo superiore" and ignores Saulino's point of locating "asininity" among the celestial "seats," instead seizing another pedantic opportunity. Adolfo Wagner's 1830 edition of Bruno's vernacular works corrected the reference of prior editions to *Meteorologica*, and Gentile questions whether "Forse W. ha fatto bene a non correggere, perché B. suole spropositare i suoi pedanti" [Perhaps W. has done well not to correct it, for B. might be making his pedants speak nonsense] (1958, 871n2). See Aristotle, *Meteorologica* 1:2, particularly the description of the "celestial element" (1952, 9).

86. See the opening of the second dialogue of *De la causa*, where Arelio Dicson asks Teofilo if he believes "that the man who knows the things thus caused and ruled by a principle, knows the cause and principle? *Teo.* Not at all easily the proximate cause and principle; and with great difficulty, even in their vestige, the first cause and principle" (Lindsay 1962, 77).

things and because of things. The first is called "cause," the second "matter," the third "knowledge."[87] The truth of the first variety exists in the ideal world archetype signified by one of the Sefirot; that of the second variety exists in the first seat where the pivot of heaven (to us supreme) is located; the third variety exists in the indicated seat of this corporeal heaven that closely influences our brains— where ignorance, insanity, and asininity are, and whence Ursa Major has been expelled. As then real and natural truth is examined by conceptual truth—the latter has the former for its object, and that former through its kind has this latter for its subject—so it is necessary that this latter be nearby and joined to the dwelling-place of that former.

SEBASTO: You put it well that, according to the order of nature, truth and ignorance or asininity are closely aligned—as sometimes the object, the act, and the power are united. But now clarify why you want to yoke and ally ignorance or asininity [with the truth], rather than knowledge or understanding. It is to be expected that ignorance and madness must be neighbors, and like cohabitants of the truth, from it they must remain at an entirely remote distance, so they must be joined to falsehood, as matters belonging to a contrary order.

SAULINO: Because wisdom created without ignorance or madness, and consequently without the asininity which signifies them and is one and the same with them, cannot comprehend the truth; and hence it is necessary that it be a mediator; because as in the act through which the extremes or ends concur—that is, object and power—so in asininity concur truth and knowledge, called by us "wisdom."

87. Bruno similarly describes cause, matter, and knowledge, respectively, in *De monade, numero et figura* (1591): "Primum est absolutum supra, extra, et ante res. Secundum adnexum rebus, in rebus, cum rebus. Tertium post res, infra res, abstractum a rebus" (1.2.367). Cf. the divisions in *De imaginum* (2.3.94–95).

SEBASTO: Briefly explain the cause.

SAULINO: Because our knowledge is ignorance, or because it is neither knowledge of anything nor the understanding of any truth, or because even if there is some entrance to that [truth], the door may not come open except by means of ignorance—which is simultaneously path, gatekeeper, and gate. Now if wisdom perceives truth through ignorance, it perceives consequently through foolishness, and consequently through asininity. Hence whoever has such knowledge has that of the ass and shares in that idea.

SEBASTO: Now show how your assumptions can be true, for I wish to concede your inferences entirely: I have no problem with holding that whoever is ignorant, inasmuch as he is ignorant, is a fool; and whoever is a fool, in as much as he is foolish, is an ass; and therefore every ignorance is asininity.

SAULINO: Others foster the contemplation of truth by means of rational study and education, through the force of the acting intellect that thrusts into the mind, awakening the inner light. And these individuals are rare; whence the poet says:

Pauci, quos ardens evexit ad aethera virtus.[88]

Still others turn in the direction of ignorance and strain themselves to arrive there. And of these some are affected by what is called ignorance of simple negation (those people neither know, nor presume to know); others by what is called ignorance of wicked disposition (and so the less they know while imbibing false information, the more they think they know)—these, to be informed of the truth, require twice as much effort, namely to cast off the one contrary aspect and to learn the other. Others [are affected] by what is cele-

---

88. Virgil, *Aeneid*, Book Six, a truncation of lines 129–131. Virgil's passage refers to the few men, favored by the gods, capable of ascending again from the underworld to the "upper air" (*aethera*) of the world above. Bruno reads this metaphorically as the attempt of individuals like himself to achieve (re)union with the divine.

brated as divine acquisition, and in this category are those who neither prefer nor think to know, who furthermore, being thought most ignorant by others, are truly learned thanks to humbling themselves to that most glorious asininity and madness. Of these some are natural, such as those who walk with their own rational light, with which they deny—with the light of sense and reason— every light of sense and reason; some others walk or, to put it better, they lead themselves with the lantern of faith, win the intellect of Him who rises above them and purposefully rectifies and guides them. And truly these are those who cannot blunder, because they don't walk according to their own fallacious understanding, but according to the infallible light of supernal intelligence. These, these are truly qualified and predestined to arrive at the Jerusalem of the Beatitude[89] and the unsealed vision of the divine truth: for on them mounts One without which rider none conducts himself worthily.[90]

SEBASTO: Now behold how the types of ignorance and asininity are distinguished, and how I come little by little to deign to concede asininity to be a necessary and divine virtue, without which the world would be lost, and by which the whole world is saved.

SAULINO: Hear, on this matter, a principle for another more particular distinction. That which unites our intellect—which is in wisdom—to the truth, which is the intelligible object, is one species

89. Cf. the simplicity, or "asininity" praised and rewarded in the Beatitudes, Matthew 5:1–12.

90. Undoubtedly thinking himself an exemplar, Bruno in the third dialogue of the *Eroici furori* praises such intellectual "overreaching": "Others, because of a custom or habit of contemplation, and because they are naturally endowed with a lucid and intellectual spirit, when under the impact of an internal stimulus and spontaneous fervor spurred on by the love of divinity, justice, truth and glory, by the fire of desire and inspired purpose, they make keen their senses and in the sulphurous cognitive faculty enkindle a rational flame which raises their vision beyond the ordinary. And these do not go about speaking and acting as mere receptacles and instruments, but as chief inventors and authors"(Memmo 1964, 107–108).

of ignorance, according to the cabalists and certain mystical theologians; a different species, according to the Pyrrhonians, Skeptics,[91] and others like them; yet another, according to Christian theologians, among whom the Tarsan proceeds to extol it the more, when to the judgment of all the world it passes for greater foolishness.[92] The first type always denies—whence it is called negative ignorance, which never dares to affirm. The second type always doubts, and never dares to determine or to define. For the third type all the principles have been recognized, approved, and with certain argument manifested without proof and likelihood. The first is denoted by the ass's colt, transient and wandering; the second by an ass that is fixed between two roads, from the middle of which it never moves, not being able to resolve along which of the two it must direct its steps; the third by the ass and its offspring, carrying the redeemer of the world on their back—where the ass, according to what the sacred doctors teach, is a type of the Jewish people, and the colt of the Gentile people who, like an ecclesiastical daughter, is delivered by the mother synagogue; hence these belong to the same generation, proceeding from the father of the believers, Abraham.[93] These three types of ignorance, like three branches, converge at a single trunk—in which asininity influences from the archetype—and which is resolute and planted upon the roots of the ten Sefirot.

CORIBANTE: O good sense! These are not rhetorical persuasions, nor catalogued sophisms, nor topical probabilities, but apodeictic demonstrations: through which the ass is not so vile an animal as is

---

91. Bruno's term *efettici* comes from the Greek *efeptikoi*, designating the followers of Pyrrho of Elis (c. 365–275 B.C.E.) and their dogma of *epoche* (suspension of judgment). See Gentile (1958, 45n1).

92. Paul—formerly Saul of Tarsus—defends his preaching in 1 Corinthians 1:18.

93. See Michel, "The Ass in Palestine and Judaism" (1967, 283–285).

commonly believed, but is rather of a far more heroic and divine condition.

SEBASTO: It isn't necessary that you wear yourself out any more coming around to conclude that which I asked you to define for me; for as you've satisfied Coribante, so also from the terms you've laid down each good listener can be satisfied easily. But please, now help me understand the reasons behind the wisdom, which consists of ignorance and asininity *iuxta* the second mode; that is, with what reason the Pyrrhonians, Skeptics, and other philosophical scholars are participants in asininity; because I have no doubt about the first and third types, that are themselves very exalted, remote from the senses and most clear, such that no eye exists that cannot see them.

SAULINO: I'll move quickly to the object of your question; but first I want you to note that the first and third modes of foolishness and asininity converge in a certain manner into one, and hence they equally dangle from an incomprehensible and ineffable principle to constitute that knowledge that is the discipline of the disciplines, doctrine of the doctrines, and art of the arts. Of their knowledge I wish to tell you how, with little or no study and without effort, each who wants or has wanted has been able to and will be able to attain it. Those holy doctors and enlightened rabbis saw and judged that the proud and presumptuous sages of the world, who had confidence in their own individual genius and with reckless and swollen presumption had the daring to raise themselves to the knowledge of divine secrets and the innermost parts of deity—no different from those who built the Tower of Babel—have been confused and scattered, themselves having shut the passage whence they became less able [to attain] to the divine wisdom and vision of the eternal truth. What did they do? Which side did they choose? They halted their steps, folded or ceased to use their arms, shut their eyes, banished every care and study of their own, censured every human thought, denied every natural sentiment; and in the end they considered themselves asses. And those who were not [previously] were transformed into this animal: they raised, distended, pointed, enlarged, and magnified their ears; and all the powers of the spirit they carried forward and united into hearing, listening only and believing, like that of whom it is said, *In auditu auris obedivit mihi* [Incline thine ear unto me and listen].[94] There concentrating and captivating the vegetative, sensitive and intellective faculties, they had manacled their five fingers in a hoof, so that they could not, as did Adam, reach their hands to pick the forbidden fruit from the tree of knowledge—for which they came to be deprived of the fruits of the tree of life—or like Prometheus (who is a metaphor for the same concept) reach their hands to steal the fire of Jove, to kindle the flame of their rational powers.[95]

Therefore, our divine asses, deprived of individual opinion and emotion, arrive at understanding only as it is whispered to their ears from the revelations—either by the gods or by their priests—and consequently they regulate themselves by no other law but their very own. Hence they turn neither to the right nor to the left, except according to the lesson and reason given by the halter or bit that holds them by the neck or by the mouth, not walking except as they are directed. They have enlarged the lips, loosened the jaws, thickened the teeth such that, though the repast placed before them be hard, thorny, bitter, and difficult to digest, it cannot fail to be accommodated to their palate. Afterward they feed on more coarse and vulgar victuals than any other beast on the shell of the earth, all by

94. Variations on this formula appear, for example, in Psalms 17:6, 45:10, 71:2, 78:1, 88:2; Proverbs 2:2, 4:20; Isaiah 37:17, 55:3; and Daniel 9:18.

95. Unreflective dominance is to Bruno the ultimate asininity. The patriarchal authority of the monotheistic God, or of the gods of antiquity's pantheons (specifically attacked through the self-revelations of Zeus in the *Spaccio*), is obstinately inflexible. For Bruno, then, Adam and Prometheus are not archetypal thieves, but archetypal liberators.

way of arriving at that most vile baseness by which they are made capable of more magnificent exaltation, *iuxta* this: *Omnis qui se humilitat exaltabitur* [All who humble themselves will be exalted].[96]

SEBASTO: But I'd like to understand how this nasty beast could be able to distinguish whether he who rides on him is God or devil, is a man or another beast not much greater or lesser—if the most certain thing that he must have is that he is an ass and wants to be an ass, cannot make a better life nor have better habits than those of the ass, must not expect a better end than that of an ass, nor is it possible, suitable, and worthy that he have glory other than an ass's?

SAULINO: Faithful is He who doesn't allow that they be tempted beyond what they can bear: He knows His own, He keeps and maintains His own as His own, and they cannot be taken from Him. O holy ignorance, O divine insanity, O superhuman asininity! That rapt, profound and contemplative Areopagite, writing to Caius, affirms that ignorance is a most perfect knowledge,[97] as if by extension he were endeavoring to say that asininity is a divinity. The erudite Areopagite, quite inebriated by this divine nectar, testifies in his *Soliloquies*[98] that ignorance rather than knowledge leads to God, and knowledge rather than ignorance merits perdition. In figure of this he determines that the redeemer of the world entered into Jerusalem with the legs and feet of asses, signifying anagogically in this service

---

96. Matthew 23:12; Luke 14:11, 18:14. Cf. 2 Chronicles 34:27.

97. Bruno similarly makes reference to Pseudo-Dionysius at the close of the Fourth Dialogue of *Gli eroici furori*: "For this reason the more profound and divine theologians say God is honored and adored more by silence than by words, and that to see him better one must close one's eyes to the species represented than open them. This is why the negative theology of Pythagoras and Dionysius is so highly renowned above the demonstrative theology of Aristotle and the schoolmen" (Memmo 1964, 257); see also Gentile (1958, 879n4). On the Areopagite's *Celestial Hierarchy*, a classification of the nine orders of spirits that bears many similarities to Bruno's configuration in the *Cabala*, see Thorndike (1923, 1:546–547).

98. See Augustine, *Soliloquies* (1910, 41–42).

what is to be verified in the triumphant city; as the psalm-singing prophet says, *Non in fortitudine equi voluntatem habebit, neque in tibiis viri beneplacitum erit ei.*[99]

CORIBANTE: *Supple tu: Sed in fortitudine et tibiis asinae et pulli filii coniugalis* [You fill in the blanks: but in strength and legs the she-ass and her colts are coequal].

SAULINO: Now, coming to show you how with nothing but asininity we can set out towards and come near that high vantage point, I desire that you understand and know that there is no possible meditation in the world better than that which denies every knowledge and every learning and judgment of truth, such that the ultimate knowledge is the assured assessment that one cannot know anything and does not know anything, consequently to recognize that one can be nothing but an ass and is nothing but an ass; to which end came the Socratics, Platonists, Epicureans, Pyrrhonians, and such others who didn't have ears so small, lips so delicate, and tails so short, that they themselves could not see them.

SEBASTO: I beg you, Saulino, not to proceed to another point by confirmation and declaration of this today: we've understood much for the present; besides, you see it's time for supper, and the matter requires more extensive discourse. Thus may it please you (if it's all the same also to Coribante) to meet tomorrow for the elucidation of this proposition; and I'll bring Onorio with me, who recalls having been an ass, and yet is Pythagorean in every sense.[100] Besides, he holds his own grand discourses with which, perhaps, he'll be able to explain to us some proposition.

SAULINO: That will be fine, and I welcome it, because he will alleviate my fatigue.

99. Psalm 147:10: "[The Lord] does not delight in the strength of a horse and takes no pleasure in a runner's speed."
100. See "The Wisdom of Asininity."

CORIBANTE: *Ego quoque huic adstipulor sententiae* [I also assent to this judgment], and the hour has arrived when I must dismiss my pupils, toward the end that *propria revistant hospitia, proprios lares* [they revisit their own proper lodging, their own hearths ("household gods")]. So then, *si lubet,* until such time as this matter be settled, I will present myself daily here to be with you promptly at these same times.

SAULINO: Nor will I fail to do the same.

SEBASTO: Then let's go.

END OF THE FIRST DIALOGUE

Second Dialogue [First Part]

Interlocutors: Sebasto, Onorio, Coribante, Saulino

SEBASTO: And you remember having carried the load?

ONORIO: The load, the burden—and "drawing the cudgel"[101] sometimes. First I was in the service of a gardener, hitched up to carry manure from the city of Thebes to the orchard near the city walls, and to return afterwards with cabbage, lettuce, onions, watermelons, parsnips, radishes, and other such things from the orchard to the city. Then [I was given over] to a coalman, who bought me from the first and who kept me alive very few days.

SEBASTO: How is it possible that you have memory of this?

ONORIO: I'll tell you then. Grazing above a certain steep and stony bank, led by the eagerness of chomping a thistle that was growing somewhat further down toward the precipice, from which I thought I could extend my neck without peril, I turned in spite of every

101. Bruno's pun derives from the ambiguity of "*tirare,*" literally "to pull," or metaphorically "to suffer," as in "*tirarla con i denti,*" "to endure hardships."

pang of conscience and instinct of native reason toward the task of clambering . . . and fell from the high cliff, whence my master realized that he had purchased me for the crows.

Bereft of my corporeal prison, I became a limbless, wandering spirit; I came to consider how, in terms of my spiritual essence, I was no different in genus nor in species from all the other spirits who had transmigrated from their animal and corruptible bodies; and I saw how in the genus of corporeal matter Fate not only fails to differentiate the human body from the ass, and the body of the animals from the body of things thought to be without soul, but even in the genus of spiritual matter Fate treats the asinine soul no differently than the human, and the spirit that constitutes those so-called animals than what is found in all things: as all humours are one humour in essence, all portions of the air are one air in essence, all spirits are of the Amphitrite of one spirit, and to that they all return.[102] Now after I was detained in such a state [of transition] for some time; behold that

> *Lethaeum ad fluvium Deus evocat agmine magno,*
> *Scilicet immemores supera ut convexa revisant,*
> *Rursus et incipiant in corpora velle reverti.*[103]

---

102. This is because each soul is originally assigned its own star by the creator, according to Plato's *Timaeus* (1961, 1170–1171). In *The Praise of Folly* Erasmus recalls "that never-sufficiently-to-be-praised Pythagorean cock, who in his own person had occupied many shapes, as of a philosopher, a man, a woman, a king, a lowly subject, a fish, a horse, a frog, even I think a sponge— after which he concluded that no animal was more wretched than man because all the others were content with the limits imposed by nature" (1989, 34–35), and Erasmus's reference is to Lucian's dialogue, *The Dream, or the Cock,* in which Micyllus is amazed to hear the fowl speak and identify himself as the former Pythagoras (1969, 179, 181).

103. Virgil, *Aeneid,* 6:749–751: "God calls all of them forth in long procession to Lethe River, and this he does so that when they again visit the sky's vault they may be without memory, and a wish to re-enter bodily life may dawn" (1956, 169).

Then, taking refuge from the fortunate fields without sipping from the waters of the swift Lethe, among the masses of whom Mercury was principal guide, I made pretense of drinking from that humour in the others' presence: but I did no more than approach it and touch it with my lips, so that the overseers were deceived because it was possible to satisfy them by seeing my mouth and chin wet. I took the cleanest path to air through the Gate of Horn,[104] and leaving the depths behind me and underfoot, I found myself on Mount Parnassus—it is no fable that its fountain, Caballinus, is property of the father Apollo, consecrated to the Muses his daughters.[105] There by the power and decree of fate I returned to being an ass, but without losing my intelligible faculties, of which the animal spirit did not remain widowed and empty: by force of which power the form and substance of two wings emerged from me on one side and the other, more than sufficient to raise my corporeal weight as far as the stars. I appeared there and was called not simply ass but flying ass or the Pegasean horse.[106] Thence I was made executor of many orders from the provident Jove, served Bellerophon, experienced many renowned and most honorable pieces of good luck, and finally

104. Virgil, *Aeneid*, 6:893–894.

105. Onorio's description here is replete with errors, and it seems most likely that Bruno is intentionally confusing the information related by his interlocutor. The spring Caballinus, also known as Hippocrene, began to flow following a stroke from the hoof of Pegasus (Ovid 1976, 1:257); it, however, is located on Mount Helicon in Boeotia, not on Mount Parnassus, which is found in Phocis. Onorio is also mistaken in believing the nine Muses were the daughters of Apollo, rather than of Zeus and Mnemosyne (Apollodorus 1921, 1:17).

106. Moving in the opposite direction, note Minerva's request to Jove in the *Spaccio* that Pegasus, "leaving his twenty brilliant spots of light, should together with Curiosity go to the equine fount, now for a long time confused, ruined, and contaminated by oxen, pigs, and donkeys. And let him see whether by means of his kicks and bites he can do enough to avenge that place against such a villainous multitude, so that the Muses may see the water of the fount settled and restored and may not disdain to return there, and there establish their schools and promotions" (Imerti 1964, 220).

was assumed into the heavens near the confines of Andromeda and the Swan [Cygnus] on one side, and the Fishes [Pisces] and Aquarius on the other.

SEBASTO: Please answer me somewhat, before making me understand these things more in detail. By experience and memory of the fact, then, do you esteem as true the opinion of the Pythagoreans, Druids, Sadducees,[107] and others similar concerning that continuous metempsychosis—namely the transformation and transmigration of all souls?

ONORIO: Indeed, sir, it's most certain.

SEBASTO: So you maintain steadfastly that the soul of the human is no different in substance than that of the beasts? And they do not vary except in representation?

ONORIO: That of the human is the same in specific and generic essence as that of flies, sea oysters, and plants, and of anything whatsoever that one finds animated or having a soul, as no body lacks a more or less lively communication of spirit within itself. Now such spirit, according to fate or providence, decree or fortune, links up now with one species of body, now with another;[108] and by reason of the diversity of constitutions and limbs, it comes to have diverse degrees and capabilities of mind and functions. Therefore, that spirit or soul that was in the spider—and there has its industry and the claws and limbs in like number, quantity, and form—the

107. Caesar, describing Druidic education in *De bello gallico,* identifies belief in metempsychosis as its foundation: "The cardinal doctrine which they seek to teach is that souls do not die, but after death pass from one to another; and this belief, as the fear of death is thereby cast aside, they hold to be the greatest incentive to valour" (1970, 339). Concerning the Sadducees and reincarnation, see Matthew 16:12–14, Mark 8:27–28 or Luke 9:18–19 (in the first reference for warning about Sadducee doctrine, and in all three for the question of Jesus being an avatar of one of the prophets of Jewish history).

108. Ovid, *Metamorphoses,* 15:167–168.

same connected to human generation acquires other intelligence, other implements, attitudes and skills.

I conclude that if it were possible, or in fact came about, that the head of a serpent were to be formed or modified into the shape of a human head, and the chest were expanded to the extent satisfactory for such species, if the tongue were enlarged, the shoulders amplified, if the arms and hands were to branch out, and the legs sprouted from the place where the tail terminates; it would understand, would appear, would breathe, would speak, would operate and would walk as none other than a man because it would be none other than man. Conversely, the man would be none other than a serpent if he were to retract his arms and legs, like a stump, and his bones were to all converge in the formation of a spine, and were to viperize and suppress all the forms of limbs and the qualities of those behaviors.[109] Then he would have a more or less lively mind: in place of speaking, he would hiss; in place of walking, he would slither; in place of building a home, he would dig a hollow (and not a room, but a hole, would suit him); and as he was formerly with one kind, now he is with another kind of limbs, organs, powers and actions— as from the same craftsman, inspired in different ways by a particular collection of materials and equipped with different tools, designs of different inspiration appear and different products result.

Hence you can imagine it possible that many animals have more understanding and a much more enlightened intellect than man (as it's no joke what Moses pronounced about the serpent, whom he called wisest among all the other beasts of the earth);[110] but through

109. The transformation of Cadmus into a serpent is described in passing by Apollodorus (1921, 335) but is elaborated considerably in 4:576–580 of Ovid's *Metamorphoses*. Dante combines the transformation of Cadmus with that of Arethusa in 25:94–135 of the *Inferno*.

110. Genesis 3:1.

lack of limbs he becomes inferior, as by wealth and gift of those same limbs one is to him [the serpent] such a degree superior. And that such be the truth, consider its subtlety a bit and examine within yourself what would be, if, supposing that man had twice the brains he has, and the active intellect would shine so much more clearly, and with all that his hands would become transformed into the shape of two feet, all the rest remaining in its ordinary whole; tell me, how might the conduct of mankind be unaltered? How could the families and leagues of such people, any more than of horses, deer, pigs, be established and continued without being devoured by innumerable species of beasts, being thus subject to greater and more certain ruin? And consequently where would be the institutions of knowledge, the inventions of disciplines, the congregations of citizens, the structures of the buildings and other things in great quantity that signify human grandeur and excellence, and make man truly the victor over the other species? All this, if you look cautiously, refers primarily not so much to the style of mind, as to that of the hand, organ of the organs.[111]

SEBASTO: What will you say about the apes and bears that—if you don't wish to say they have a hand—have no worse tool than the hand?

ONORIO: They don't have a constitution ample enough for such genius, because the universal intelligence, in similar and many other animals, due to the bulk or lewdness of their material constitution, cannot inculcate so much power of understanding into such spirits. However, the comparison made must be understood within the genus of the cleverest animals.

SEBASTO: Doesn't the parrot have his organ attuned to uttering al-

---

111. Onorio is distorting Aristotle, *De anima*, 3:8:432a: "The soul, then acts like a hand; for the hand is an instrument which employs instruments, and in the same way the mind is a form which employs forms, and sense is a form which employs the forms of sensible objects" (1964, 181).

most any kind of articulate speech? Now why with such hard work can it speak so little, furthermore, without understanding what it says?

ONORIO: Because it lacks apprehension, retention adaptable and of the same quality as that of man, but conforms exactly to that of its species; for which reason it has no need for others to teach it about flying, searching for food, differentiating nourishment from poison, breeding, building a nest, changing habitations, and warding off the outrages of weather, seeing to the necessities of life no less well—and sometimes better and more easily—than man.

SEBASTO: This, say the scholars, not being by intellect or by discourse, but by natural instinct.

ONORIO: Make those scholars speak: is such natural instinct sense or intellect? If it is sense, is it internal or external? Now, not being external, as is evident, they say that according to that internal sense [the parrots] have insights, know-how, skills, foresights, and quick thoughts concerning not only present, but also future occasions far better than man.

SEBASTO: They are moved by unerring intelligence.

ONORIO: The latter, if it is a natural and related principle applicable to related and individual operations, cannot be universal and extrinsic, but particular and intrinsic, and is consequently the power of the soul and master in the breast of that [creature].

SEBASTO: You don't mean, then, that it is the universal intelligence that moves [it]?

ONORIO: I say that the efficient, universal intelligence is one of all, and that it moves and gives understanding; furthermore, in all it is the particular intelligence through which they are moved, enlightened, and led to understand; and this is multiplied according to the number of individuals. As visual potency is multiplied according to the number of eyes, moved and illuminated generally by a fire, by a lamp, by a sun: thus the intellective power is multiplied according to the number of subjects sharing in spirit, over all of whom shines an intellectual sun. So, therefore, above all the animals is an acting sense, namely that which makes everything feel and through which all creatures are sensitive in action; and one acting intellect, namely that which makes everything understand and through which all creatures are intellectual in action; and at hand there are as many senses and as many particular passive or potential intellects as there are subjects, and there are accordingly as many specific and numeral grades of constitutions, as there are specific and numeral constitutions of body.

SEBASTO: Say what you please, and understand it as you wish; but where the animals are concerned, I don't want to get into the habit of calling that instinct rational intellect.

ONORIO: Now if you can't call it sense, you need to imagine some other cognitive power in the animals beyond the sensory and intellective power.

SEBASTO: I will say that it is an efficacy of inner senses.

ONORIO: Yet such efficacy enables us to say that it is the human intellect; whence man naturally discourses, and it is in our freedom to name as it pleases us, and to limit the definitions and names as we please, as did Averroës.[112] And it's also in my freedom to say that your understanding isn't understanding, and whatever you do, to think it is not by intellect, but by instinct; since the works of the other animals more worthy than yours (like those of the bees and the

112. Averroës rationalizes this when he writes, "It is self-evident that things have essences and attributes which determine the specific acts of each existent and through which the essences, names, and definitions of things differ. If each existent did not have its specific act, it would not have a specific name nor a definition, and all things would be one [and the same] thing and not one [and the same] thing" (Kogan 1985, 107). Rather than Averroës's participating in a cavalier method of semiosis, as Onorio suggests, the philosopher recognized that if "there are no longer formal structures of reflexive and relational powers constituting and disclosing the *ousiae* of individual particulars, then there can be no distinctive content in things to formulate in definitions" (Kogan 1985, 125).

ants) do not have the reputation of intellect, but of instinct. Or I'll say as well that the instinct of those little creatures is more worthy than your intellect.

SEBASTO: For now let's leave off discussing this more thoroughly and return to us. Do you mean then that as diverse and contrary figures are formed from one common wax or other material, so all bodies are made from the same corporeal matter, and all spirits from the same spiritual substance?

ONORIO: Most certainly; and add to this that due to various reasons, habits, orders, measures and numbers of body and spirit there exist various dispositions and constitutions that yield diverse organs and make up the various genera of things.

SEBASTO: To me that seems not very far off, nor does it abolish from this opinion that prophetic dogma, when it says that everything is in the hand of the universal cause; as the same mud in the hand of the same potter—that with the wheel of this dizziness of the stars comes to be composed and decomposed according to the vicissitudes of the generation and corruption of things—is now an honored vessel, now a contemptuous vessel of the same stuff.[113]

113. Sebasto is reiterating fundamental Aristotelian arguments concerning original causes and the transformation of matter. The archetypal sense of cause in *De generatione et corruptione* 2:8 is threefold, including matter, form, and "originative source" (1958, 436). The *Metaphysics* (1:3) notes the four fundamental distinctions between causes: substance / essence, matter / substratum, the "source of the change," and "the purpose and the good" (1952, 501); the *Physics* (2:3) identifies the four respectively as material cause, formal cause, efficient cause ("the agent that produces the effect and starts the material on its way to the product"), and final cause (1957, 131). Bruno's *De la causa, principio e uno* extends this by differentiating between extrinsic and intrinsic cause: "I call a cause extrinsic when as an efficient it does not form a part of things composed and things produced. I call a cause intrinsic insofar as it does not operate around matter and outside it. . . . Hence a cause is extrinsic through being distinct from the substance and essence of its effects, and because its being does not resemble that of things capable of generation and decay, although it embraces them" (Lindsay 1962, 82–83). Sebasto's analogy of "the hand of the

ONORIO: Many of the more learned among the rabbis have understood and declared so. Thus it was understood of Him who said "Thou wilt save men and beasts according as thou wilt multiply thy mercy"; such is made clear in the metamorphosis of Nebuchadnezzar.[114] Hence some Sadducees wondered whether the Baptist was Elias, not, indeed, on account of the same body, but on account of the same spirit in another body.[115] Some people expect the execution of divine justice in precisely such a revivification, according to the emotions and actions they have exercised in another body.

SEBASTO: Please, let's not reason more of this, because unfortunately I'm beginning to like your opinion, and to judge it more than credible; and I want to keep myself in that faith in which I have been instructed by my forefathers and teachers.[116] And speak of events that are historical, or fantastic, or metaphorical, and leave alone demonstrations and authorities—which I believe are more quickly twisted by you than by others.

ONORIO: You're quite right, my brother. Besides, I must needs return to complete what I had started to tell you, if you don't suspect that

efficient universal" to the "hand of the potter" recalls Aristotelian speculation on the *primum mobile* (e.g., *Metaphysics* 12:7 [1952, 602]) and may allude as well to Romans 9:20.

114. Daniel 4:29. King Nebuchadnezzar is shown the error of his "bestially" obstinate, prideful ways in Daniel 4:26–37.

115. See Jesus' words to his disciples and the subsequent acknowledgment of his popular identification with Elias, John the Baptist, Jeremiah, and the like in Matthew 16:12–17.

116. Sebasto refers to his Christian heritage, though his provisional acceptance of Onorio's dissertation on metempsychosis—in the context of Alfonso Ingegno's analysis of Bruno's antichristian doctrines—suggests that in the *Cabala del cavallo pegaseo* the dialogist himself was pursuing "il criterio per giudicare correttamente della fonte dell'ispirazione ricevuta, per decidere dell'origine divina o demonica di tale ispirazione" [the criterion for correctly judging the source of received inspiration, for determining the divine or demonic origin of such inspiration] (1985, 25).

with this same subject I will come to subvert your mind and to trouble your honest conscience.

SEBASTO: No, no, certainly not, I'm listening to this more willingly than I have listened to a fable ever before.

ONORIO: If, then, you are not listening to me for quality of doctrine and discipline, listen to me for amusement.

Second Part of the [Second] Dialogue

SEBASTO: Don't you see Saulino and Coribante coming?

ONORIO: It's about time that they came. Better late than never, Saulino.

CORIBANTE: *Si tardus adventus, citior expeditio* [If the arrival was slow, the campaign was more swift].

SEBASTO: Thanks to your lingering you've missed some fine arguments, which I would wish repeated by Onorio.

ONORIO: No, please, for I'd regret it; instead let's pursue our theme— we'll discuss the other matter privately, at a more convenient time, as it will require much more discussion, and I wouldn't wish to interrupt the thread of my argument.

SAULINO: Yes, yes; so be it. Go right ahead.

ONORIO: Being, as I have already said, in the celestial region entitled to Pegasus the horse, by the command of fate it happened to me that through the conversion into lesser things (which caused a certain feeling that I acquired afterward, which is quite well described by the Platonist Plotinus),[117] as though inebriated by nectar, I was banished to being now a philosopher, now a poet, now a pedant, leaving

---

117. Onorio is referring to the "sympathy existing between souls" that in Plotinus's *Enneads* (4:8) is "explained by the fact that all souls are derived from the same principle from which the universal Soul also is derived. . . . [T]here is one Soul (the universal) and several souls (human souls)" (1918, 400).

behind my image in the heavens; to which seat I returned, at the times of my transmigrations, carrying back the memory of the species, which I had acquired while in corporeal habitation; and these I left there, as in a library, when it so happened that I had to return to some other terrestrial habitation.[118] Of these memorable species the latest are those that I had begun to absorb at the time of the life of Macedonian Philip, after I was engendered, as is believed, from the seed of Nichomachus.[119]

Here, after having been a disciple of Aristarchus,[120] Plato and others, I was promoted through the favor of my father—who was Philip's counselor—to being the pedant of Alexander the Great, under whom I entered into the presumption (although very learned in the humanist sciences, in which I was more distinguished than all of my predecessors) of being a natural philosopher, as it's ordinary in pedants always to be rash and presumptuous; and with this, the science of philosophy extinct, Socrates dead, Plato banished, and

118. Plotinus explains this "depositing" of memories in *Enneads* 4:12 (1918, 409).

119. Onorio is now recalling his incarnation as Aristotle, who at the age of seventeen (367 B.C.E.) studied in Athens at Plato's Academy during the early years of Philip II of Macedonia's reign (359–336 B.C.E.), until Plato's death in 348 B.C.E. In *Lives* (7:2), Plutarch reports that Philip, sensing his son Alexander's great potential, "sent for the most famous and learned of philosophers, Aristotle, and paid him a noble and appropriate tuition-fee. The city of Stageira, that is, of which Aristotle was a native, and which he had himself destroyed, he peopled again, and restored to it those of its citizens who were in exile or slavery" (1958, 241) in return for three years of tutoring for the future Alexander the Great. Aristotle's father was a Macedonian court physician named Nichomachus; the *Nichomachean Ethics*, however, are not named for the philosopher's father, but are "so called because Aristotle's son Nichomachus is said to have edited the work after his father's death" (1962, xii–xiii).

120. Again, this must represent either misinformation on Bruno's part or another indictment of Onorio as an intellectual, for both the grammarian and Homeric scholar Aristarchus of Samothrace (c. 217–145 B.C.E.) and the astronomer Aristarchus of Samos (c. 310–230 B.C.E.) postdate the death of Aristotle in 322 B.C.E. See Jaki (1975, 69n55).

others in various manners dispersed, I alone was one-eyed among the blind and easily gained the reputation not only of rhetorician, politician, logician—but even of philosopher.

Thence reporting the opinions of the ancients badly and foolishly, in such obscene manner that not even children and crazy old women would speak and understand as I described those gallant men understanding and speaking, I became cast as the reformer of that discipline about which I had no information. I was called the Prince of the Peripatetics; I taught in Athens in the Lyceum's porch where, according to the light—and to speak truthfully, according to the darkness that reigned within me—I comprehended and taught perversely about the nature of precepts and substance of things, I raved in more of the same delirium about the essence of the soul, unable to understand anything correctly about the nature of motion and of the universe; and in conclusion I am the tool by which natural and divine knowledge is stuck on the lowest point of the wheel, as in the time of the Chaldeans and Pythagoreans[121] it was at its highest point.

SEBASTO: Nevertheless we've seen you retain the world's admiration since then; among other marvels is found a certain Arab who has indicated the nature of your work to have been the ultimate effort to express how much more clearly, purely, loftily and truthfully genius can be expressed;[122] and generally you are called "the daemon of nature."

---

121. Reflecting the Roman interchangeability of the terms *Chaldaei* and *mathematici* (see Suetonius, *The Twelve Caesars*, Tiberius: 69 [1979, 149]; Domitian: 14, 15 [1979, 309–311]; cf. Daniel 1:4, 2:2), Bruno employs "Chaldean" both to signify a practicing astrologer and to recall the ancient Semitic people of Babylon.

122. Averroës's Aristotelian commentaries arrived in Paris between 1230 and 1234 and were literal in contrast to Avicenna's paraphrases, for he "approached the writings of Aristotle more as a philosopher than a syncretist," considering "philosophical truth the highest kind of human truth" (Roensch 1964, 6). Although as an Aristotelian defender Averroës frequently cited the clarity of Aris-

ONORIO: There'd be no blockheads if there were no faith; and if there were none, there would be no changes in knowledge and virtues, bestialities and sloth, and other occurrences of contrary impressions—as night and day, the heat of summer and the severity of winter.

SEBASTO: Proceeding now to what is relevant to the concept of the soul (putting aside the other propositions at present), I have perused and contemplated your three books[123] in which you speak more stammeringly than could ever be understood from another stammerer; as you can well imagine of such diverse opinions, extravagant designs and questions, maxims concerning untying and unbridling that you declaim in such muddled and frivolous propositions that if they really conceal something it can't be anything but pedantic or peripatetic levity.

ONORIO: It's no wonder, brother, given that it couldn't be of any count that others are able to perceive my understanding regarding those things about which I had no understanding, or that they sift to find interpretation or argument about what I wish to tell them, when I myself didn't know what I was wanting to say. What difference do you suppose there to be between such people and those who search for the horns of the cat and the legs of the eel? None, of course. As to arranging so that no one else would realize this thing— and for that, I proceed to lose the reputation of protosophist—I directed matters in such a way that whoever should examine me in

---

totle's philosophy, at times his admiration even led him to adopt elements of the Stagirite's *imprecision* (particularly of the sort demonstrated in some of Aristotle's cosmological treatises) in his writing (Leaman 1988, 63–71). Toward verifying the degree of Averroës's intellectual debts to Aristotle, even in limited examination of the latter's *Physics, Metaphysics,* and *Categories,* see Kogan (1985, 86–142).

123. That is, the three books making up Aristotle's *De anima.*

light of natural philosophy[124] (in which I was, and felt myself, most ignorant) should perceive something, however difficult or confusing, and if he lacked some enlightenment of mind would have to think and believe that [obfuscation] was not my profound intention, but rather that thereby he could, according to his capacity, superficially comprehend my meanings. Therefore I sent to be published that *Letter to Alexander,*[125] where I was protesting that physical books were placed in the light while not being brought to the light.

SEBASTO: And so far it seems to me you have unburdened your conscience; and these many great asses are wrong to get ready to complain on the judgment day about you as the one who has

124. As Aristotle explains in the *Physics* (2:2), the natural philosopher's teleology focuses on "the form primarily and essentially, as the physician is with health" and on "the material up to a certain point, as the physician is with sinew and the smith with bronze. For his main concern is with the goal, which is formal; but he deals with such forms as are conceptually, but not factually, detachable from the material in which they occur" (1957, 125, 127). Praising the insights of Aristotle's *Meteorologica* rather backhandedly—and reflecting precisely what Onorio confesses were personal faults in his philosophy while Aristotle—Bruno writes in *La cena* that "he spoke as one who prophesies and divines; though he himself did not in such cases really mean it; yet, he says by and large and by its principal part the truth, as if somewhat limping, and always adding something of his own error to the divine furor" (Jaki 1975, 157).

125. The *Rhetorica ad Alexandrum* opens, "You write to me that you have again sent people to me to speak about my composing for you a treatise on the principles of political oratory" (*Problems* 1957, 267), yet in the *Moralia*, 4:329:6, Plutarch records that "Alexander did not follow Aristotle's advice to treat the Greeks as if he were their leader, and other peoples as if he were their master; to have regard for the Greeks as for friends and kindred, but to conduct himself toward other peoples as though they were plants or animals; for to do so would have been to cumber his leadership with numerous battles and banishments and festering seditions" (1969, 397, 399). Cf. W. D. Ross's reference, in *The Works of Aristotle, Vol. XII: Select Fragments*, to the *Vita Aristotelis Marciana:* "In order to confer a benefit on all men, Aristotle writes a book addressed to Alexander on kingship, instructing him how he should rule. This had such an effect on Alexander's mind that when he had failed to confer a benefit on anyone he said: 'Today I have not been king; I have done good to no one'" (1952, 65).

deceived and seduced them, and with sophistical flourishes diverted them from the path of any truth that could have been reacquired by other principles and methods. You've also taught them that which they should have rightly thought: that if you have published, as if you've not published, they, after having read you, must reason that have not read you, as you had thus written, as if you had not written—to such a degree that they who teach your doctrine have to be listened to as to one who speaks, as though he hasn't spoken. And finally no more must be expected from you, than as from one who reasons and casts forth an opinion about that which he's never understood.

ONORIO: This much is certain, to tell you candidly as I understand it at present. No one ought to be understood more than he himself wishes to be, and we must not with that same intellect go following after those who flee from our intellect—which is to say that some speak certainties through riddle or metaphor, some because they don't want the ignorant understanding them, some so the multitude doesn't despise them, others so that pearls aren't trampled by swine. We have become such that every satyr, faun, melancholic—intoxicated and infected with black bile—in reckoning visions and voicing tirades without any structure and sense, desire to produce suspicions of great prophecy, of hidden mystery, of lofty secrets and divine arcana for raising the dead, of philosopher's stones and other idleness by directing them at those who have little brains, to make fools of them all in gambling away their time, intellect, reputation, and possessions, and spending so miserably and ignobly the course of their life.

SEBASTO: A certain friend of mine understood this well: who, having I know not if it was a particular book of one obscure prophet or another, after having mulled over a good deal of its humour, with a gracefulness and beautiful charm went to throw it into the latrine, saying to it, "Brother, you don't want to be understood; I don't want to understand you"; adding that it should go with a hundred devils,[126] and leave my friend in peace with his own affairs.

ONORIO: And what's worthy of pity and laughter is that in these published libels and sheepish tractates you see Salvio become astonished, Ortensio melancholic, Serafino thin, Cammaroto pale, Ambruggio aged, Gregorio insane, Reginaldo abstracted, Bonifacio swollen;[127] and the very reverend Don Cocchiarone,[128] full of infinite and noble wonder,[129] leaves for the open space of his hall where, removed from the coarse, ignoble mob he takes a stroll; and shaking

126. A favorite Bruno curse ("andare con cento diavoli"), with "cento" [one hundred] employed as an intensifier.

127. This parodic catalogue seems to indicate how completely Bruno has severed his ties with the Dominicans. Gentile explains that these men are "Tutti domenicani regnicoli, vecchie conoscenze del B., del convento di S. Domenico di Napoli" [All Dominican veterans, old acquaintances of Bruno, from the convent of San Domenico di Napoli] (1958, 897–898), and relates Vincenzo Spampanato's identifications of them (1958, 898) as Fra Ambrogio Salvio of Bagnoli, a doctor of theology appointed Bishop of Nardò, and spiritual advisor of Pius V; Fra Giambattista Ortensio of Campagna, a renowned preacher; Fra Serafino Maio of Napoli, a lecturer in theology and two-time regent of the Office of San Domenico; Fra Antonino of Camerota, revered by his contemporaries as one of the greatest of the Dominicans, a theologian and also regent of the Office; Master Ambrogio Pasqua, by whom Bruno was invested, later occupant of the Office of Napoli; Fra Gregorio of Bagnoli; and Fra Reginaldo Accetto of Massalubrense, a theologian and grammarian. Gentile omits Bonifacio, the foolish husband—who pursues a courtesan, Vittoria / Porzia, though he already has a beautiful young wife, Carubina—from Bruno's comedy Il candelaio. A similarly structured list of comic allusions to contemporaries appears in the sixth of Ariosto's Satires (Ariosto 1976, 159).

128. Apparently another nonsense name like Don Sapatino; a cocchia is a trawling net. For Gentile's etymological speculations, see (1958, 898n1).

129. Bruno's original, "pien d'infinità e nobil maraviglia," is the opening line of the second canto of Petrarch's Triumph of Fame (post-1348), translated by Ernest Hatch Wilkins as "Filled with amazement endless and profound" (1962, 78). This is an apt allusion with which to follow Onorio's parodic list of names, inasmuch as Petrarca in the preceding canto has included his own catalogue of famous Romans: Scipio, Caesar, Claudius, Metaurus, the Catos, Crassus, Torquatus, and many others, concluding with Marcus Aurelius.

from here to there the fringes of his literary gown, shaking now this foot, now that, thrusting his chest now to the right, now to the left side, with the glossed text under his armpit and with a gesture like wanting to fling to the ground that flea which he has between his first two fingers, musing with his furrowed forehead, with eyebrows inclined and eyes rounded in the image of a man powerfully amazed, concluding with a grave and emphatic sigh he will make this sentence reach the ear of those nearby: *Hoc usque alii philosophi non pervenerunt* [The other philosophers have not come all the way here]. If, in respect to the lesson of a book composed by some demonic or possessed person, he comes across where it's unclear and hence can squeeze out no more sensibility than may be encountered in an equine spirit, to demonstrate his having hit the nail on the head he will exclaim, "*O magnum mysterium* [O great mystery]!" If by chance he finds a book of—

SEBASTO: Please, no more of these subjects of which we are, alas, only too well informed; and let's return to our topic.

CORIBANTE: *Ita ita, sodes* [So thus, with your leave]. Explain with what order and manner you have recovered the memory you lost of your imagined Peripatetic and other hypostatic existences.

ONORIO: I believe I said to Sebasto that whenever I migrated from the body, before I would enter thoroughly into another, I returned to the vestige of my asinine image (that for the honor and faculty of its wings has not pleased some, who hold such an animal in infamy by calling it an ass, though Pegasus the horse): and from there—after having described to you the acts and fortunes I had undergone—I was always destined to reappear human, rather than something else, the privilege I earned by having had the shrewdness and continence that one time not to send the humour of the Lethe's waters down my gullet. Besides, through the jurisdiction of that celestial court, it has happened that I've never again taken the path toward the Plutonian kingdom to see the Elysian Fields; rather, upon departing from bodies, I head toward the illustrious and august empire of Jove.

CORIBANTE: To the abode of the winged quadruped.

ONORIO: Up until now, pleasing the senate of the gods, it has been convenient for me to transmigrate with the other beasts below, leaving only the impression of my virtue on high; whence, by the grace and worthy favor of the gods, I come there adorned and girded about with my library, carrying not only the memory of the opinionated, sophisticated, superficial, probable and demonstrative species, but also the distinct discernment of those things that are true from those that are false. And in addition to those things that indifferently constituted bodies which I conceived of by means of various kinds of disciplines, I still retain the habit and many other truths to which—without administration of the senses, with unadulterated intellectual eye—the path opens; and they don't escape me, though one finds me trapped beneath this skin and walls whence, through the doors of the senses, as through certain extremely narrow openings, we can ordinarily contemplate some species of being: as otherwise it becomes permissible for us to see, clear and open, the whole prospect of natural forms—finding ourselves outside of prison.

SEBASTO: So you remain informed about everything in such a manner that you acquire more than the habit of so many philosophies, of so many philosophical hypotheses that you have presented to the world, obtaining as well judgment superior to that darkness and that light under which you've grown, felt, understood—either in act or in power—living now in the terrestrial, now in the infernal, now in the celestial abodes.

ONORIO: True: and from such retention I'm better able to consider and comprehend, better than in a mirror, that which is true of the essence and substance of the soul.

Third Part of the [Second] Dialogue

SEBASTO: Let's postpone this for now, and let's hear your opinion concerning the question that was raised yesterday between me and Saulino, here present, concerning the opinion of some sects that desire us not to come to any learning.

SAULINO: I made it certainly clear that beneath the eminence of the truth we have nothing more eminent than ignorance and asininity: therefore, this is the medium by which one unites with, and with which one tames, wisdom; and there is no other virtue ample enough to have its room joined wall-to-wall with that. Considering that human intellect has some access to the truth: if it is not through knowledge and cognition, that access must necessarily be through ignorance and asininity.

CORIBANTE: *Nego sequelam* [I deny that this follows].

SAULINO: The consequence is shown by the fact that in the rational intellect there is no mean between ignorance and knowledge; being two opposites, like deprivation and surfeit, only one of the two must exist.

CORIBANTE: *Quid de assumptione, sive antecedente* [What of the assumption, or antecedent]?

SAULINO: That, as I said, is placed at the forefront by many very famous philosophers and theologians.

CORIBANTE: The argument *ab humana authoritate* [from human authority] is most feeble.

SAULINO: Such assertions are not without demonstrative discourses.

SEBASTO: Therefore, if such an opinion is true, it's true by demonstration; demonstration is a scientific syllogism; therefore, according to those who deny the knowledge and understanding of truth, it comes after the understanding of truth and scientific discourse; and consequently they are scolded by their own sense and words. I arrive at this: if one knows no truth, these same don't know what they're talking about and can't be certain whether they're speaking or braying, whether they're men or asses.

SAULINO: You can expect the resolution of this from what you will hear of me next; for the mystery will be first to understand the thing, and afterward the mode and manner of that.

CORIBANTE: Fine. *Modus enim rei rem praesupponat oportet* [It is fitting that the measure of the thing replace the thing (itself)].

SEBASTO: Now make us understand these things in whatever order pleases you.

SAULINO: I shall do so. Among the sects of philosophers are found some generally called Academicians, and more properly Skeptics or even Realists, who distrust determining anything; banishing every expression, not daring to affirm or to negate—nevertheless they desire to be called inquisitors, investigators, and scrutinizers of things.

SEBASTO: Why did these vain beasts inquire, investigate, and scrutinize without hope of finding anything? Now these are those types who weary themselves purposelessly.

CORIBANTE: In order to prove that Vulgate sentence a lie: *Omne agens est propter finem* [Every action has a purpose]. But *edepol* [by Pollux], *mehercle* [by Hercules], I persuade myself that as Onorio depends on the influence of Pegasus the ass, or even is that very Pegasus, even so those philosophers have been the very Belides[130]—or at least the Belides did affect them in the head.

SAULINO: Permit me to finish. Now those people put no faith in what they said, nor in what they heard: for they esteemed the truth a thing confused and incomprehensible, placed in the nature and composition of every variety, diversity, and contrariety; each thing being a

---

130. To Bruno the project of skeptic philosophy is as futile as the task described in Ovid's *Metamorphoses* 4:463, given to forty-nine of the fifty daughters of Egyptian king Belus, the Belides (or Danaïdes) as punishment in Hades "for daring to work destruction on their cousin-husbands, with unremitting toil [to] seek again and again the waters, only to lose them" (1976, 1:211).

mixture, nothing consistent within itself, nothing being of its own nature and virtue, and objects appearing to the powers of understanding not as themselves, but according to the relation they acquire through their species, that somehow deviating from this and that matter they come to unite and create new models for our senses.

SEBASTO: Oh, in truth, without much toil such people, in very little time, can be philosophers and show themselves more wise than others.

SAULINO: To these succeeded the Pyrrhonians,[131] much less scarcely placing faith in individual sense and intellect than the Realists; for where the others think to have comprehended something and to be made participants in some wisdom by having information about this truth—that is, that nothing can be understood or determined— these even esteemed themselves lacking of such wisdom, saying that they could not even be certain of this: namely, that nothing can be determined.

SEBASTO: Behold the diligence of this other Academy, that—having seen the pattern of its genius and having noted the industry of that which with ease and laziness it wished to leave its mark—by spilling the other philosophies on the ground—armed with greater stupidity, fortifying [this] with a smidgeon more of the salt of insipidity— wants to give the push both to all of those and these together, making themselves much more wise about everything generally, so that with little expense and racking of their brains they invest [i.e., entoga] themselves and make themselves doctors. Come now, let's go one further. Now what must I do, being ambitious to form a new sect and to seem wisest of all, and of those even who surpass all others? I will make a third tabernacle here, will set up a more learned Academy by cinching up my belt a bit. But shall I, perchance, want

---

131. Here "pirroni" is Bruno's own variation on "pirronici" or "pirronisti," the followers of Pyrrho of Elis (c. 360–275 B.C.E.). See Popkin (1979, 35, 259).

so much to repress the voice of the Realists and to constrain the breath of the Pyrrhonians that I must give up my own spirit and die?

SAULINO: What are you trying to say by this?

SEBASTO: These sluggards—by escaping the labor of providing reasons behind things, by not acknowledging their laziness and the envy they have toward the industry of others, wishing to appear better than they are, and not satisfying themselves with concealing their own unworthiness, unable to move ahead of others either by running with their peers or by possessing the means of doing something of their own, by not risking their vain presumption, confessing the imbecility of their own mind, their coarseness of sense, and privation of intellect, and their own blindness, by making others seem to be without proper illumination of judgment—lay the blame on nature for the evil things they represent, and not principally on the bad understanding of the Dogmatics; for with this method of proceeding they would have been obliged to place their good understanding upon the field of comparison, which would have produced better faith after having generated a better conception in the souls of those who delight in the contemplations of natural things. Therefore, wishing to seem more sagacious than others with less toil and thought, and small risk of losing credit, the Realists said that nothing can be determined, because nothing is known: whence those who believe they understand and speak assertively wander more clumsily than those who do not understand and do not speak.

The next ones, then, called Pyrrhonians, in order to appear to be archscholars, said that not even this (which the Realists suppose themselves to understand) can be understood: that nothing can be determined or known. Thus where the Realists understood that others, who were thinking to understand, were not understanding, the Pyrrhonians on the other hand understood that the Realists were not understanding—whether any others, who were thinking to understand, understood or not. Now that which remains of it, to arrive at the advantage of the wisdom of these people, is that we know that the Pyrrhonians did not know, that the Realists did not know, that the Dogmatics, who thought they knew, did not know; and so with ease this noble ladder of philosophies comes always more and more to enlarge, until demonstratively one concludes the ultimate degree of the supreme philosophy and perfect contemplation to belong to those who not only neither affirm nor deny knowing or not knowing, but are not even able to affirm nor to deny; such that the asses are the most divine animals, and asininity—its sister—is the companion and secretary of truth.

SAULINO: If this which you say abusively and in anger were said speaking from good sense and assertively, I would say that your inference is most excellent and splendidly divine and that you've arrived at that finish for which the great Dogmatics and great Academics compete, by staying far behind the pack of them.

SEBASTO: I pray (since we've come to this) you make me understand with what persuasion the Academics deny the possibility of said understanding.

SAULINO: I would wish that this had been related by Onorio, since, by virtue of standing in the hypostasis of so many great anatomists of the viscera of nature, it isn't beyond reason that some time he had been an Academic.

ONORIO: As a matter of fact, I have been that Xenophanes of Colophon, who said in all and of all that things are nothing but what they are believed.[132] Leaving my own thoughts to one side now, concerning the proposition, I declare the Pyrrhonians' reason to be trite,[133]

---

132. Xenophanes of Colophon (c. 520 B.C.E.) preceded Heraclitus as the first of the Eleatic School; "less a philosopher than a religious reformer who declaimed against traditional mythology and preached a pantheism which identified the One Universe with God" (Sextus Empiricus 1955, viii).

133. In *Adversus Mathematicos* (1:5), Sextus Empiricus explains that the School of Pyrrho was "not moved either by the view that these subjects are of no

who have said that comprehending the truth requires doctrine; and to put doctrine into effect requires one who teaches, one who is taught, and something to be taught: namely, the master, the disciple, the art; but none of these three can be found, in effect; consequently it is not doctrine, and it is not understanding of truth.

SEBASTO: With what reason do they say first that there is no thing of which there will be doctrine or discipline?

ONORIO: With this. That thing, they say, must be either true or false. If it is false, it cannot be taught, because the false can be neither doctrine nor discipline: considering that nothing can happen to something that doesn't exist, and for that reason it can't even happen to be taught. If it's true, it still can't very well be taught: for either it's a quality that is equally obvious to everybody, thus in itself cannot be doctrine, and consequently there can be no teacher of it, as neither of white that it is "white," of the horse that it's a "horse," of the tree that it's a "tree"; or it's something that otherwise appears unequally to others, thus in itself can have nothing but controversy, and one can't form anything about it but opinion. Besides, if that which one must be taught and informed is true, it's necessary that it be taught by some cause or medium: which cause or medium is necessarily hidden or known. If it is hidden, it cannot be told anyone. If it is known, it must be so by cause of medium; and thus, proceeding further and further, we'll come to perceive that one

---

help to gaining wisdom (for that is a 'dogmatic' assertion) or by any lack of culture attaching to themselves; for in addition to their culture and their superiority to all other philosophers in breadth of experience they are also indifferent to the opinion of the multitude" (1949, 5). An example of the philosophical paralysis that Bruno seeks to challenge and refute here can be found in Sextus's *Pyrroneion Hypotyposes*, 3:28, on Cause: "For if Cause as a relative notion cannot be conceived as causative in its effect, it must be conceived before its effect, while it is impossible for anything to be conceived before that which the conception of it cannot precede,—then it is impossible for the Cause to be conceived" (1955, 343).

cannot arrive at the principle of knowledge, if every knowledge exists by cause.

Furthermore, they say—such is the nature of things that are, that some might be bodies, others incorporeals—that it's necessary that of the things that are taught, some belong to the one genus and some to the other. Now the body can't be taught, since it can be judged by neither sense nor intellect. Certainly not by the judgment of the senses: seeing that according to all doctrines and sects, the body consists of more sizes, reasons, differences and circumstances; and not only is it not a definite chance that something be objectionable to a particular sense or to common sense—nay, it's a composition and congregation of countless properties and individuals. And granted, if such is pleasing, that the body is a perceptible thing, this doesn't make it a thing of doctrine or discipline; for it's not necessary to find the disciple and master to make it known that white is white and hot is hot. Neither can the body be subject to the judgment of the mind, because it is widely conceded, following all the Dogmatics and Academics, that the subject of the intellect cannot exist other than as an incorporeal thing. From here one infers secondarily that there cannot be a teacher; nor, thirdly, someone that can be taught; because, as observed, the one has nothing to understand or conceive, and the other has nothing to teach or impart.

They reach another point. If it happens that one teaches, or one without skill teaches another without skill—and this isn't possible, because neither one has less need to be taught; or one artist instructs another artist—and this would become a joke, for neither has the position of master; or that one who doesn't know teaches one who does—and this would be as if a blind man wished to guide one who sees. If none of these methods is feasible, it'll remain, then, that he who knows, teaches him who doesn't know; and thus there's more trouble than anyone can imagine in each of the other three ways of imagining; for he who is unskilled can't be made a craftsman without the skill, assuming that it could happen that one could be a craftsman when he's not one. (In addition, he is similar to one born deaf and blind, who can never conceive of voices and colors. I offer what is said in the *Meno*[134] with the example of the runaway slave, that, when found out, it cannot be known it was he, if he weren't already known. Whence they desire by equal and similar reason that no new wisdom and doctrine of knowable species be able to exist, except as recollection.) Neither can be made a craftsman when he has the skill; for in that case he can't say that he's making himself or can be made a craftsman, but that he is a craftsman.

SEBASTO: What do you think of these reasonings, Onorio?

ONORIO: I say that in examining such discourses there will be no mystery as to what is entertaining us. It's enough that I call them good, as certain herbs are "good" to certain tastes.

SEBASTO: But I would like to know from Saulino (who extols asininity so much, as though science and speculation, knowledge and discipline can't be extolled at all) whether asininity can take place in other than asses themselves; that is to say, if someone who wasn't an ass could become an ass through doctrine and discipline. Because it's

134. Although Gentile reports that he is led "sospettare che il B. non avesse mai letto questo dialogo di Platone" [to suspect that Bruno had never read this dialogue by Plato] (1957, 909n1), he also posits the imprecision of Bruno's allusion as the much more likely "vago ricordo d'una lontana lettura" [vague recollection of a distant reading]. The passage in question involves Socrates' description to Meno of "the statues of Daedalus," reputed to be capable of independent motion:

SOCRATES. They too, if no one ties them down, run away and escape. If tied, they stay where they are put.
MENO. What of it?
SOCRATES. If you have one of his works untethered, it is not worth much; it gives you the slip like a runaway slave. But a tethered specimen is very valuable, for they are magnificent creations. (1961, 381)

essential that of these, one who teaches or one who's taught, either both, or neither, be asses. Do they say whether only the one who teaches will be an ass, or only the one who's taught, or neither, or both together? For here with the same rule one can see that one can't make an ass of one's self in any case. Hence, there can be no learning of asininity whatsoever, as it is not of arts nor of knowledge.

ONORIO: We'll reason of this at the table after supper. Let's go, then— it's time.

CORIBANTE: *Propere eamus* [We need to hurry].

SAULINO: Come on!

END OF THE SECOND DIALOGUE

Third Dialogue

Interlocutors: Saulino, Alvaro

SAULINO: I have just strolled a fair piece while waiting, and I perceive the hour of beginning our discussion to be past—yet the others have not come. Oh, I see Sebasto's servant.

ALVARO: Good to find you, Saulino! I come to inform you on behalf of my master that you will not be able to convene another meeting for at least a week. His wife is dead, and he stays in preparing for the execution of the will—in order to be free of that concern as well. Coribante is attacked by the gout, and Onorio is gone to the baths. Good-bye.

SAULINO: Go in peace. Now I believe the time for constructing other arguments about the cabala of the so-called horse is passing. For as I see it, the order of the universe decrees that as this divine horse in the celestial region cannot show itself except to the navel (where the star that terminates there is placed in dispute and in question whether it belongs to the head of Andromeda or simply to the trunk of this splendid brute), thus analogically it happens that this descriptory horse cannot achieve perfection:

So goes Fortune, changing style.[135]

But we must not despair due to this; since, if it chances that the others return to meet together another time, I shall shut up all three of them inside the conclave, from whence they cannot get out until they have spun the creation of an illustrious Cabala of Pegasus the horse. *Interim,* these two dialogues are selected for a small, inexperienced, introductory, microcosmic Cabala.[136] And so as not to let the present time get the better of me by passing it foolishly in strolling through this atrium, I wish to read this dialogue that I have in hand.

END OF THE THIRD DIALOGUE OF
THE CABALA OF PEGASUS

To the Cillenican Ass

O blessed that womb and the teats
2   That ha[ve] borne you and on earth nursed you,[137]
Divinest brute, dear to the world,
4   That dwells here and among the stars!
May your back never again with burdens and saddle be pressed;
6   Against the ungrateful world and heavenly greed
May fortune and nature defend your need,

135. This is 1:135 of Petrarch's *Triumph of Death,* and Gentile notes that it is one of those verses "già nel Cinquecento diventati proverbiali" (912) [that had already become proverbial in the Cinquecento]. Ernest Hatch Wilkins translates Petrarch's "Come Fortuna va cangiando stile!" as "Surely the ways of fate are strange indeed!" (1962, 58).

136. That is, the preceding two dialogue segments of the *Cabala.* More Brunist complication: these portions of the *Cabala* serve as the "microcosmic Cabala" of Pegasus that the author tantalizingly claims *hasn't* yet been written.

137. Luke 11:27.

8   With such a happy mind and a good hide.
      Your head shows natural good,
10   As your nostrils [show] sober judgment,
      Your long ears a regal hearing,
12   Your thick lips the mode of great fashion,
      That organ something to make the gods envious,
14   Such a neck whose constance I praise.
      I rejoice only in praising you:
16   But, alas, they describe your conditions
      Not [in] one sonnet, but [in] a thousand sermons.

The Nolan's Cillenican Ass[138]

Interlocutors: The Ass, Pythagorean Fool, Mercury

ASS: Now why must I abuse your lofty, rare and exotic gift, O dazzling Jove? Why shall I keep such talent—given to me by you, when you gazed at me with a personal eye (*indicante fato* [indicating (thy) will])—buried under the black and gloomy earth of a most ungrateful silence? Shall I suffer more in being urged to speak, to not let that extraordinary bray out of my mouth that your bounty, in this most muddled age, has sown in my inner spirit (so that it would act externally)? Open, open then the asinine palate with the key of

---

138. Mercury (also known as Cyllenius), benefactor of the "Ass" appearing in this dialogue, was born on Cyllene, a mountain in Arcadia. In a section of *De imaginum, signorum et idearum compositione* (1591) headed "Asinus Cyllenicus," Bruno describes the ass as spare transportation should the messenger of the gods ever need it, for if he ever found himself grounded, "Nullum sane esset Mercurii numen, nisi equitabile pecus aliquod subesset" [Mercury's majesty would not be sound, unless he could mount some horselike beast] (2:3:237). The "Pythagorean Fool," among this dialogue's three interlocutors, is a translation of Bruno's *Micco,* which Salvatore Battaglia defines figuratively as "Persona goffa, impacciata, minchione, babbeo, stupido. —Anche: zerbinotto, bellimbusto" [An awkward, clumsy, foolish, silly, stupid person. —Also: a fop, a coxcomb] (1978, 346). The *NED* notes that this figurative usage derives from apelike imitation of human behavior (i.e., inferior or spurious imitation). "God's ape" is a "natural born fool"—not in the sense of a purely unbiased or uninformed intellect, but in the animal sense of being incapable of intellectual response.

opportunity, loose the tongue through the diligence of supposition, gather by the hand of care, straightened by the arm of understanding: the fruits of the trees and the flowers of the herbs that are in the garden of the asinine memory.

FOOL: O uncommon portent, O stupendous prodigy, O incredible marvel, O miraculous event! May the gods drive away any misfortune! Speaks the ass? The ass speaks? O Muses, O Apollo, O Hercules, articulate voices issue from such a head? Hold your tongue, Fool; perhaps you're deceived; perhaps some man stands masquerading beneath this hide, to make fun of us.

ASS: Think rather, Fool, not that I am false, but that I am most naturally a talking ass; and as such I remember having had other human faces, as now you see me having bestial limbs.

FOOL: Soon enough, O demon incarnate, I will demand of you who, what, and how you are. For now, and first of all, I would like to know what you want here. What omen do you bring us? What command do you carry from the gods? What will this scene come to? To what end have you placed your feet under this, our portico, to show yourself decidedly vocal?

ASS: First off, I want you to know that I seek to be a member and to declare myself a doctor of some college or academy, that my adequacy may be authenticated until my concepts have been understood, my words weighed, and my doctrine esteemed with less faith than—

FOOL: O Jove! is it possible that *ab aeterno* an event, an issue, a case like this has never been registered?

ASS: Leave the wonders for now, and answer me quickly, either you or one of these astonished others who are assembling to listen to me. O gowned, sealed, capped[139] instructors, archinstructors, the heroes and demigods of wisdom: do you wish, does it please you, do you

139. Bruno's term is *"pileati"*; that is, the *"berreta"* (*pileum*) of the doctoral uniform. The Nolan's point is that the clothes do not make the professor.

have in your heart to accept into your consortium, society, fraternity, under the banner and ensign of your communion, this ass you see and hear? Because of you, some who are laughing marvel, others who are marveling laugh, and astonished others (who are the majority) are biting their lips; and no one responds?

FOOL: You see that, stupefied, they do not speak, and all being turned to me, they signal for me to respond to you: to which, as president, it's my duty to give you a decision, and from which, as from all, you must await the dispatch.

ASS: What academy is this, that keeps *lineam ne pertransito* [don't cross the line] written above its door?

FOOL: It is a school of Pythagoreans.

ASS: Can one enter?

FOOL: For an academic, not without difficult, and many, conditions.

ASS: Now what are these "conditions"?

FOOL: They're quite numerous.

ASS: I asked *what*, not *how many*.

FOOL: I'll answer you better, reporting our principles. First, that anyone proposing himself to be admitted, before being accepted, must be well adjusted in the disposition of his body, physiognomy, and mind, due to the great contingent effect that we recognize the body to have on and with the soul.

ASS: *Ab Iove, principium, Musae,*[140] if one wishes to join.

FOOL: Second, once he is admitted, he is given a fixed time (no less than two years)[141] during which time he must be silent and it is not permissible for him to dare to ask about any point—even about things not understood—not even to debate and examine propositions; and during that time he is called "auditor." Third, once past

---

140. From Virgil, *Eclogues* 3:60: "With Jove the Muse begins" (1984, 49).

141. The discipline of the Pythagorean disciple—and the rationale for the Fool's adamant refusal to admit the Ass—is described in the second-century C.E. work *The Attic Nights of Aulus Gellius,* 1:9 (1927, 45, 47, 49).

this time, he is permitted to speak, to inquire, to write down the things heard, and to explain his own opinions; and at this time he is named "mathematician" or "Chaldean." Fourth, informed about similar things, and adorned by those studies, he turns to contemplation of the workings of the world and principles of nature; and here he stops his passage, calling himself "physicist."

ASS: Doesn't he proceed further?

FOOL: One cannot be more than physicist: for supernatural things cannot be reasoned except in how they are reflected in natural things, and there cannot be further understanding than through the correct and superior consideration of these things themselves.

ASS: You have no metaphysics among you?

FOOL: No; and that which others glorify as metaphysics is none other than part of logic. But let's ignore what's irrelevant to our purpose. Such, in conclusion, are the conditions and rules of our academy.

ASS: These?

FOOL: Yes, sir.

ASS: O honored school, eminent study, beautiful sect, venerated college, most illustrious gymnasium, unconquerable recreation and academy most principal among the principals! The wandering ass, like a thirsty deer, [presents himself] unto you, as to most limpid and fresh waters; the humble and supplicant ass presents himself to you, most benign receivers of pilgrims, eager to be registered in your consortium.

FOOL: In our consortium, eh?

ASS: Yes, yes, yes, sir—in your consortium.

FOOL: Go through that other door, mister, because asses are banned from this one.

ASS: Tell me, brother, by which door did you enter?

FOOL: Heaven can make asses speak, but not enroll them in the Pythagorean school.

ASS: Don't be so proud, O Fool, and recall that your Pythagoras teaches not to disdain anything found in the bosom of nature. Although I am an ass in form at present, I may have been and may yet be in form a great man; and although you are a man, you may have been and may yet be a great ass, according to what will seem expedient to the distributor of clothes and abodes, and the dispatcher of transmigrant souls.

FOOL: Tell me, brother, have you understood the principles and conditions of the academy?

ASS: Very well.

FOOL: Have you conversed with yourself as to whether on account of your defect you can be prevented from entering?

ASS: Plenty, in my judgment.

FOOL: Then make yourself understood.

ASS: The principal condition that has made me doubt is the first. It is simple truth that I lack that one characteristic, that soft flesh, that delicate, neat and genteel skin, which the diligent physiognomists understand [as essential] to the reception of the doctrine; because the toughness of mine is contrary to the agility of the intellect. But given such condition it seems to be that the principle could be dispensed with; because someone should not be rejected when many other facets petition on behalf of such a defect, like the sincerity of manners, the quickness of the mind, the efficacy of the intelligence and other companion conditions, sisters and daughters of these. I submit that one must not take it as universal that the souls follow the constitution of the body; since it may be that some more efficacious spiritual principle can vanquish and surmount the insult made to him by the crassness or other indisposition of that principle.

To that proposition I bring you the example of Socrates, judged by the physiognomist Zopiro as a dissolute, stupid, dull, effeminate man, enamored of young boys and inconstant; all of which was conceded by the philosopher, but I don't mean that the act of such inclinations was all-consuming; seeing that he was tempered by the continual study of philosophy, he carried in hand his firm rudder against the violent waves of natural indispositions, being that nothing cannot be overcome by study.[142] As, then, to the other principal physiognomical issue that is based not in the complexion of temperaments but in the harmonious proportion of limbs, I inform you that when it will be judged fairly, it will not be possible to find any defect in me. You know the pig cannot be a fine horse, or the ass a fine man; but the ass a fine ass, the pig a fine pig, the man a fine man. What if, carrying this argument further, the horse doesn't seem handsome to the pig, nor the pig handsome to the man, and the man isn't enamored with the ass; conversely, suppose the man doesn't seem beautiful to the ass, and the ass isn't enamored of the man.

Therefore, by this rule, once things are examined and weighed with reason, the one will concede to the other, according to their individual manners, that their beauties are diverse according to diverse proportionalities; and nothing is truly and absolutely beautiful if not one that is of the same beauty—or is beautiful by essence rather than by participation. I leave aside that in the same human species that which is said of the flesh must be attached *respectu habito* to twenty-five circumstances and glosses that classify them; for otherwise your physiognomical rule about soft fleshes is false,[143]

142. This "firm rudder against the violent waves of indisposition" was found by Christian humanists and neostoics in texts like Cicero's *Tusculan Disputations*, 4:37 (1960, 367).

143. Aristotle, *On Breath*, 9:20ff, parallels the Ass's argument (1964, 515). The Ass acknowledges the academic acceptance of Aristotelian ontology and epistemology as norms, particularly as they are codified in the *Categories* (esp. Chapter 8, on quality), the *Posterior Analytics*, and the *Topics* (esp. Book 6); at the same time, Bruno invents a counterproof that, by virtue of its very simplicity, is meant to undermine the logic and authority of Aristotelian rhetoric.

seeing that children are not more fit for knowledge than adults, nor women more skillful than men—unless that possibility farthest from practice can be called greater aptitude.

FOOL: So far that fellow displays vast, vast learning. Listen, Sir Ass, and make your reasons stronger, as pleases you, for

> You plough in the waves, and sow in the desert sands,
> And the wandering wind in a net you hope to gather,
> You found your hopes in the hearts of women,[144]

if you expect that the gentlemen academicians of this or that sect can or must concede you entrance. But if you are learned, content yourself by keeping your doctrine to yourself.

ASS: O fools, do you believe that I recited my reasons to you in order that you validate them for me? Do you believe that I've done this for any other purpose than accusing and rendering you unpardonable before Jove? Jove, in making me learned, made me a scholar. I well expected that from the fine judgment of your pride would be spit out this sentence: "It is not acceptable that asses enter into the academy together with us men." Whether or not a student of any other sect can say it, this cannot reasonably be said by you Pythagoreans, who with this—who deny me entrance—destroy the principles, foundations, and body of your philosophy. Now what difference do you discover between us asses and you men, not judging things by their surface, countenance and appearance? Moreover, inept judges, tell how many of you used to be in the academy of the asses. How many acquire knowledge in the academy of the asses? How many profit in the academy of the asses? How many are made doctors, rot, and die in the academy of the asses? How many are chosen, exalted, magnified, canonized, glorified, and deified in the academy of the

144. Ralph Nash's translation of Jacopo Sannazaro, *Arcadia*, Eclogue 8:10–12 (1966, 86).

asses? If they had not been and were not asses, I don't know how it would have gone and would go for them.

Are there not many extremely honorable and splendid studies, where one is given the lesson of learning to become ignorant, toward attaining not only the good of the temporal life but also of the eternal? Speak, to how many and to which faculties and honors does one enter via the door of asininity? Exclaim how many are impeded, excluded, rejected, and disgraced by not being participants in the asinine faculty and perfection. Now then, won't some of the asses, or at least one of the asses, be allowed entrance into the academy of the humans? Why should I not be accepted by having the favor of the majority of voices and votes in whatever academy, being that, if not all, at least the majority are enrolled and recorded in our greatly universal academy? If we asses are so liberal and effusive in receiving everyone, why must you be so stubborn about accepting at least one of us?

FOOL: One encounters greater difficulty in more worthy and important matters: one is not greatly concerned and one's eyes are not open much to things of such small moment. However, without repugnance—and much scruple of conscience—all are received into the academy of the asses, and it must not be thus in the academy of the humans.

ASS: But speak knowledgeably and resolve me a little, O sir, which thing of the two is more worthy: that a man becomes asinine, or that an ass becomes human? Why, here in truth is my Cyllenius: I know him by his caduceus and wings.

Welcome wandering winged one, messenger of Jove, faithful interpreter of the will of all the gods, generous donor of the sciences, defender of the arts, continuous oracle of mathematicians, admirable accountant, elegant orator, handsome visage, comely appearance, engaging demeanor, gracious personage, man among men, woman among women, unfortunate among the unfortunates, blessed among the blessed, everything among all things; who rejoices with those rejoicing, who with the weeping weeps; however, you are favorably viewed and accepted everywhere you go and stay. What good news do you bring?

MERCURY: Since, ass, you hope to call yourself an academician, I, who have given you other gifts and favors, once again with complete authority ordain, constitute and confirm you universal academician and dogmatician, so you may enter and reside anywhere, without anyone able to bar the door to you or to give any sort of insult or impediment, *quibuscumque in oppositum non obstantibus* [those in opposition are no obstruction]. Enter, then, wherever pleases you. Nor do we desire that you be obligated by the stipulation of the two-year silence one finds in the Pythagorean order, and by whatever other customary laws: for *novis intervenientibus causis, novae condendae sunt leges, proque ipsis condita non intelliguntur iura: iterimque ad optimi iudicium iudicis referenda est sententia, cuius intersit iuxta necessarium atque commodum providere* [new cases having intervened, new laws must be established, and before these the established laws are not understood: and meanwhile judgments must be left to the discretion of the best judge, whose concern it is to foresee what seems most necessary and beneficial]. Speak, then, among the auditors; consider and contemplate among the mathematicians; discuss, question, teach, declare, and determine among the physicists; mix with everyone; discourse with everyone; fraternize, unite, and identify with everyone; rule over everyone; be everything.

ASS: Have you understood this?

FOOL: We're not deaf.

THE END

Cabala del cavallo pegaseo
con l'aggiunta
dell'Asino cillenico

Descritta dal Nolano
Dedicata al
Vescovo di Casamarciano

Parigi,
Appresso
Antonio Baio,
Anno 1585

Epistola Dedicatoria Sopra la Seguente Cabala
Al Reverendissimo Signor Don Sapatino,
abbate successor di San Quintino
e vescovo di Casamarciano.

Reverendissime in *Christo Pater,*

Non altrimente che accader suole a un figolo, il qual gionto al termine del suo lavoro (che non tanto per trasmigrazion de la luce, quanto per difetto e mancamento della materia spacciata è gionto al fine) e tenendo in mano un poco di vetro, o di legno, o di cera, o altro che non è sufficiente per farne un vase, rimane un pezzo senza sapersi né potersi risolvere, pensoso di quel che n'abbia fare, non avendolo a gittar via disutilmente, e volendo al dispetto del mondo che serva a qualche cosa; ecco che a l'ultimo il mostra predestinato ad essere una terza manica, un orlo, un coperchio di fiasco, una forzaglia, un empiastro, o una intacconata che risalde, empia o ricuopra qualche fessura pertuggio o crepatura; è avvenuto a me, dopo aver dato spaccio non a tutti miei pensieri, ma a un certo fascio de scritture solamente, che al fine, non avendo altro da ispedire, piú per caso che per consiglio, ho volti gli occhi ad un cartaccio che avevo altre volte spreggiato e messo per copertura di que' scritti: trovai che conteneva in parte quel tanto che vi vederete presentato. Questo primo pensai di donarlo a un cavalliero; il quale avendovi aperti gli occhi, disse che non avea tanto studiato che potesse intendere gli misterii, e per tanto non gli possea piacere. L'offersi appresso ad un di questi *ministri verbi Dei;* e disse che era amico della lettera, e che non si delettava de simili esposizioni proprie a Origene, accettate da scolastici ed altri nemici della lor professione. Il misi avanti ad una dama; e disse che non gli aggradava per non esser tanto grande quanto conviene al suggetto d'un cavallo ed un asino. Il presentai ad un'altra; la quale, quantunque gustandolo gli piacesse, avendolo gustato, disse che ci volea pensar su per qualche giorno. Viddi se vi potesse accoraggiar una pizocchera; e la me disse: Non lo accetto, se parla d'altro che di rosario, della vertú de granelli benedetti e de l'agnusdei.

Accostailo al naso d'un pedante, il qual, avendo torciuto il viso in altra parte, mi disse che aboliva ogni altro studio e materia eccetto che qualche annotazione, scolia ed interpretazione sopra Vergilio, Terenzio e Marco Tullio. Udivi da un versificante che non lo volea, se non era qualche copia d'ottave rime o de sonetti. Altri dicevano che gli meglior trattati erano stati dedicati a persone che non erano megliori che essi loro. Altri co' l'altre raggioni mi parevan disposti a dovermene ringraziar o poco o niente, se io gli l'avesse dedicato; e questo non senza caggione, perché, a dir il vero, ogni trattato e considerazione deve essere speso, dispensato e messo avanti a quel tale che è de la suggetta professione o grado.

Stando dunque io con gli occhi affissi su la raggion della materia enciclopedica, mi ricordai dell'enciclopedico vostro ingegno, il qual non tanto per fecondità e ricchezza par che abbraccie il tutto, quanto per certa pelegrina eccellenza par ch'abbia il tutto a meglio ch' il tutto. Certo nessun potrà piú espressamente che voi comprendere il tutto, perché siete fuor del tutto; possete entrar per tutto, perché non è cosa che vi tegna rinchiuso; possete aver il tutto, perché non è cosa che abbiate. (Non so se mi dechiararò meglio co' descrivere il vostro ineffabile intelletto). Io non so se siete teologo, o filosofo, o cabalista; ma so ben che siete tutti, se non per essenza, per partecipazione; se non in atto, in potenza; se non d'appresso, da lontano. In ogni modo credo che siate cossí sufficiente nell'uno come nell'altro. E però eccovi cabala, teologia e filosofia: dico una cabala di teologica filosofia, una filosofia di teologia kaballistica, una teologia di cabala filosofica, di sorte ancora che non so se queste tre cose avete o come tutto, o come parte, o come niente; ma questo so ben certo che avete tutto del niente in parte, parte del tutto nel niente, niente de la parte in tutto.

Or per venire a noi, mi dimandarete: che cosa è questa che m'inviate? quale è il suggetto di questo libro? di che presente m'avete fatto degno? Ed io vi rispondo, che vi porgo il dono d'un Asino, vi si presenta l'Asino il quale vi farà onore, vi aumentarà dignità, vi metterà nel libro de l'eternità. Non vi costa niente per ottenerlo da me ed averlo per vostro; non vi costarà altro per mantenerlo, perché non mangia, non beve, non imbratta la casa; e sarà eternamente vostro, e duràravi piú che la vostra mitra, croccia, piovale, mula e vita; come, senza molto discorrere, possete voi medesmo ed altri comprendere. Qua non dubito, reverendissimo monsignor mio, che il dono de l'asino non sarà ingrato alla vostra prudenza e pietà: e questo non dico per caggione che deriva dalla consuetudine di presentar a gran maestri non solamente una gemma, un diamante, un rubino, una perla, un cavallo perfetto, un vase eccellente; ma ancora una scimia, un papagallo, un gattomammone, un asino; e questo, allora che è necessario, è raro, è dottrinale; e non è de gli ordinarii. L'asino indico è prezioso e duono papale in Roma; l'asino d'Otranto è duono imperiale in Costantinopoli; l'asino di Sardegna è duono regale in Napoli; e l'asino kaballistico, il qual è ideale e per conseguenza celeste, volete voi che debba esser men caro in qualsivoglia parte de la terra a qualsivoglia principal personaggio, che per certa benigna ed alta repromissione sappiamo che si trova in cielo il terrestre? Son certo dunque che verrà accettato da voi con quell'animo, con quale da me vi vien donato.

Prendetelo, o padre, se vi piace, per ucello, perché è alato ed il piú gentil e gaio che si possa tener in gabbia. Prendetelo, se 'l volete, per fiera, perché è unico, raro e pelegrino da un canto, e non è cosa piú brava che possiate tener ferma in un antro o caverna. Trattatelo, se vi piace, come domestico; perché è ossequioso, comite e servile, ed è il meglior compagno che possiate aver in casa. Vedete che non vi scampe di mano; perché è il meglior destriero che possiate pascere, o, per dir meglio, vi possa pascere in stalla; meglior familiare che vi possa esser contubernale e trattenimento in camera. Maneggiatelo come una gioia e cosa preciosa; perché non possete aver tesoro piú eccellente nel vostro ripostiglio. Toccatelo come cosa sacra, e miratelo come cosa da gran considerazione; perché non possete aver meglior libro, meglior imagine e meglior specchio nel vostro cabinetto.

[no paragraph break at this point in the original]

Tandem, se per tutte queste raggioni non fa per il vostro stomaco, lo potrete donar ad alcun altro che non ve ne debba essere ingrato. Se l'avete per cosa ludicra, donatelo ad qualche buon cavalliero, perché lo metta in mano de suoi paggi, per tenerlo caro tra le scimie e cercopitechi. Se lo passate per cosa armentale, ad un contadino che li done ricetto tra il suo cavallo e bue. Se 'l stimate cosa ferina, concedetelo a qualche Atteone che lo faccia vagar con gli capri e gli cervi. Se vi par ch'abbia del mignone, fatene copia a qualche damigella che lo tegna in luogo di martora e cagnuola. Se finalmente vi par ch'abbia del matematico, fatene grazia ad un cosmografo, perché gli vada rependo e salticchiando tra il polo artico ed antartico de una di queste sfere armillari, alle quali non men comodamente potrà dar il moto continuo, ch'abbia possuto donar l'infuso mercurio a quella d'Archimede, ad esser piú efficacemente tipo del megacosmo, in cui da l'anima intrinseca pende la concordanza ed armonia del moto retto e circolare.

Ma se siete, come vi stimo, sapiente, e con maturo giudicio considerate, lo terrete per voi, non stimando a voi presentata da me cosa men degna, che abbia possuto presentar a papa Pio quinto, a cui consecrai l'*Arca di Noè;* al re Errico terzo di Francia, il quale immortaleggio con l'*Ombre de le Idee;* al suo legato in Inghilterra, a cui ho conceduti *Trenta sigilli;* al cavallier Sidneo, al quale ho dedicata la *Bestia trionfante.* Perché qua avete non solamente la bestia trionfante viva; ma, ed oltre, gli trenta sigilli aperti, la beatitudine perfetta, le ombre chiarite e l'arca governata; dove l'asino (che non invidia alla vita delle ruote del tempo, all'ampiezza de l'universo, alla felicità de l'intelligenze, alla luce del sole, al baldachino di Giove) è moderatore, dechiaratore, consolatore, aperitore e presidente.

[no paragraph break in the original]

Non è, non è asino da stalla o da armento, ma di que' che possono comparir per tutto, andar per tutto, entra per tutto, seder per tutto, comunicar, capir, consegliar, definir e far tutto. Atteso che se lo veggio zappar, inaffiar ed inacquare, perché non volete ch' il dica ortolano? S'ei solca, pianta e semina, perché non sarà agricoltore? Per qual caggione non sarà fabro, s'ei è manipolo, mastro ed architettore? Chi m'impedisce che non lo dica artista, se è tanto inventivo, attivo e reparativo? Se è tanto esquisito argumentore, dissertore ed apologetico, perché non vi piacerà che lo dica scolastico?

Essendo tanto eccellente formator di costumi, institutor di dottrine e riformator de religioni, chi si farà scrupolo de dirlo academico, e stimarlo archimandrita di qualche archididascalia? Perché non sarà monastico, stante ch'egli sia corale, capitolare e dormitorale? S'egli è per voto povero, casto ed ubediente, mi biasimarete se lo dirò conventuale? Mi impedirete voi che non possa chiamarlo conclavistico, stante ch'egli sia per voce attiva e passiva graduabile, eligibile, prelatibile? Se è dottor sottile, irrefragabile ed illuminato, con qual conscienza non vorrete che lo stime e tegna per degno consegliero? Mi terrete voi la lingua, perché non possa bandirlo per domestico, essendo che in quel capo sia piantata tutta la moralità politica ed economica? Potrà far la potenza de canonica autoritade ch' io non lo tegna ecclesiastica colonna, se mi si mostra di tal maniera pio, devoto e continente? Se lo veggio tanto alto, beato e trionfante, potrà far il cielo e mondo tutto che non lo nomine divino, olimpico, celeste?

In conclusione (per non piú rompere il capo a me ed a voi) mi par che sia l'istessa anima del mondo, tutto in tutto, e tutto in qualsivoglia parte.

[no paragraph break in the original]

Or vedete, dunque, quale e quanta sia la importanza di questo venerabile suggetto, circa il quale noi facciamo il presente discorso e dialogi: nelli quali se vi par vedere un gran capo o senza busto o con una picciola coda, non vi sgomentate, non vi sdgenate, non vi maravigliate; perché si trovano nella natura molte specie d'animali che non hanno altri membri che testa, o par che siano tutto testa, avendo questa cossí grande e l'altre parti come insensibili; e per ciò non manca che siano perfettissime nel suo geno. E se questa raggione non vi sodisfa, dovete considerar oltre, che questa operetta contiene una descrizione, una pittura; e che ne gli ritratti suol bastar il piú de le volte d'aver ripresentata la testa sola senza il resto. Lascio che tal volta si mostra eccellente artificio in far una sola mano, un piede, una gamba, un occhio, una svelta orecchia, un mezo volto che si spicca da dietro un arbore, o dal cantoncello d'una fenestra, o sta come sculpito al ventre d'una tazza, la qual abbia per base un piè d'oca, o d'acquila, o di qualch'altro animale; non però si danna, né però si spreggia, ma piú viene accettata ed approvata la manifattura. Cossí mi persuado, anzi son certo, che voi accettarete questo dono come cosa cossí perfetta, come con perfettissimo cuore vi vien offerta. *Vale.*

Sonetto in Lode de l'Asino

O sant'asinità, sant'ignoranza,
   Santa stolticia e pia divozione,
   Qual sola puoi far l'anime sí buone,
   Ch'uman ingegno e studio non l'avanza;
Non gionge faticosa vigilanza
   D'arte qualunque sia, o 'nvenzione,
   Né de sofossi contemplazione
   Al ciel dove t'edifichi la stanza.
Che vi val, curiosi, il studïare,
   Voler saper quel che fa la natura,
   Se gli astri son pur terra, fuoco e mare?

La santa asinità di ciò non cura;
Ma con man gionte e 'n ginocchion vuol stare,
Aspettando da Dio la sua ventura.
Nessuna cosa dura,
Eccetto il frutto de l'eterna requie,
La qual ne done Dio dopo l'essequie.

Declamazione al Studioso, Divoto e Pio Lettore.

Oimè, auditor mio, che senza focoso suspiro, lubrico pianto e tragica querela, con l'affetto, con gli occhi e le raggioni non può rammentar il mio ingegno, intonar la voce e dechiarar gli argumenti, quanto sia fallace il senso, turbido il pensiero ed imperito il giudicio, che con atto di perversa, iniqua e pregiudiciosa sentenza non vede, non considera, non definisce secondo il debito di natura, verità di raggione e diritto di giustizia circa la pura bontade, regia sinceritade e magnifica maestade della santa ignoranza, dotta pecoragine e divina asinitade! Lasso! a quanto gran torto da alcuni è sí fieramente essagitata quest'eccellenza celeste tra gli uomini viventi, contra la quale altri con larghe narici si fan censori, altri con aperte sanne si fan mordaci, altri con comici cachini si rendono beffeggiatori.
Mentre ovunque spreggiano, burlano e vilipendeno qualche cosa, non gli odi dir altro che: Costui è un asino, quest'azione è asinesca, questa è una asinitade;—stante che ciò absolutamente convegna dire dove son piú maturi discorsi, piú saldi proponimenti e piú trutinate sentenze.
[no paragraph break in the original]
Lasso! perché con ramarico del mio core, cordoglio del spirito ed aggravio de l'alma mi si presenta a gli occhi questa imperita, stolta e profana moltitudine che sí falsamente pensa, sí mordacemente parla, sí temerariamente scrive per paturir que' scelerati discorsi de tanti monumenti che vanno per le stampe, per le librarie, per tutto, oltre gli espressi ludibrii, dispreggi e biasimi: *l'asino d'oro*, le *lodi de*

l'asino, l'*encomio de l'asino*; dove non si pensa altro che con ironiche sentenze prendere la gloriosa asinitade in gioco, spasso e scherno? Or chi terrà il mondo che non pensi ch' io faccia il simile? Chi potrà donar freno alle lingue che non mi mettano nel medesimo predicamento, come colui che corre appo gli vestigii de gli altri che circa cotal suggetto democriteggiano? Chi potrà contenerli che non credano, affermino e confermino che io non intendo vera- e seriosamente lodar l'asino ed asinitade, ma piú tosto procuro di aggionger oglio a quella lucerna la quale è stata da gli altri accesa? [no paragraph break in the original] Ma, o miei protervi e temerarii giodici, o neghittosi e ribaldi calunniatori, o foschi ed appassionati detrattori, fermate il passo, voltate gli occhi, prendete la mira; vedete, penetrate, considerate se gli concetti semplici, le sentenze enunciative e gli discorsi sillogistici ch'apporto in favor di questo sacro, impolluto e santo animale, son puri, veri e demostrativi, o pur son finti, impossibili ed apparenti. Se le vedrete in effetto fondati su le basi de fondamenti fortissimi, se son belli, se son buoni, non le schivate, non le fuggite, non le rigettate; ma accettatele, seguitele, abbracciatele, e non siate oltre legati dalla consuetudine del credere, vinti dalla sufficienza del pensare e guidati dalla vanità del dire, se altro vi mostra la luce de l'intelletto, altro la voce della dottrina intona ed altro l'atto de l'esperienza conferma.

L'asino ideale e kaballistico, che ne vien proposto nel corpo de le sacre lettere, che credete voi che sia? Che pensate voi essere il cavallo pegaseo, che vien trattato in figura de gli poetici figmenti? De l'asino cillenico degno d'esser messo *in croceis* nelle piú onorate academie che v'imaginate? Or lasciando il pensier del secondo e terzo da canto, e dando sul campo del primo, platonico parimente e teologale, voglio che conosciate che non manca testimonio dalle divine ed umane lettere, dettate da sacri e profani dottori, che parlano con l'ombra de scienze e lume della fede. Saprà, dico, ch' io non mentisco colui ch'è anco mediocremente perito in queste dottrine, quando avien ch' io dica l'asino ideale esser principio prodottivo, formativo e perfettivo sopranaturalmente della specie asinina; la quale quantunque nel capacissimo seno della natura si vede ed è dall'altre specie distinta, e nelle menti seconde è messa in numero, e con diverso concetto appresa, e non quel medesimo con cui l'altre forme s'apprendeno; nulla di meno (quel ch' importa tutto) nella prima mente è medesima che la idea de la specie umana, medesima che la specie de la terra, della luna, del sole, medesima che la specie dell'intelligenze, de gli demoni, de gli dei, de gli mondi, de l'universo; anzi è quella specie da cui non solamente gli asini, ma e gli uomini e le stelle e gli mondi e gli mondani animali tutti han dependenza: quella dico, nella quale non è differenza di forma e suggetto, di cosa e cosa; ma è semplicissima ed una.

[no paragraph break in the original]

Vedete, vedete dunque, d'onde derive la caggione che senza biasimo alcuno il santo de santi or è nominato non solamente leone, monocorno, rinoceronte, vento, tempesta, aquila, pellicano, ma e non uomo, opprobrio de gli uomini, abiezion di plebe, pecora, agnello, verme, similitudine di colpa, sin ad esser detto peccato e peggio. Considerate il principio della causa, per cui gli cristiani e giudei non s'adirano, ma piú tosto con glorioso trionfo si congratulano insieme, quando con le metaforiche allusioni della santa scrittura son figurati per titoli e definizioni asini, son appellati asini, son definiti per asini: di sorte che, dovunque si tratta di quel benedetto animale, per moralità di lettera, allegoria di senso ed anagogia di proposito s'intende, l'uomo giusto, l'uomo santo, l'uomo de Dio.

Però, quando ne l'*Exodo* si fa menzione della redenzione e mutazion dell'uomo, in compagnia di quello vien fatta la menzion de l'asino. *Il primogenito dell'asino,* dice, *cangiarai con la pecora; il primogenito dell'uomo redimerai col prezzo.* Quando nel medesimo libro è donata legge al desiderio dell'uomo che non si stenda alla moglie, alla servente, vedi nel medesimo numero messo il bue e l'asino: come che non meno importe proporsi materia di peccato l'uno che l'altro appetibile. Però quando nel libro de *Giudici* cantò Debora e Barac, figlio d'Abinoen, dicendo: *Udite, o regi, porgete l'orecchie, o principi, li quali montate su gli asini nitenti e sedete in giudicio,* interpretano gli santi rabini: O governatori de la terra, li quali siete superiori a gli generosi popoli, e con la sacra sferza le governate, castigando gli rei, premiando gli buoni e dispensando giustamente le cose.

[no paragraph break in the original]

—Quando ordina il *Pentateuco* che devi ridur ed addirizzar al suo camino l'asino e bue errante del prossimo tuo, intendeno moralmente gli dottori, che l'uomo del nostro prossimo Idio, il quale è dentro di noi ed in noi, s'aviene che prevariche dalla via della giustizia, debba essere da noi corretto ed avertito. Quando l'archisinagogo riprese il Signor che curava nel sabbato, ed egli rispose che *non è uomo da bene che in qualunque giorno non vegna a cavar l'asino o bue dal pozzo dove è cascato*; intendeno gli divini scrittori che l'asino è l'uomo semplice, il bue è l'uomo che sta sul naturale, il pozzo è il peccato mortale, quel che cava l'asino dal pozzo è la divina grazia e ministero che redime gli suoi diletti da quell'abisso. Ecco, dunque, qualmente il popolo redemuto, preggiato, bramato, governato, addirizzato, avertito, corretto, liberato e finalmente predestinato, è significato per l'asino, è nominato asino. E che gli asini son quelli per gli quali la divina benedizione e grazia piove sopra gli uomini, di maniera che guai a color che vegnon privi del suo asino, certamente molto ben si può veder nell'importanza di quella maledizione che impiomba nel *Deuteronomio,* quando minacciò Dio dicendo: *L'asino tuo ti sia tolto d'avanti, e non ti sia reso!*

Maladetto il regno, sfortunata la republica, desolata la città, desolata la casa, onde è bandito, distolto ed allontanato l'asino! Guai al senso, conscienza ed anima dove non è participazion d'asinità! Ed è pur trito adagio: *ab asino excidere,* per significar l'esser destrutto, sfatto, spacciato. Origene Adamanzio, accettato tra gli ortodoxi e sacri dottori, vuole che il frutto de la predicazione de' settanta doi discepoli è significato per li settanta doi milia asini che il popolo israleita guadagnò contra gli Moabiti: atteso che de quei settanta doi ciascuno guadagnò mille, cioè un numero perfetto, d'anime predestinate, traendole da le mani de Moab, cioè liberandole dalla tirannia de Satan. Giongasi a questo che gli uomini piú divoti e santi, amatori ed exequitori dell'antiqua e nova legge, absolutamente e per particolar privilegio son stati chiamati asini. E se non me 'l credete, andate a studiar quel ch' è scritto sopra quell'Evangelico: *L'asina ed il pulledro sciogliete e menateli a me.*

[no paragraph break in the original]

Andate a contemplar su gli discorsi che fanno gli teologi ebrei, greci e latini sopra quel passo che è scritto nel libro de *Numeri: Aperuit, Dominus os asinae, et locuta est.* E vedete come concordano tanti altri luoghi delle sacrate lettere, dove sovente è introdotto il providente Dio aprir la bocca de diversi divini e profetici suggetti, come di quel che disse: *Oh oh oh, Signor, ch'io non so dire.* E là dove dice: *Aperse il Signor la sua bocca.* Oltre tante volte ch' è detto: *Ego ero in ore tuo;* tante volte che'gli è priegato: *Signor, apri le mie labra, e la mia bocca ti lodarà.* Oltre nel testamento novo: *Li muti parlano, li poveri evangelizano.*

Tutto è figurato per quello che il Signor aperse la bocca de l'asina, ed ella parlò. Per l'autorità di questa, per la bocca, voce e paroli di questa è domata, vinta e calpestrata la gonfia, superba e temeraria scienza secolare; ed è ispianata al basso ogni altezza che ardisce di levar il capo verso il cielo: perché Dio av'elette le cose inferme per confondere le forze del mondo; le cose stolte ave messe in riputazione; atteso che quello, che per la sapienza non posseva essere restituito, per la santa stoltizia ed ignoranza è stato riparato: però è riprovata la sapienza de sapienti e la prudenza de prudenti è rigettata. Stolti del mondo son stati quelli ch' han formata la religione, gli ceremoni, la legge, la fede, la regola di vita; gli maggiori asini del mondo (che son quei che, privi d'ogni altro senso e dottrina, e voti d'ogni vita e costume civile, marciti sono nella perpetua pedanteria) son quelli che per grazia del cielo riformano la temerata e corrotta fede, medicano le ferite de l'impiagata religione, e togliendo gli abusi de le superstizioni, risaldano le scissure della sua veste; non son quelli che con empia curiosità vanno, o pur mai andâro perseguitando gli arcani della natura, computâro le vicissitudini de le stelle.

[no paragraph break in the original]

Vedete se sono o furon giamai solleciti circa le cause secrete de le cose; se perdonano a dissipazion qualunque de regni, dispersion de popoli, incendii, sangui, ruine ed esterminii; se curano che perisca il mondo tutto per essi loro: purché la povera anima sia salva, purché si faccia l'edificio in cielo, purché si ripona il tesoro in quella beata patria, niente curando della fama e comodità e gloria di questa frale ed incerta vita, per quell'altra certissima ed eterna. Questi son stati significati per l'allegoria de gli antiqui sapienti (alli quali non ha voluto mancar, il divino spirito di revelar qualche cosa, almeno per farli inescusabili) in quello sentenzioso apologo de gli dei che combattirono contra gli rubelli giganti, figli de la terra ed arditi predatori del cielo; che con la voce de gli asini confusero, atterrirono, spaventâro, vinsero e domorno.

[no paragraph break in the original]

Il medesimo è sufficientemente espresso dove, alzando il velo de la sacrata figura, s'affigono gli occhi all'anagogico senso di quel divin Sansone, che con l'asinina mascella tolse la vita a mille Filistei; perché dicono gli santi interpreti, che nella mascella de l'asina, cioè de gli predicatori de la legge e ministri della sinagoga, e nella mascella del pulledro de gli asini, cioè de' predicatori della nova legge e ministri de l'ecclesia militante, *delevit eos,* cioè scancellò, spinse que' mille, quel numero compito, que' tutti, secondo che è scritto: *Cascarono dal tuo lato mille, e dalla tua destra diece milia;* ed è chiamato il luogo

Ramath-lechi, cioè exaltazion de la mascella. Dalla quale per frutto di predicazione non solo è seguita la ruina delle avversarie ed odiose potestadi, ma anco la salute de regenerati: perché dalla medesima mascella, cioè per virtú di medesima predicazione, son uscite e comparse quelle acqui, che promulgando la divina sapienza, diffondeno la grazia celeste e fanno gli suoi abbeverati capaci de vita eterna.

O dunque forte, vittoriosa e trionfatrice mascella d'un asino morto, o diva, graziosa e santa mascella d'un polledro defunto, or che deve essere della santità, grazia e divinità, fortezza, vittoria e trionfo dell'asino tutto, intiero e vivente,—asino, pullo e madre,—se di quest'osso e sacrosanta reliquia la gloria ed exaltazion è tanta? E mi volto a voi, o dilettissimi ascoltatori; a voi, a voi mi rivolto, o amici lettori de mia scrittura ed ascoltatori de mia voce; e vi dico, e vi avertisco, e vi esorto, e vi scongiuro, che ritorniate a voi medesimi. Datemi scampo dal vostro male, prendete partito del vostro bene, banditevi dalla mortal magnificenza del core, ritiratevi alla povertà del spirito, siate umili di mente, abrenunziate alla raggione, estinguete quella focosa luce de l'intelletto che vi accende, vi bruggia e vi consuma; fuggite que' gradi de scienza che per certo aggrandiscono i vostri dolori; abnegate ogni senso, fatevi cattivi alla santa fede, siate quelle benedetta asina, riducetevi a quei glorioso pulledro, per li quali soli il redentor del mondo disse a gli ministri suoi: *Andate al castello ch'avete a l'incontro;* cioè andate per l'universo mondo sensibile e corporeo il quale come simulacro è opposto e supposto al mondo intelligibile ed incorporeo. *Trovarete l'asina ed il pulledro legati:* v'occorrerà il popolo ebreo e gentile, sottomesso e tiranneggiato dalla captività di Belial.

Dice ancora: *Scioglietele:* levateli de la cattività, per la predicazion dell' Evangelio ed effusion de l'acqua battismale; e *menatele a me,* perché mi servano, perché siano miei: perché portando il peso del mio corpo, cioè della mia santa instituzione e legge sopra le spalli, ed essendo guidati dal freno delli miei divini consegli, sian fatti degni e capabili d'entrar meco nella trionfante Ierusalem, nella città celeste. Qua vedete chi son li redemuti, chi son gli chiamati, chi son gli predestinati, chi son gli salvi: l'asina, l'asinello, gli semplici, gli poveri d'argumento, gli pargoletti, quelli ch'han discorso de fanciulli; quelli, quelli entrano nel regno de' cieli; quelli, per dispreggio del mondo e de le sue pompe, calpestrano gli vestimenti, hanno bandita da sé ogni cura del corpo, de la carne che sta avolta circa quest'anima, se l'han messa sotto gli piedi, l'hanno gittata via a terra, per far piú gloriosa- e trionfalmente passar l'asina ed il suo caro asinello. Pregate, pregate Dio, o carissimi, se non siete ancora asini, che vi faccia dovenir asini. Vogliate solamente; perché certo certo, facilissimamente vi sarà conceduta la grazia: perché, benché naturalmente siate asini, e la disciplina commune non sia altro che una asinitade, dovete avertire e considerar molto bene se siate asini secondo Dio; dico, se siate quei sfortunati che rimagnono legati avanti la porta, o pur quegli altri felici li quali entran dentro. Ricordatevi, o fideli, che gli nostri primi parenti a quel tempo piacquero a Dio, ed erano in sua grazia, in sua salvaguardia, contenti nel terrestre paradiso, nel quale erano asini, cioè semplici ed ignoranti del bene e male; quando posseano esser titillati dal desiderio di sapere bene e male, e per consequenza non ne posseano aver notizia alcuna; quando possean credere una buggia che gli venesse detta dal serpente; quando se gli possea donar ad intendere sin a questo: che, benché Dio avesse detto che morrebono, ne potesse essere il contrario: in cotal disposizione erano grati, erano accetti, fuor d'ogni dolor, cura e molestia. Sovvegnavi ancora ch'amò Dio il popolo ebreo, quando era afflitto, servo, vile, oppresso, ignorante, onerario, portator de còfini, somarro, che non gli possea mancar altro che la coda ad esser asino naturale sotto il domíno de l'Egitto: allora fu detto da Dio suo popolo, sua gente, sua scelta generazione. Perverso, scelerato, reprobo, adultero fu detto quando fu sotto le discipline, le dignitadi, le grandezze e similitudine de gli altri popoli e regni onorati secondo il mondo.

[no paragraph break in the original]

Non è chi non loda l'età de l'oro, quando gli uomini erano asini, non sapean lavorar la terra, non sapean l'un dominar a l'altro, intender piú de l'altro, avean per tetto gli antri e le caverne, si donavano a dosso come fan le bestie, non eran tante coperte e gelosie e condimenti de libidine e gola; ogni cosa era commune, il pasto eran le poma, le castagne, le ghiande in quella forma che son prodotte dalla madre natura. Non è chi non sappia qualmente non solamente nella specie umana, ma ed in tutti gli geni d'animali la madre ama piú, accarezza piú, mantien contento piú ed ocioso, senza sollecitudine e fatica, abbraccia, bacia, stringe, custodisce il figlio minore, come quello che non sa male e bene, ha dell'agnello, ha de la bestia, è un asino, non sa cossí parlare, non può tanto discorrere; e come gli va crescendo il senno e la prudenza, sempre a mano a mano se gli va scemando l'amore, la cura, la pia affezione che gli vien portata da gli suoi parenti.

[no paragraph break in the original]

Non è nemico che non compatisca, abblandisca, favorisca a quella età, a quella persona che non ha del virile, non ha del demonio, non ha de l'uomo, non ha del maschio, non ha de l'accorto, non ha del barbuto, non ha del sodo, non ha del maturo. Però quando si vuol mover Dio a pietà e comiserazione il suo Signore, disse quel profeta: *Ah ah ah, Domine, quia nescio loqui;* dove, col ragghiare e sentenza, mostra esser asino. Ed in un altro luogo dice: *Quia puer sum.* Però quando si brama la remission della colpa, molte volte si presenta la causa nelli divini libri, con dire: *Quia stulte egimus, stulte egerunt, quia nesciunt quid faciant, ignoramus, non intellexerunt.* Quando si vuol impetrar da lui maggior favore ed acquistar tra gli uomini maggior fede, grazia ed autorità, si dice in un loco, che li apostoli eran stimati imbreachi; in un altro loco, che non sapean quel che dicevano, perché non erano essi che parlavano: ed un de piú eccellenti, per mostrar quanto avesse del semplice, disse che era stato rapito al terzo cielo, uditi arcani ineffabili, e che non sapea s'era morto o vivo, se era in corpo o fuor di quello. Un altro disse che vedeva gli cieli aperti, e tanti e tanti altri propositi che tegnono gli diletti de Dio, alli quali è revelato quello che è occolto a la sapienza umana, ed è asinità esquisita a gli occhi del discorso razionale: perché queste pazzie, asinitadi e bestialitadi son sapienze, atti eroici ed intelligenze appresso il nostro Dio; il qual chiama li suoi pulcini, il suo grege, le sue pecore, li suoi parvuli, li suoi stolti, il suo pulledro, la sua asina que' tali che li credeno, l'amano, il siegueno.

[no paragraph break in the original]

Non è, non è, dico, meglior specchio messo avanti gli occhi umani che l'asinitade ed asino, il qual piú esplicatamente secondo tutti gli numeri dimostre qual esser debba colui, che faticandosi nella vigna del Signore deve aspettar la retribuzion del danaio diurno, il gusto della beatifica cena, il riposo che segue il corso di questa transitoria vita. Non è conformità megliore o simile che ne amene, guide e conduca alla salute eterna piú attamente che far possa questa vera sapienza approvata dalla divina voce: come, per il contrario, non è cosa che ne faccia piú efficacemente impiombar al centro ed al baratro tartareo, che le filosofiche e razionali contemplazioni, quali nascono da gli sensi, crescono nella facultà discorsiva e si maturano nell'intelletto umano. Forzatevi, forzatevi dunque ad esser asini, o voi, che siete uomini. E voi, che siete già asini, studiate, procurate, adattatevi a proceder sempre da bene in meglio, a fin che perveniate a quel termine, a quella dignità, la quale, non per scienze ed opre, quantunque grandi, ma per fede s'acquista; non per ignoranza e misfatti, quantunque enormi, ma per la incredulità (come dicono, secondo l'Apostolo) si perde. Se cossí vi disporrete, se tali sarete e talmente vi governarete, vi trovarete scritti nel libro de la vita, impetrarete la grazia in questa militante, ed otterrete la gloria in quella trionfante ecclesia, nella quale vive e regna Dio per tutti secoli de secoli. Cossí sia!

FINIS

Un Molto Pio Sonetto Circa la Significazione de l'Asina e Pulledro.

—Ite al castello ch'avete d'avanti,
E trovarete l'asina col figlio:
Quelli sciogliete, e dandogli de piglio,
L'amenarete a me, servi miei santi.
S'alcun, per impedir misterii tanti,
Contra di voi farà qualche bisbiglio,
Risponderete lui con alto ciglio,
Ch' il gran Signor le vuol far trionfanti.—
Dice cossí la divina scrittura,
Per notar la salute de' credenti
Al redentor dell'umana natura.
Gli fideli di Giuda e de le genti
Con vita parimente sempia e pura
Potran montar a que' scanni eminenti.
Divoti e pazienti
Vegnon a fars' il pullo con la madre
Contubernali a l'angeliche squadre.

Dialogo Primo

Interlocutori: Sebasto, Saulino, Coribante
Sebasto. È il peggio che diranno che metti avanti metaffore, narri favole, raggioni in parabola, intessi enigmi, accozzi similitudini, tratti misterii, mastichi tropologie.

Saulino. Ma io dico la cosa a punto come la passa; e come la è propriamente, la metto avanti gli occhi.

Cor. *Id est, sine fuco, plane, candide*; ma vorrei che fusse cossí, come dite, da dovero.

Saul. Cossí piacesse alli dei, che fessi tu altro che fuco con questa tua gestuazione, toga, barba e supercilio: come, anco quanto a l'ingegno, *candide, plane et sine fuco,* mostri a gli occhi nostri la idea della pedantaria.

Cor. *Hactenus haec?* Tanto che Sofia loco per loco, sedia per sedia vi condusse?

Saul. Sí.

Seb. Occórevi de dir altro circa la provisione di queste sedie?

Saul. Non per ora, se voi non siete pronto a donarmi occasione di chiarirvi de piú punti circa esse col dimandarmi e destarmi la memoria, la quale non può avermi suggerito la terza parte de notabili propositi degni di considerazione.

Seb. Io, a dir il vero, rimagno sí suspeso dal desio de saper qual cosa sia quella ch' il gran padre de gli dei ha fatto succedere in quelle due sedie, l'una Boreale e l'altra Australe, che m' ha parso il tempo di mill'anni per veder il fine del vostro filo, quantunque curioso, utile e degno: perché quel proposito tanto piú mi vien a spronar il desio d'esserne fatto capace, quanto voi piú l'avete differito a farlo udire.

Cor. *Spes etenim dilata affligit animum, vel animam, ut melius dicam; haec enim mage significat naturam passibilem.*

Saul. Bene. Dunque, perché non piú vi tormentiate su l'aspettar della risoluzione, sappiate che nella sedia prossima immediata e gionta al luogo dove era l'Orsa minore, e nel quale sapete essere exaltata la Veritade, essendone tolta via l'Orsa maggiore nella forma ch'avete inteso, per providenza del prefato consiglio vi ha succeduto l'Asinità in abstratto: e là dove ancora vedete in fantasia il fiume Eridano, piace a gli medesimi che vi si trove l'Asinità in concreto, a fine che da tutte tre le celesti reggioni possiamo contemplare l'Asinità, la quale in due facelle era come occolta nella via de' pianeti, dov' è la coccia del Cancro.

Cor. Procul, o procul este, profani! Questo è un sacrilegio, un profanismo, di voler fingere (poscia che non è possibile che cossí sia in fatto) vicino a l'onorata ed eminente sedia de la Verità essere l'idea de sí immonda e vituperosa specie, la quale è stata da gli sapienti Egizii ne gli lor ieroglifici presa per tipo de l'ignoranza, come ne rende testimonio Oro Apolline, piú volte replicando: qualmente gli Babiloni sacerdoti con l'asinino capo compiuto al busto e cervice umana volsero designar un uomo imperito ed indisciplinabile.

Seb. Non è necessario andar al tempo e luogo d'Egizii, se non è né fu mai generazione, che con l'usato modo di parlare non conferme quel che dice Coribante.

Saul. Questa è la raggione, per cui ho differito al fine di raggionar circa queste due sedie: atteso che dalla consuetudine del dire e credere m'areste creduto parabolano, e con minor fede ed attenzione arreste perseverato ad ascoltarmi nella descrizione della riforma de l'altre sedie celesti, se prima con prolissa infilacciata de propositi non v'avesse resi capaci di quella verità; stante che queste due sedie da per esse meritano almeno altretanto de considerazione, quanto vedete aver ricchezza di tal suggetta materia. Or non avete voi unqua udito, che la pazzia, ignoranza ed asinità di questo mondo è sapienza, dottrina e divinità in quell'altro?

Seb. Cossí è stato riferito da primi e principali teologi; ma giamai è stato usato un cossí largo modo de dire, come è il vostro.

Saul. È perché giamai la cosa è stata chiarita ed esplicata cossí, come io son per esplicarvela e chiarirvela al presente.

Cor. Or dite, perché staremo attenti ad ascoltarvi.

Saul. Perché non vi spantiate, quando udite il nome d'asino, asinità, bestialità, ignoranza, pazzia, prima voglio proporvi avanti gli occhi della considerazione, e rimenarvi a mente il luogo de gl' illuminati cabalisti, che con altri lumi che di Linceo, con altri occhi che di Argo, profondorno, non dico sin al terzo cielo, ma nel profondo abisso del sopramondano ed ensofico universo: per la contemplazione di quelle diece Sefirot che chiamiamo in nostra lingua *membri ed idumenti,* penetrorno, veddero, concepirno *quantum fas est homini loqui.*

[no paragraph break in the original]

Ivi son le dimensioni *Ceter, Hocma, Bina, Hesed, Geburah, Tipheret, Nezah, Hod, Iesod, Malchuth;* de quali la prima da noi è detta *Corona,* la seconda *Sapienza,* la terza *Providenza,* la quarta *Bontà,* la quinta *Fortezza,* la sesta *Bellezza,* la settima *Vittoria,* la ottava *Lode,* la nona *Stabilimento,* la decima *Regno.* Dove dicono rispondere diece ordini d' intelligenze; de quali il primo vien da essi chiamato *Haioth heccados,* il secondo *Ophanim,* il terzo *Aralin,* il quarto *Hasmalin,* il quinto *Choachin,* il sesto *Malachim,* il settimo *Elohim,* l'ottavo *Benelohim,* il nono *Maleachim,* il decimo *Issim;* che noi nominiamo il primo *Animali santi* o *Serafini,* il secondo *Ruote formanti* o *Cherubini,* il terzo *Angeli robusti* o *Troni,* il quarto *Effigiatori,* il quinto *Potestadi,* il sesto *Virtudi,* il settimo *Principati* o *dei,* l'ottavo *Arcangeli* o *figli de dei,* il nono *Angeli* o *Imbasciatori,* il decimo *Anime separate* o *Eroi.* Onde nel mondo sensibile derivano le diece sfere: 1. il primo mobile, 2. il cielo stellato o ottava sfera o firmamento, 3. il cielo di Saturno, 4. di Giove, 5. di Marte, 6. del Sole, 7. di Venere, 8. di Mercurio, 9. della Luna, 10. del Chaos sublunare diviso in quattro elementi.

[no paragraph break in the original]

Alli quali sono assistenti diece motori, o insite diece anime: la prima *Metattron* o principe de faccie, la seconda *Raziel,* la terza *Zaphciel,* la quarta *Zadkiel,* la quinta *Camael,* la sesta *Raphael,* la settima *Aniel,* l'ottava *Michael,* la nona *Gabriel,* la decima *Samael;* sotto il quale son quattro terribili principi, de quali il primo domina nel fuoco ed è chiamato da Iob *Behemoth,* il secondo domina nell'aria ed è nomato da cabalisti e comunmente *Beelzebub,* cioè principe de mosche, *idest* de volanti immondi, il terzo domina nell'acqui ed è nomato da Iob *Leviathan*, il quarto è presidente ne la terra, la qual spasseggia e circuisse tutta, ed è chiamato da Iob *Sathan*. Or contemplate qua, che secondo la kaballistica revelazione Hocma, a cui rispondeno le forme o ruote nomate *Cherubini*, che influiscono nell'ottava sfera, dove consta la virtú dell'intelligenza de Raziele, l'asino o asinità è simbolo della sapienza.

Cor. Parturient montes.

Saul. Alcuni thalmutisti apportano la raggione morale di cotale influsso, arbore, scala o dependenza, dicendo che però l'asino è simbolo della sapienza nelli divini Sefirot, perché a colui che vuoi, penetrare entro gli secreti ed occolti ricetti di quella, sia necessariamente de mistiero d'esser sobrio e paziente, avendo mustaccio, testa e schena d'asino; deve aver l'animo umile, ripremuto e basso, ed il senso che non faccia differenza tra gli cardi e le lattuche.

Seb. Io crederei piú tosto, che gli Ebrei abbiano tolti questi misterii da gli Egizii; li quali per cuoprir certa ignominia loro hanno voluto in tal maniera esaltar al cielo l'asino e l'asinità.

Cor. Declara.

Seb. Oco, re de Persi, essendo notato da gli Egizi, suoi nemici, per il simulacro d'asino, ed appresso essendo lui vittorioso sopra de loro, ed avendoseli fatti cattivi, le costrinse ad adorar l'imagine de l'asino e sacrificargli il bove già tanto adorato da essi, con rimproverargli che a l'asino il lor bove Opin o Apin verrebbe immolato. Questi dunque, per onorar quel loro vituperoso culto, e cuoprir quella machia, hanno voluto fingere raggioni sopra il culto de l'asino; il quale da quel che gli fu materia di biasimo e burla, gli venne ad esser materia di riverenza. E cossí poi, in materia d'adorazione, admirazione, contemplazione, onore e gloria, se l'hanno fatto kaballistico, archetipo, sephirotico, metafisico, ideale, divino. [no paragraph break in the original]
Oltre, essendo l'asino animal de Saturno e della Luna, e gli Ebrei di natura, ingegno e fortuna saturnini e lunari, gente sempre vile,

servile, mercenaria, solitaria, incomunicabile ed inconversabile con l'altre generazioni, le quali bestialmente spregiano, e da le quali per ogni raggione son degnamente dispreggiate; or questi si trovâro nella cattività e servizio de l'Egitto, dove erano destinati ad esser compagni a gli asini con portar le some e servire alle fabriche; e là parte per esserno leprosi, parte perché intesero gli Egizii, che in essi pestilanziati regnava l'impression saturnia ed asinina, per la conversazione ch'aveano con questa razza; vogliono alcuni che le discacciassero dagli lor confini con lasciargli l'idolo dell'asino d'oro alle mani; il quale tra tutti li dei se mostrava più propisiabile a questa gente, cossí a tutte l'altre nemica e ritrosa, come Saturno a tutti gli pianeti. Onde rimanendo con il proprio culto, lasciando da canto l'altre feste egiziane, celebravano per il lor Saturno, demostrato nell'idolo de l'asino, gli sabbati, e per la lor Luna le neomenie, di sorte che non solamente uno, ma, ed oltre, tutti gli sephiroti possono essere asinini ai cabalisti giudei.

Saul. Voi dite molte cose autentiche, molte vicine all'autentiche, altre simili a l'autentiche, alcune contrarie a l'autentiche ed approvate istorie. Onde dite alcuni propositi veri e boni, ma nulla dite bene e veramente, spreggiando e burlandovi di questa santa generazione, dalla quale è proceduta tutta quella luce che si trova sin oggi al mondo, e che promette de donar per tanti secoli. Cossí perseveri nel tuo pensiero ad aver l'asino ed asinità per cosa ludibriosa; quale, qualunque sia stata appresso Persi, Greci e Latini, non fu però cosa vile appresso gli Egizii ed Ebrei. Là onde è falsità ed impostura questa tra l'altre, cioè che quel culto asinino e divino abbia avuto origine dalla forza e violenza, e non più tosto ordinato dalla raggione, e tolto principio dalla elezione.

Seb. Verbi gratia, forza, violenza, raggion ed elezione di Oco.

Saul. Io dico divina inspirazione, natural bontade ed umana intelligenza. Ma prima che vengamo al compimento di questa demostrazione, considerate un poco se mai ebbero, o denno aver avuto, o tener a vile la idea ed influenza de gli asini questi Ebrei ed altri partecipi e consorti de la lor santimonia. Il patriarca Iacob, celebrando la natività e sangue della sua prole, e padri de le dodici tribú con la figura de le dodici bestie, vedete se ebbe ardimento di lasciar l'asino. Non avete notato che come fe' Ruben montone, Simone orso, Levi cavallo, Giuda leone, Zabulon balena, Dan serpente, Gad volpe, Aser bove, Nettalim cervio, Gioseffo pecora, Beniamin lupo, cossí fece il sesto genito Isachar asino, insoffiandoli per testamento quella bella nuova e misteriosa profezia nell'orecchio: *Isachar, asino forte, che poggia tra gli termini, ha trovato il riposo buono ed il fertilissimo terreno; ha sottoposte le robuste spalli al peso, ed èssi destinato al tributario serviggio.*

[no paragraph break in the original]

Queste sacrate dodici generazioni rispondeno da qua basso a gli alti dodici segni del zodiaco, che son nel cingolo del firmamento, comme vedde e dechiarò il profeta Balaam, quando dal luogo eminente d'un colle le scòrse disposte e distinte in dodici castramentazioni alla pianura, dicendo: —Beato e benedetto popolo d'Israele, voi sète stelle, voi li dodici segni messi in sí bell'ordine di tanti generosi greggi. Cossí promese il vostro Giova che moltiplicarebbe il seme del vostro gran padre Abraamo come le stelle del cielo, cioè secondo la raggione delli dodici segni del zodiaco, li quali venite a significar per li nomi de dodici bestie. —Qua vedete qualmente quel profeta illuminato, dovendole benedire in terra, andò a presentarseli montato sopra l'asino, per la voce de l'asino venne instrutto della divina volontà, con la forza de l'asino vi pervenne, da sopra l'asino stese le mani alle tende, e benedisse quel popolo de Dio santo e benedetto, per far evidente che quelli asini saturnini ed altre bestie, che hanno influsso, dalle dette Sefirot, da l'asino archetipo, per mezzo de l'asino naturale e profetico, doveano esser partecipi de tanta benedizione.

Cor. Multa igitur asinorum genera: aureo, archetipo, indumentale, celeste, intelligenziale, angelico, animale, profetico, umano, bestiale, gentile, etico, civile ed economico; *vel* essenziale, subsistenziale, metafisico, fisico, ipostatico, nozionale, matematico, logico e morale; *vel* superno, medio ed inferno; *vel* intelligibile, sensibile e fantastico; *vel* ideale, naturale e nozionale; *vel ante multa, in multis et post multa.* Or seguíte, perché *paulatim, gradatim atque pedetentim,* piú chiaro, alto e profondo venite a riuscirmi.

Saul. Per venir dunque a noi, non vi deve parer strano che la asinità sia messa in sedia celeste nella distribuzione delle catedre, che sono nella parte superna di questo mondo ed universo corporeo; atteso che esso deve esser corrispondente e riconoscere in se stesso certa analogia al mondo superiore.

Cor. Ita contiguus hic illi mundus, ut omnis eius virtus inde gubernetur, come oltre promulgò il prencipe de' peripatetici nel principio del primo della *Metorologica* [sic] *contemplazione.*

Seb. O che ampolle, o che parole sesquipedali son le vostre, o dottissimo ed altritonante messer Coribante!

Cor. Ut libet.

Seb. Ma permettiate che si proceda al proposito, e non ne interrompete!

Cor. Proh!

Saul. A la verità nulla cosa è piú prossima e cognata che la scienza; la quale si deve distinguere, come è distinta in sé, in due maniere: cioè in superiore ed inferiore. La prima è sopra la creata verità, ed è l'istessa verità increata, ed è causa del tutto; atteso che per essa le cose vere son vere, e tutto quel che è, è veramente quel tanto che è. La seconda è verità inferiore, la quale né fa le cose vere, né è le cose vere, ma pende, è prodotta, formata ed informata da le cose vere, ed apprende quelle non in verità, ma in specie e similitudine: perché nella mente nostra, dove è la scienza dell'oro, non si trova l'oro in verità, ma solamente in specie e similitudine.

[no paragraph break in the original]

Sí che è una sorte de verità, la quale è causa delle cose, e si trova sopra tutte le cose; un'altra sorte che si trova nelle cose ed è delle cose; ed è un'altra terza ed ultima, la quale è dopo le cose e dalle cose. La prima ha nome di causa, la seconda ha nome di cosa, la terza ha nome di cognizione. La verità nel primo modo è nel mondo archetipo ideale significata per un de' Sefirot; nel secondo modo è nella prima sedia dove è il cardine del cielo a noi supremo; nel terzo modo è nella detta sedia che prossimamente da questo corporeo cielo influisce ne gli cervelli nostri, dove è l'ignoranza, stoltizia, asinità, ed onde è stata discacciata l'Orsa maggiore. Come dunque la verità reale e naturale è essaminata per la verità nozionale, e questa ha quella per oggetto, e quella mediante la sua specie ha questa per suggetto, cossí è bisogno che a quella abitazione questa sia vicina e congionta.

Seb. Voi dite bene, che secondo l'ordine della natura sono prossimi la verità e l'ignoranza o asinità: come sono talvolta uniti l'oggetto, l'atto e la potenza. Ma fate ora chiaro, perché piú tosto volete far gionta e vicina l'ignoranza o asinità, che la scienza o cognizione: atteso che tanto manca che l'ignoranza e pazzia debbano esser prossime e come coabitatrici della verità, che ne denno essere a tutta distanza lontane, perché denno esser gionte alla falsità, come cose appartenenti ad ordine contrario.

Saul. Perché la sofia creata senza l'ignoranza o pazzia, e per consequenza senza l'asinità che le significa ed è medesima con esse, non può apprendere la verità; e però bisogna che sia mediatrice; perché come nell'atto mediante concorreno gli estremi o i termini, oggetto e potenza, cossí nell'asinità concorreno la verità e la cognizione, detta da noi sofia.

Seb. Dite brevemente la caggione.

Saul. Perché il saper nostro è ignorare, o perché non è scienza di cosa alcuna e non è apprensione di verità nessuna, o perché se pur a quella è qualche entrata, non è se non per la porta che ne viene aperta da l'ignoranza, la quale è l'istesso camino, portinaio e porta. Or se la sofia scorge la verità per l'ignoranza, la scorge per la stoltizia consequentemente, e consequentemente per l'asinità. Là onde chi ha tal cognizione, ha de l'asino, ed è partecipe di quella idea.

Seb. Or mostrate come siano vere le vostre assumpzioni: perché voglio concedere le illazioni tutte; perché non ho per inconveniente che chi è ignorante, per quanto è ignorante, è stolto; e chi è stolto, per quanto è stolto, è asino: e però ogni ignoranza è asinità.

Saul. Alla contemplazion de la verità altri si promuoveno per via di dottrina e cognizione razionale, per forza de l'intelletto agente che s'intrude nell'animo, excitandovi il lume interiore. E questi son rari; onde dice il poeta:

Pauci, quos ardens evexit ad aethera virtus.

Altri per via d'ignoranza vi si voltano e forzansi di pervenirvi. E di questi alcuni sono affetti di quella che è detta ignoranza di semplice negazione: e costoro né sanno, né presumeno di sapere; altri di quella che è detta ignoranza di prava disposizione: e tali, quanto men sanno e sono imbibiti de false informazioni, tanto piú pensano di sapere: quali, per informarsi del vero, richiedeno doppia fatica, cioè de dismettere l'uno abito contrario e di apprender l'altro. Altri di quella ch' è celebrata come divina acquisizione; ed in questa son color che né dicendo, né pensando di sapere, ed oltre essendo creduti da altri ignorantissimi, son veramente dotti, per ridursi a quella gloriosissima asinitade e pazzia. E di questi alcuni sono naturali, come quei che caminano con il lume suo razionale, con cui negano col lume del senso e della raggione ogni lume di raggione e senso; alcuni altri caminano, o per dir meglio si fanno guidare con la lanterna della fede, cattivando l'intelletto a colui che gli monta sopra ed a sua bella posta l'addirizza e guida. E questi veramente son quelli che non possono essi errare, perché non caminano col proprio fallace intendimento, ma con infallibil lume di superna intelligenza.

Questi, questi son veramente atti e predestinati per arrivare alla Ierusalem della beatitudine e vision aperta della verità divina: perché gli sopramonta quello, senza il qual sopramontante non è chi condurvesi vaglia.

Seb. Or ecco come si distingueno le specie dell'ignoranza ed asinitade, e come vegno a mano a mano a condescendere per concedere l'asinitade essere una virtú necessaria e divina, senza la quale sarrebe perso il mondo, e per la quale il mondo tutto è salvo.

Saul. Odi a questo proposito un principio per un'altra piú particular distinzione. Quello ch'unisce l'intelletto nostro, il qual è nella sofia, alla verità, la quale è l'oggetto intelligibile, è una specie d'ignoranza, secondo gli cabalisti e certi mistici teologi; un'altra specie, secondo gli pirroniani, efettici ed altri simili; un'altra, secondo teologi cristiani, tra' quali il Tarsense la viene tanto piú a magnificare, quanto a giudicio di tutt' il mondo è passata per maggior pazzia. Per la prima specie sempre si niega; onde vien detta ignoranza negativa, che mai ardisce affirmare. Per la seconda specie sempre si dubita, e mai ardisce determinare o definire. Per la terza specie gli principii tutti s'hanno per conosciuti, approvati e con certo argumento manifesti, senza ogni demostrazione ed apparenza.

[no paragraph break in the original]

La prima è denotata per l'asino pullo, fugace ed errabondo; la seconda per un'asina, che sta fitta tra due vie, dal mezo de quali mai si parte, non possendosi risolvere per quale delle due piú tosto debba muovere i passi; la terza per l'asina con il suo pulledro, che portano su la schena il redentor del mondo: dove l'asina, secondo che gli sacri dottori insegnano, è tipo del popolo giudaico, ed il pullo del popolo gentile, che, come figlia ecclesia, è parturito dalla madre sinagoga; appartenendo cossí questi come quelli alla medesima generazione, procedente dal padre de' credenti, Abraamo. Queste tre specie d'ignoranza, come tre rami, si riducono ad un stipe, nel quale da l'archetipo influisce l'asinità, e che è fermo e piantato su le radici delli diece Sefirot.

Cor. O bel senso! Queste non sono retorice persuasioni, né elenchici sofismi, né topice probabilitadi, ma adodiptice demostrazioni; per le quali l'asino non è sí vile animale come comunmente si crede, ma di tanto piú eroica e divina condizione.

Seb. Non è d'uopo ch'oltre t'affatichi, o Saulino, per venir a conchiudere quel tanto che io dimandavo che da te mi fusse definito: sí perché avete sodisfatto a Coribante, sí anco perché da li posti mezi termini ad ogni buono intenditore può esser facilmente sodisfatto. Ma di grazia, fatemi ora intendere le raggioni della sapienza, che consiste nell'ignoranza ed asinitade *iuxta* il secondo modo: cioè con qual raggione siano partecipi dell'asinità gli pirroniani, efettici ed altri academici filosofi; perché non dubito della prima e terza specie, che medesime sono altissime e remotissime da' sensi e chiarissime, di sorte che non è occhio che non le possa conoscere.

Saul. Presto verrò al proposito della vostra dimanda; ma voglio che prima notiate il primo e terzo modo di stoltizia ed asinitade concorrere in certa maniera in uno; e però medesimamente pendeno da principio incomprensibile ed ineffabile, a constituir quella cognizione, ch' è disciplina delle discipline, dottrina delle dottrine ed arte de le arti. Della quale voglio dirvi in che maniera con poco o nullo studio e senza fatica alcuna ognun che vuole e volse, ne ha possuto e può esser capace.

[no paragraph break in the original]

Veddero e considerorno que' santi dottori e rabini illuminati, che gli superbi e presumptuosi sapienti del mondo, quali ebbero fiducia nel proprio ingegno, e con temeraria e gonfia presunzione hanno avuto ardire d'alzarsi alla scienza de secreti divini e que' penetrali della deitade, non altrimente che coloro ch'edificâro la torre di Babelle, son stati confusi e messi in dispersione, avendosi essi medesimi serrato il passo, onde meno fussero abili alla sapienza divina e visione della veritade eterna. Che fêro? qual partito presero? Fermâro i passi, piegâro o dismisero le braccia, chiusero gli occhi, bandiro ogni propria attenzione e studio, riprovâro qualsivoglia uman pensiero, riniegâro ogni sentimento naturale: ed in fine si tennero asini. E quei che non erano, si transformâro in questo animale: alzâro, distesero, acuminâro, ingrossâro e magnificorno l'orecchie; e tutte le potenze de l'anima riportorno e uniro nell'udire, con ascoltare solamente e credere: come quello, di cui si dice: *In auditu auris obedivit mihi.* Là concentrandosi e cattivandosi la vegetativa, sensitiva ed intellettiva facultade, hanno inceppate le cinque dita in un'unghia, perché non potessero, come l'Adamo, stender le mani ad apprendere il frutto vietato dall'arbore della scienza, per cui venessero ad essere privi de frutti de l'arbore della vita, o come Promoteo (che è metafora di medesimo proposito), stender le mani a suffurar il fuoco di Giove, per accendere il lume nella potenza razionale.

[no paragraph break in the original]

Cossí li nostri divi asini, privi del proprio sentimento ed affetto, vegnono ad intendere non altrimente che come gli vien soffiato a l'orecchie dalle revelazioni o de gli dei o de' vicarii loro; e per consequenza a governarsi non secondo altra legge che di que' medesimi. Quindi non si volgono a destra o a sinistra, se non secondo la lezione e raggione che gli dona il capestro o freno che le tien per la gola o per la bocca, non caminano se non come son toccati. Hanno ingrossate le labbra, insolidate le mascelle, incotennuti gli denti, a fin che, per duro, spinoso, aspro a forte a digerir che sia il pasto che gli vien posto avante, non manche d'essere accomodato al suo palato. Indi si pascono de piú grossi e materialacci appositorii, che altra qualsivoglia bestia che si pasca sul dorso de la terra; e tutto ciò per venire a quella vilissima bassezza, per cui fiano capaci de piú magnifica exaltazione, *iuxta* quello: *Omnis qui se humiliat exaltabitur.*

Seb. Ma vorrei intendere come questa bestiaccia potrà distinguere che colui che gli monta sopra, è Dio o diavolo, è un uomo o un'altra bestia non molto maggiore o minore, se la piú certa cosa ch'egli deve avere, è che lui è un asino e vuole essere asino, e non può far meglior vita ed aver costumi megliori che di asino, e non deve aspettar meglior fine che di asino, né è possibile, congruo e condigno ch'abbia altra gloria che d'asino?

Saul. Fidele colui che non permette che siano tentati sopra quel che possono: lui conosce li suoi, lui tiene e mantiene gli suoi per suoi, e non gli possono esser tolti. O santa ignoranza, o divina pazzia, o sopraumana asinità! Quel rapto, profondo e contemplativo Areopagita, scrivendo a Caio, afferma che la ignoranza è una perfettissima scienza; come per l'equivalente volesse dire che l'asinità è una divinità. Il dotto Agostino, molto inebriato di questo divino nettare, nelli suoi *Soliloquii* testifica che la ignoranza piú tosto che la scienza ne conduce a Dio, e la scienza piú tosto che l'ignoranza ne mette in perdizione. In figura di ciò vuole ch' il redentor del mondo con le gambe e piedi de gli asini fusse entrato in Gerusalemme, significando anagogicamente in questa militante quello che si verifica nella trionfante cittad; come dice il profeta salmeggiante: *Non in fortitudine equi voluntatem habebit, neque in tibiis viri beneplacitum erit ei.*

Cor. Supple tu: *Sed in fortitudine et tibiis asinae et pulli filii coniugalis.*

Saul. Or, per venire a mostrarvi come non è altro che l'asinità quello con cui possiamo tendere ed avvicinarci a quell'alta specola, voglio che comprendiate e sappiate non esser possibile al mondo meglior contemplazione che quella che niega ogni scienza ed ogni apprension e giudicio di vero; di maniera che la somma cognizione è certa stima che non si può saper nulla e non si sa nulla, e per consequenza di conoscersi di non posser esser altro che asino e non esser altro che asino; allo qual scopo giunsero gli socratici, platonici, efettici, pirroniani ed altri simili, che non ebbero l'orecchie tanto picciole, e le labbra tanto delicate, e la coda tanto corta, che non le potessero lor medesimi vedere.

Seb. Priegoti, Saulino, non procedere oggi ad altro per confirmazion e dechiarazion di questo: perché assai per il presente abbiamo inteso; oltre che vedi esser tempo di cena, e la materia richiede piú lungo discorso. Per tanto piacciavi (se cosí pare anco al Coribante) di rivederci domani per la elucidazione di questo proposito; ed io menarò meco Onorio, il quale si ricorda d'esser stato asino, e però è a tutta divozione pitagorico; oltre che ha de grandi proprii discorsi con gli quali forse ne potrà far capaci di qualche proposito.

Saul. Sarà bene, e lo desidero; perché lui allevierà la mia fatica,

Cor. *Ego quoque huic adstipulor sententiae,* ed è gionta l'ora, in cui debbo licenziar gli miei discepoli, a fin che *propria revistant hospitia, proprios lares.* Anzi, *si lubet,* per sin tanto che questa materia fia compita, quotidianamente io m'offero pronto in queste ore medesime farmi qua vosco presente.

Saul. Ed io non mancarò di far il medesimo.

Seb. Usciamo dunque.

FINE DEL PRIMO DIALOGO.

Dialogo Secondo [Parte Prima]

Interlocutori, Sebasto, Onorio, Coribante, Saulino.

Sebasto. E tu ti ricordi d'aver portata la soma?

Onorio. La soma, la carga, e tirato il manganello qualche volta. Fui prima in serviggio d'un ortolano, aggiuntandolo a portar lettame dalla cittade di Tebe a l'orto vicino le mura, ed a riportar poi cauli, lattuche, cipolle, cocumeri, pastinache, ravanelli ed altre cose simili dall'orto alla cittad. Appresso ad un carbonaio, che mi comprò da quello, ed il qual pochissimi giorni mi ritenne vivo.

Seb. Come è possibile ch'abbi memoria di questo?

Onor. Ti dirò poi. Pascendo io sopra certa precipitosa e sassosa ripa, tratto dall'avidità d'addentar un cardo ch'era cresciuto alquanto piú giú verso il precipizio, che io senza periglio potesse stendere il collo, volsi al dispetto d'ogni rimorso di conscienza ed instinto di raggion naturale piú del dovero rampegarvi; e caddi da l'alta rupe; onde il mio signore s'accorse d'avermi comprato per gli corvi.

[no paragraph break in the original]

Io privo de l'ergastulo corporeo dovenni vagante spirto senza membra; e venni a considerare come io, secondo la spiritual sustanza, non ero differente in geno, né in specie da tutti gli altri spiriti che dalla dissoluzione de altri animali e composti corpi transmigravano; e viddi come la Parca non solamente nel geno della materia corporale fa indifferente il corpo dell'uomo da quel de l'asino ed il corpo de gli animali dal corpo di cose stimate senz'anima; ma ancora nel geno della materia spirituale fa rimaner indifferente l'anima asina da l'umana, e l'anima che constituisce gli detti animali, da quella che si trova in tutte le cose: come tutti gli umori sono uno umore in sustanza, tutte le parti aeree son un aere in sustanza, tutti gli spiriti sono dall'Anfitrite d'un spirito, ed a quello ritornan tutti. Or dopo che qualche tempo fui trattenuto in cotal stato, ecco che

> *Lethaeum ad fluvium Deus evocat agmine magno,*
> *Scilicet immemores supera ut convexa revisant,*
> *Rursus et incipiant in corpora velle reverti.*

Allora, scampando io da' fortunati campi, senza sorbir de l'onde del rapido Lete, tra quella moltitudine di cui era principal guida Mercurio, io feci finta de bevere di quell'umore in compagnia de gli altri: ma non feci altro ch'accostarvi e toccarvi con le labbra, a fin che venessero ingannati gli soprastanti a' quali poté bastare di vedermi la bocca e 'l mento bagnato. Presi il camino verso l'aria piú puro per la porta Cornea, e lasciandomi a le spalle e sotto gli piedi il profondo, venni a ritrovarmi nel Parnasio monte, il qual non è favola che per il suo fonte Caballino sia cosa dal padre Apolline consecrata alle Muse sue figlie. Ivi per forza ed ordine del fato tornai ad essere asino, ma senza perdere le specie intelligibili, delle quali non rimase vedovo e casso il spirito animale, per forza della cui virtude m'uscirno da l'uno e l'altro lato la forma e sustanza de due ali sufficientissime ad inalzar in sino a gli astri il mio corporeo pondo. Apparvi e fui nomato non asino già semplicemente, ma o asino volante, o ver cavallo Pegaseo. Indi fui fatto exequitor de molti ordini del provido Giove, servii a Bellerofonte, passai molte celebri ed onoratissime fortune, ed alla fine fui assumpto in cielo circa gli confini d'Andromeda ed il Cigno d'un canto, e gli Pesci ed Aquario da l'altro.

Seb. Di grazia, rispondetemi alquanto, prima che mi facciate intendere queste cose piú per il minuto. Dunque, per esperienza e memoria del fatto estimate vera l'opinion de' Pitagorici, Druidi, Saduchimi ed altri simili, circa quella continua metamfisicosi, cioè transformazione e trancorporazione de tutte l'anime?

Spiritus eque feris humana in corpora transit,
Inque feras noster, nec tempore deperit ullo.

Onor. Messer sí, cossí è certissimamente.

Seb. Dunque, constantemente vuoi che non sia altro in sustanza l'anima de l'uomo e quella de le bestie? e non differiscano se non in figurazione?

Onor. Quella de l'uomo è medesima in essenza specifica e generica con quella de le mosche, ostreche marine e piante, e di qualsivoglia cosa che si trove animata o abbia anima: come non è corpo che non abbia o piú o meno vivace- e perfettamente communicazion di spirito in se stesso. Or cotal spirito, secondo il fato o providenza, ordine o fortuna, viene a giongersi or ad una specie di corpo, or ad un'altra; e secondo la raggione della diversità di complessioni e membri, viene ad avere diversi gradi e perfezioni d'ingegno ed operazioni. Là onde quel spirito o anima che era nell'aragna, e vi avea quell'industria e quelli artigli e membra in tal numero, quantità e forma; medesimo, gionto alla prolificazione umana, acquista altra intelligenza, altri instrumenti, attitudini ed atti.

[no paragraph break in the original]

Giongo a questo che, se fusse possibile, o in fatto si trovasse che d'un serpente il capo si formasse e stornasse in figura d'una testa umana, ed il busto crescesse in tanta quantità quanta può contenersi nel periodo di cotal specie, se gli allargasse la lingua, ampiassero le spalli, se gli ramificassero le braccia e mani, ed al luogo dove è terminata coda, andassero ad ingeminarsi le gambe; intenderebbe, apparirebbe, spirarebbe, parlarebbe, oprarebbe e caminarebbe non altrimente che l'uomo; perché non sarebbe altro che uomo. Come, per il contrario, l'uomo non sarebbe altro che serpente, se venisse a contraere, come dentro un ceppo, le braccia e gambe, e l'ossa tutte concorressero alla formazion d'una spina, s'incolubrasse e prendesse tutte quelle figure de membri ed abiti de complessioni. Allora arrebe piú o men vivace ingegno; in luogo di parlar, sibilarebbe; in luogo di caminare, serperebbe; in luogo d'edificarsi palaggio, si cavarebbe un pertuggio; e non gli converrebe la stanza, ma la buca; e come già era sotto quelle, ora è sotto queste membra, instrumenti, potenze ed atti: come dal medesimo artefice diversamente inebriato dalla contrazion di materia e da diversi organi armato, appaiono esercizii de diverso ingegno e pendeno esecuzioni diverse.

[no paragraph break in the original]

Quindi possete capire esser possibile che molti animali possono aver piú ingegno e molto maggior lume d'intelletto che l'uomo (come non è burla quel che proferí Mosè del serpe, che nominò sapientissimo tra tutte l'altre bestie de la terra); ma per penuria d'instrumenti gli viene ad essere inferiore, come quello per ricchezza e dono de medesimi gli è tanto superiore. E che ciò sia la verità, considera un poco al sottile, ed essamina entro a te stesso quel che sarrebe, se, posto che l'uomo avesse al doppio d'ingegno che non ave, e l'intelletto agente gli splendesse tanto piú chiaro che non gli splende, e con tutto ciò le mani gli venesser transformate in forma de doi piedi, rimanendogli tutto l'altro nel suo ordinario intiero; dimmi, dove potrebbe *impune* esser la conversazion de gli uomini? Come potrebero instituirsi e durar le fameglie ed unioni di costoro parimente, o piú, che de cavalli, cervii, porci, senza esserno devorati da innumerabili specie de bestie, per essere in tal maniera suggetti a maggiore e piú certa ruina? E per conseguenza dove sarrebono le instituzioni de dottrine, le invenzioni de discipline, le congregazioni de cittadini, le strutture de gli edificii ed altre cose assai che significano la grandezza ed eccellenza umana, e fanno l'uomo trionfator veramente invitto sopra l'altre specie? Tutto questo, se oculatamente guardi, si referisce non tanto principalmente al dettato de l'ingegno, quanto a quello della mano, organo de gli organi.

Seb. Che dirai de le scimie ed orsi che, se non vuoi dir ch'hanno mano, non hanno peggior instrumento che la mano?

Onor. Non hanno tal complessione che possa esser capace di tale ingegno; perché l'universale intelligenza in simili e molti altri animali per la grossezza o lubricità della material complessione non può imprimere tal forza di sentimento in cotali spiriti. Però la comparazion fatta si deve intendere nel geno de' piú ingegnosi animali.

Seb. Il papagallo non ha egli l'organo attissimo a proferir qualsivoglia voce articulata? Or perché è tanto duro e con tanta fatica può parlar sí poco, senza oltre intendere quel che dice?

Onor. Perché non ha apprensiva, retentiva adequabile e congenea a quella de l'uomo, ma tal quale conviene alla sua specie; in raggion della quale non ha bisogno ch'altri gl'insegne di volare, cercare il vitto, distinguere il nutrimento dal veleno, generare, nidificare, mutar abitazioni, e riparar alle ingiurie del tempo, e provedere alle necessitadi della vita non men bene, e tal volta meglior- e piú facilmente che l'uomo.

Seb. Questo dicono li dotti non esser per intelletto o per discorso, ma per istinto naturale.

Onor. Fatevi dire da cotesti dotti: cotal instinto naturale è senso o intelletto? Se è senso, è interno o esterno? Or non essendo esterno, come è manifesto, dicano secondo qual senso interno hanno le providenze, tecne, arti, precauzioni ed ispedizioni circa l'occasioni non solamente presenti, ma ancora future, megliormente che l'uomo.

Seb. Son mossi da l'intelligenza non errante.

Onor. Questa, se è principio naturale e prossimo applicabile all'operazione prossima ed individuale, non può essere universale ed estrinseco, ma particolare ed intrinseco, e per consequenza potenza dell'anima e presidente nella poppa di quella.

Seb. Non volete dunque che sia l'intelligenza universale che muove?

Onor. Dico che la intelligenza efficiente universale è una de tutti; e quella muove e fa intendere; ma, oltre, in tutti è l'intelligenza particulare, in cui son mossi, illuminati ed intendono; e questa è moltiplicata secondo il numero de gli individui. Come la potenza visiva è moltiplicata secondo il numero de gli occhi, mossa ed illuminata generalmente da un fuoco, da un lume, da un sole: cossí la potenza intellettiva è moltiplicata secondo il numero de suggetti partecipi d'anima, alli quali tutti sopra splende un sole intellettuale. Cossí dunque sopra tutti gli animali è un senso agente, cioè quello che fa sentir tutti, e per cui tutti son sensitivi in atto; ed uno intelletto agente, cioè quello che fa intender tutti, e per cui tutti sono intellettivi in atto; ed appresso son tanti sensi e tanti particolari intelletti passivi o possibili, quanti son suggetti: e sono secondo tanti specifici e numerali gradi di complessioni, quante sono le specifice e numerali figure e complessioni di corpo.

Seb. Dite quel che vi piace, ed intendetela come volete; ché io negli animali non voglio usar di chiamar quello instinto raggionevole intelletto.

Onor. Or se non lo puoi chiamar senso, bisogna che ne gli animali, oltre la potenza sensitiva ed intellettiva, fingi qualch'altra potenza cognoscitiva.

Seb. Dirò ch' è un'efficacia de sensi interiori.

Onor. Tal efficacia possiamo ancor dire che sia lo intelletto unamo; onde naturalmente discorre l'uomo, ed è in nostra libertà di nominar come ci piace e limitar le diffinizioni e nomi a nostra posta, come fe' Averroe. Ed anco è in mia libertà de dire che il vostro intendere non è intendere, e qualunque cosa che facciate, pensare che non sia per intelletto, ma per instinto; poiché l'operazioni de altri animali piú degne che le vostre (come quelle dell'api e de le formiche) non hanno nome d'intelletto ma d'instinto. O pur dirò che l'instinto di quelle bestiole è piú degno che l'intelletto vostro.

Seb. Lasciamo per ora de discorrere piú ampiamente circa questo, e torniamo a noi. Vuoi dunque che come d'una medesima cera o altra materia si formano diverse e contrarie figure, cossí di medesima materia corporale si fanno tutti gli corpi, e di medesima sustanza spirituale sono tutti gli spiriti?

Onor. Cossí certo; e giongi a questo che per diverse raggioni, abitudini, ordini, misure e numeri di corpo e spirito sono diversi temperamenti, complessioni, si producono diversi organi ed appaiono diversi geni de cose.

Seb. Mi par che non è molto lontano, né abborrisce da questo parere quel profetico dogma, quando dice il tutto essere in mano dell'universale efficiente, come la medesima luta in mano del medesimo figolo, che con la ruota di questa vertigine de gli astri viene ad esser fatto e disfatto secondo le vicissitudini della generazione e corrozione delle cose, or vase onorato, or vase contumelioso di medesima pezza.

Onor. Cossí hanno inteso e dechiarato molti de piú savii tra gli rabini. Cossí par ch'intendesse colui che disse: *uomini e giumenti salverai secondo che moltiplicarai la misericordia*; cossí si fa chiaro nella metamorfose di Nabuchodonosor. Quindi dubitorno alcuni Saduchimi del Battista, se lui fusse Elia, non già per medesimo corpo, ma per medesimo spirito in un altro corpo. In cotal modo di resuscitazione alcuni si prometteno l'execuzione della giustizia divina secondo gli affetti ed atti ch' hanno exercitati in un altro corpo.

Seb. Di grazia, non raggioniamo piú di questo, perché pur troppo mi comincia a piacere e parermi piú che verisimile la vostra opinione; ed io voglio mantenermi in quella fede nella quale son stato instrutto da miei progenitori e maestri. E però parliate de successi istorici, o favoleschi, o metaforici, e lasciate star le demostrazioni ed autoritadi, le quali credo che sono piú tosto storciute da voi che da gli altri.

Onor. Hai buona raggione, fratel mio. Oltre che conviene ch' io torne a compire quel ch'avevo cominciato a dirti, se non dubiti che con ciò medesimamente non ti vegna a sobvertere l'ingegno e perturbar la conscienza intemerata.

Seb. Non non, certo, questo ascolto piú volontiera che mai posso aver ascoltata favola alcuna.

Onor. Se dunque non m'ascolti sotto specie di dottrina e disciplina, ascoltami per spasso.

Seconda Parte del [Secondo] Dialogo

Seb. Ma non vedete Saulino e Coribante che vegnono?

Onor. È ora che doveano esser venuti. Meglio il tardi che mai, Saulino.

Cor. *Si tardus adventus, citior expeditio.*

Seb. Col vostro tardare avete persi de bei propositi, quali desidero che siano replicati da Onorio.

Onor. Non, di grazia, perché mi rincrescerebbe; ma seguitamo il nostro proposito, perché quanto a quello che sarà bisogno de riportar oltre, ne raggionarremo privatamente con essi a meglior comodità, perché ora non vorrei interrompere il filo del mio riporto.

Saul. Sí, sí; cossí sia. Andate pur seguitando.

Onor. Or essendo io, come ho già detto, nella region celeste in titolo di cavallo Pegaseo, mi è avvenuto per ordine del fato, che per la conversione alle cose inferiori (causa di certo affetto, ch' io indi venevo ad acquistare, la qual molto bene vien descritta dal platonico Plotino), come inebriato di nettare, venea bandito ad esser or un filosofo, or un poeta, or un pedante, lasciando la mia imagine in cielo; alla cui sedia a tempi a tempi delle trasmigrazioni ritornavo, riportandovi la memoria delle specie le quali nell'abitazion corporale avevo acquistate; e quelle medesime, come in una biblioteca, lasciavo là quando accadeva ch' io dovesse ritornar a qualch'altra terrestre abitazione. Delle quali specie memorabili le ultime son quelle ch' ho cominciate a imbibire a tempo della vita de Filippo macedone, dopo che fui ingenerato dal seme de Nicomaco, come si crede.

[no paragraph break in the original]

Qua, appresso esser stato discepolo d'Aristarco, Platone ed altri, fui promosso col favor di mio padre, ch'era consegliero di Filippo, ad esser pedante d'Alexandro Magno: sotto il quale, benché erudito molto bene nelle umanistiche scienze, nelle quali ero piú illustre che tutti li miei predecessori, entrai in presunzione d'esser filosofo naturale, come è ordinario nelli pedanti d'esser sempre temerarii e presuntuosi; e con ciò, per esser estinta la cognizione della filosofia, morto Socrate, bandito Platone, ed altri in altre maniere dispersi, rimasi io solo lusco intra gli ciechi; e facilmente possevi aver riputazion non sol di retorico, politico, logico, ma ancora de filosofo.

[no paragraph break in the original]

Cossí malamente e scioccamente riportando le opinioni de gli antiqui, e de maniera tal sconcia, che né manco gli fanciulli e le insensate vecchie parlarebono ed intenderebono come io introduco quelli galant'uomini intendere e parlare, mi venni ad intrudere come riformator di quella disciplina della quale io non avevo notizia alcuna. Mi dissi principe de' peripatetici: insegnai in Atene nel sottoportico Liceo: dove, secondo il lume, e per dir il vero, secondo le tenebre che regnavano in me, intesi ed insegnai perversamente circa la natura de li principii e sustanza delle cose, delirai piú che l'istessa delirazione circa l'essenza de l'anima, nulla possevi comprendere per dritto circa la natura del moto e de l'universo; ed in conclusione son fatto quello per cui la scienza naturale e divina è stinta nel bassissimo della ruota, come in tempo de gli Caldei e Pitagorici è stata in exaltazione.

Seb. Ma pur ti veggiamo esser stato tanto tempo in admirazion del mondo; e tra l'altre maraviglie è trovato un certo Arabo ch' ha detto la natura nella tua produzione aver fatto l'ultimo sforzo, per manifestar quanto piú terso, puro, alto e verace ingegno potesse stampare; e generalmente sei detto *demonio della natura.*

Onor. Non sarebbono gli ignoranti, se non fusse la fede; e se non la fusse, non sarebbono le vicissitudini delle scienze e virtudi, bestialitadi ed inerzie ed altre succedenze de contrarie impressioni, come son de la notte ed il giorno, del fervor de l'estade e rigor de l'inverno.

Seb. Or per venire a quel ch'appartiene alla notizia de l'anima (mettendo per ora gli altri propositi da canto), ho letti e considerati que' tuoi tre libri nelli quali parli piú balbamente, che possi mai da altro balbo essere inteso; come ben ti puoi accorgere di tanti diversi pareri ed estravaganti intenzioni e questionarii, massime circa il dislacciar e disimbrogliar quel che ti vogli dire in que' confusi e leggieri propositi, gli quali se pur ascondono qualche cosa, non può esser altro che pedantesca o peripatetica levitade.

Onor. Non è maraviglia, fratello; atteso che non può in conto alcuno essere, che essi loro possano apprendere il mio intelletto circa quelle cose nelle quali io non ebbi intelletto: o che vagliano trovar construtto o argumento circa quel ch' io vi voglia dire, se io medesimo non sapevo quel che mi volesse dire. Qual differenza credete voi essere tra costoro e quei che cercano le corna del gatto e gambe de l'anguilla? Nulla certo. Della qual cosa precavendo ch'altri non s'accorgesse, ed io con ciò venesse ad perdere la riputazion di protosofosso, volsi far de maniera, che chiunque mi studiasse nella natural filosofia (nella qual fui e mi sentivi a fatto ignorantissimo), per inconveniente o confusion che vi scorgesse, se non avea qualche lume d'ingegno, dovesse pensare e credere ciò non essere la mia intenzion profonda, ma piú tosto quel tanto che lui, secondo la sua capacità, posseva da gli miei sensi superficialmente comprendere. Là onde feci che venesse publicata quella *Lettera ad Alexandro*, dove protestavo gli libri fisicali esser messi in luce, come non messi in luce.

Seb. E per tanto voi mi parete aver isgravata la vostra conscienza; ed hanno torto questi tanti asinoni a disporsi di lamentarsi di voi nel giorno del giudicio, come di quel che l'hai ingannati e sedutti, e con sofistici apparati divertiti dal camino di qualche veritade che per altri principii e metodi arrebono possuta racquistarsi. Tu l'hai pure insegnato quel tanto ch'a diritto doveano pensare: che se tu hai publicato, come non publicato, essi, dopo averti letto, denno pensare di non averti letto, come tu avevi cossí scritto, come non avessi scritto: talmente quei cotali ch' insegnano la tua dottrina, non altrimente denno essere ascoltati che un che parla come non parlasse. E finalmente né a voi deve piú essere atteso, che come ad un che raggiona e getta sentenza di quel che mai intese.

Onor. Cossí è certo, per dirti ingenuamente come l'intendo al presente. Perché nessuno deve essere inteso piú ch'egli medesimo mostra di volersi far intendere; e non doviamo andar preseguitando con l'intelletto color che fuggono il nostro intelletto, con quel dir che parlano certi per enigma o per metafora, altri perché vuolen che non l'intendano gl'ignoranti, altri perché la moltitudine non le spreggie, altri perché le margarite non sieno calpestrate da porci; siamo dovenuti a tale ch'ogni satiro, fauno, malenconico, embreaco ed infetto d'atra bile, in contar sogni e dir de pappolate senza construzione e senso alcuno, ne vogliono render suspetti ed profezia grande, de recondito misterio, de alti secreti ed arcani divini da risuscitar morti, da pietre filosofali ed altre poltronarie da donar volta a quei ch' han poco cervello, a farli dovenir al tutto pazzi con giocarsi il tempo, l'intelletto, la fama e la robba, e spendere sí misera- ed ignobilmente il corso di sua vita.

Seb. La intese bene un certo mio amico; il quale, avendo non so se un certo libro de profeta enigmatico o d'altro, dopo avervisi su lambiccato alquanto dell'umor del capo, con una grazia e bella leggiadria andò a gittarlo nel cesso, dicendogli: —*Fratello, tu non voi esser inteso; io non ti voglio intendere;*—e soggionse ch'andasse con cento diavoli, e lo lasciasse star con fatti suoi in pace.

Onor. E quel ch' è degno di compassione e riso, è che su questi editi libelli e trattati pecoreschi vedi dovenir attonito Salvio, Ortensio melanconico, smagrito Serafino, impallidito Cammaroto, invecchiato Ambruogio, impazzito Gregorio, abstratto Reginaldo, gonfio Bonifacio; ed il molto reverendo Don Cocchiarone, *pien d'infinita e nobil maraviglia,* sen va per il largo della sua sala, dove, rimosso dal rude ed ignobil volgo, se la spasseggia; e rimenando or quinci, or quindi de la litteraria sua toga le fimbrie, rimenando or questo, or quell'altro piede, rigettando or vers' il destro, or vers' il sinistro fianco il petto, con il texto commento sotto l'ascella, e con gesto di voler buttar quel pulce, ch' ha tra le due prime dita, in terra, con la rugata fronte cogitabondo, con erte ciglia ed occhi arrotondati, in gesto d'un uomo fortemente maravigliato, conchiudendola con un grave ed emfatico suspiro, farà pervenir a l'orecchio de circonstanti questa sentenza: *Huc usque alii philosophi non pervenerunt.* Se si trova in proposito di lezion di qualche libro composto da qualche energumeno o inspiritato, dove non è espresso e donde non si può premere piú sentimento che possa ritrovarsi in un spirito cavallino, allora per mostrar d'aver dato sul chiodo, exclamarà: —*O magnum mysterium!*— Se per avventura si trovasse un libro de—

Seb. Non piú, di grazia, di questi propositi delli quali siamo pur troppo informati; e torniamo al nostro proposito.

Cor. Ita ita, sodes. Fatene intendere con qual ordine e maniera avete repigliata la memoria la qual perdeste nel supposito peripatetico ed altre ipostatiche sussistenze.

Onor. Credo aver detto a Sebasto, che quante volte io migravo dal corpo, prima che m' investisse d'un altro, ritornavo a quel mio vestigio dell'asinina idea (che per l'onor e facultà de l'ali non ha piaciuto ad alcuni, che tegnono tal animale in opprobrio, di chiamarlo asino, ma cavallo Pegaseo): e da là, dopo avervi descritti gli atti e le fortune ch'avevo passate, sempre fui destinato a ritornar piú tosto uomo che altra cosa, per privilegio che mi guadagnai per aver avuto astuzia e continenza quella volta con non mandar giú per il gorgazuolo de l'umor de l'onde letee. Oltre, per la giurisdizione di quella piazza celeste, è avvenuto che, partendo io da corpi, mai oltre ho preso il camino verso il plutonio regno per riveder gli campi Elisii, ma vêr l'illustre ed augusto imperio di Giove.

Cor. Alla stanza dell'aligero quadrupede.

Onor. Sin tanto che a questi tempi, piacendo al senato de gli dei, m' ha convenuto de transmigrar con l'altre bestie a basso, lasciando solamente l'impression de mia virtude in alto; onde, per grazia e degno favor de gli dei, ne vegno ornato e cinto de mia biblioteca, portando non solamente la memoria delle specie opinabili, sofistiche, apparenti, probabili e demostrative, ma, ed oltre, il giudicio distintivo di quelle cose che son vere, da l'altre che son false. Ed oltre de quelle cose che in diversamente complessionati diversi corpi per varie sorti de discipline ho concepute, ritegno ancora l'abito, e de molte altre veritadi alle quali, senza ministerio de sensi, con puro occhio intellettuale vien aperto il camino; e non mi fuggono, quantumque mi trove sotto questa pelle e pareti rinchiuso, onde per le porte de' sensi, come per certi strettissimi buchi, ordinariamente possiamo contemplar qualche specie di enti: sí come altrimente ne vien lecito di veder chiaro ed aperto l'orizonte tutto de le forme naturali, ritrovandoci fuor de la priggione.

Seb. Tanto che restate di tutto sí fattamente informato, che ottenete piú che l'abito di tante filosofie, di tanti suppositi filosofici, ch'avete presentati al mondo, ottenendo oltre il giudicio superiore a quelle tenebre e quella luce sotto le quali avete vegetato, sentito, inteso, o in atto o in potenza, abitando or nelle terrene, or nell'inferne, or nelle stanze celesti.

Onor. Vero: e da tal retentiva vegno a posser considerar, e conoscer meglio che come in specchio, quel tanto ch' è vero dell'essenza e sustanza de l'anima.

Terza Parte del [Secondo] Dialogo

Seb. Soprasediamo circa questo per ora, e venemo a sentir il vostro parere circa la questione qual ieri fu mossa tra me e Saulino qua presente; il quale referisce l'opinion d'alcune sette le quali vogliono non esser scienza alcuna appo noi.

Saul. Feci a certa bastanza aperto, che sotto l'eminenza de la verità non abbiam noi cosa piú eminente che l'ignoranza ed asinitade: perciò che questa è il mezzo per cui la sofia si congionge e si domestica con essa; e non è altra virtude che sia capace ad aver la stanza gionta muro a muro con quella. Atteso che l'umano intelletto ha qualch'accesso a la verità; il quale accesso se non è per la scienza e cognizione, necessariamente bisogna che sia per l'ignoranza ed asinità.

Cor. Nego sequelam.

Saul. La consequenza è manifesta da quel che nell'intelletto razio-

nale non è mezzo tra l'ignoranza e scienza; perché bisogna che vi sia
l'una de due, essendo doi oppositi circa tal suggetto, come priva-
zione ed abito.

Cor. *Quid de assumptione, sive antecedente?*

Saul. Quella, come dissi, è messa avanti da tanti famosissimi filosofi
e teologi.

Cor. Debilissimo è l'argumento *ab humana authoritate.*

Saul. Cotali asserzioni non son senza demostrativi discorsi.

Seb. Dunque, se tal opinione è vera, è vera per demostrazione; la
demonstrazione è un sillogismo scientifico; dunque, secondo quei
medesimi che negano la scienza ed apprension di verità, viene ad
esser posta l'apprension di verità e discorso scienziale; e consequentemente sono dal suo medesimo senso e paroli redarguiti. Giongo a
questo che se non si sa verità alcuna, essi medesimi non sanno quel
che dicono, e non possono esser certi se parlano o ragghiano, se son
omini o asini.

Saul. La risoluzion di questo la potrete attendere da quel che vi farò
udire appresso; perché prima fia mistiero intendere la cosa, e poi il
modo e maniera di quella.

Cor. Bene. *Modus enim rei rem praesupponat oportet.*

Seb. Or fatene intendere le cose con quell'ordine che vi piace.

Saul. Farò. Son trovati tra le sette de filosofi alcuni nomati generalmente academici, e piú propriamente sceptici o ver efettici, li quali
dubitavano determinar di cosa veruna; bandito ogni enunciazione,
non osavano affirmare o negare, ma si faceano chiamare inquisitori,
investigatori e scrutatori de le cose.

Seb. Perché queste vane bestie inquirevano, investigavano e scru-
tavano senza speranza di ritrovar cosa alcuna? Or questi son de quei
che s'affaticano senza proposito.

Cor. Per far buggiarda quella vulgata sentenza: *Omne agens est agens*
est propter finem. Ma *edepol, mehercle,* io mi persuado che come
Onorio ha dependenza da l'influsso de l'asino Pegaseo, o pur è il

Pegaseo istesso, talmente cotai filosofi sieno stati le Belide istesse, se almeno quelle non gl' influivano nel capo.

Saul. Lasciatemi compire. Or costoro non porgean fede a quel che vedeano, né a quel ch'udivano: perché stimavano la verità cosa confusa ed incomprensibile, e posta nella natura e composizione d'ogni varietà, diversità e contrarietà; ogni cosa essere una mistura, nulla costar di sé, niente esser di propria natura e virtude, e gli oggetti presentarsi alle potenze apprensive non in quella maniera con cui sono in se medesimi, ma secondo la relazione ch'acquistano per le lor specie, che in certo modo partendosi da questa e quella materia vegnono a giuntarsi e crear nuove forme ne gli nostri sensi.

Seb. Oh in verità costoro con non troppa fatica in pochissimo tempo possono esser filosofi e mostrarsi piú savii de gli altri.

Saul. A questi succesero gli pirroni, molto piú scarsi in donar fede al proprio senso ed intelletto, che gli efettici; perché, dove quelli altri credeno aver compresa qualche cosa ed esser fatti partecipi di qualche giudicio per aver informazion di questa verità, cioè che cosa alcuna non può esser compresa né determinata, questi anco di cotal giudicio se stimâro privi, dicendo che né men possono esser certi di questo, cioè che cosa alcuna non si possa determinare.

Seb. Guardate l'industria di quest'altra Academia, ch'avendo visto il modello de l'ingegno e notato l'industria di quella che con facilità ed atto di poltronaria volea dar de calci, per versar a terra l'altre filosofie, essa armata di maggior pecoraggine, con giongere un poco piú di sale della sua insipidezza, vuol donar la spinta ed a quelle tutte ed a cotesta insieme, con farsi tanto piú savia de tutte generalmente, quanto con manco spesa e lambiccamento di cervello in essa s'intogano ed addottorano. Via via, andiam piú oltre. Or che debbo far io, essendo ambizioso di formar nuova setta, e parer piú savio de tutti, e di costoro ancora che sono oltre gli tutti? Farò qua un terzo tabernaculo, piantarò un'Academia piú dotta, con stringermi alquanto la cintura. Ma vorrò forse tanto raffrenar la voce con gli efettici,

e stringere il fiato con gli pirroni, che per me poi non exali spirito
e crepi?

Saul. Che volete dir per questo?

Seb. Questi poltroni per scampar la fatica di dar raggioni delle cose,
e per non accusar la loro inerzia, ed invidia ch' hanno all'industria
altrui, volendo parer megliori, e non bastandoli d'occultar la propria
viltade, non possendoli passar avanti né correre al pari né aver modo
di far qualche cosa del suo, per non pregiudicar alla lor vana presunzione confessando l'imbecillità del proprio ingegno, grossezza di
senso e privazion d'intelletto, e per far parer gli altri senza lume di
giudicio della propria cecitade, donano la colpa alla natura, alle cose
che mal si rapresentano, e non principalmente alla mala apprensione de gli dogmatici; perché con questo modo di procedere sarrebono stati costretti di porre in campo al paragone la lor buona
apprensione, la quale avesse parturito meglior fede, dopo aver gen-
erato meglior concetto ne gli animi de quei che si delettano delle
contemplazioni de cose naturali. Or dunque essi, volendo con minor fatica ed intelletto, e manco rischio de perdere il credito, parer
piú savii che gli altri, dissero, gli efettici, che nulla si può determinare, perché nulla si conosce: onde quelli che stimano d'intendere
e parlano assertivamente, delirano piú in grosso che quei che non
intendeno e non parlano.

[no paragraph break in the original]

Gli secondi poi, detti pirroni, per parer essi archisapienti, dissero
che né tampoco questo si può intendere (il che si credeano intendere
gli efettici): che cosa alcuna non possa esser determinata o conosciuta. Sí che dove gli efettici intesero che gli altri, che pensavano
d'intendere, non intendevano, ora gli pirroni intesero che gli efettici
non intendevano, se gli altri, che si pensavano d'intendere, inten-
dessero o non. Or quel che ne resta per giongere di vantaggio alla
sapienza di costoro, è che noi sappiamo che gli pirroni non sapevano, che gli efettici non sapevano, che gli dogmatici, che pensavano

di sapere, non sapevano; e cossí, con aggevolezza, sempre piú e piú vegna a prendere aumento questa nobil scala de filosofie, sin tanto che demostrativamente si conchiuda l'ultimo grado della somma filosofia ed ottima contemplazione essere di quei che non solamente non affermano né niegano di sapere o ignorare, ma né manco possono affirmare né negare; di sorte che gli asini sono li piú divini animali, e l'asinitade sua sorella è la compagna e secretaria della veritade.

Saul. Se questo che dici improperativamente ed in colera, lo dicessi da buon senno ed assertivamente, direi che la vostra deduzione è eccellentissima ed egregiamente divina; e che sei pervenuto a quel scopo, al quale gli tanti dogmatici e tanti academici hanno concorso, con rimanerti di gran lunga a dietro tanti quanti sono.

Seb. Vi priego (poi che siamo venuti sin a questo) che mi facciate intendere con qual persuasione gli academici niegano la possibilità di detta apprensione.

Saul. Questa vorrei che ne fusse riferita da Onorio, percioché, per esser egli stato in ipostasi de sí molti e gran notomisti de le viscere de la natura, non è fuor di raggione che tal volta si sia trovato academico.

Onor. Anzi io son stato quel Xenofane Colofonio, che disse in tutte e de tutte le cose non esser altro che opinione. Ma, lasciando ora que' miei proprii pensieri da canto, dico, circa il proposito, essere raggion trita quella de' pirroni, li quali dicevano che per apprendere la verità bisogna la dottrina; e per mettere in effetto la dottrina, è necessario quel che insegna, quel ch' è insegnato e la cosa la quale è per insegnarsi: cioè il mastro, il discepolo, l'arte; ma di queste tre non è cosa che si trove in effetto; dunque non è dottrina e non è apprension di veritade.

Seb. Con qual raggione dicono prima, non esser cosa de cui fia dottrina o disciplina?

Onor. Con questa. Quella cosa, dicono, o devrà esser vera o falsa. Se è falsa, non può essere insegnata, perché del falso non può esser dottrina né disciplina: atteso che a quel che non è, non può accader cosa alcuna, e perciò non può accader anco d'essere insegnato. Se è vera, non può pure piú che tanto essere insegnata: perché o è cosa la quale equalmente appare a tutti, e cossí di lei non può esser dottrina, e per consequenza non può esserne alcun dottore, come né del bianco che sia bianco, del cavallo che sia cavallo, de l'arbor che sia arbore; o è cosa, che altrimente ed inequalmente ad altri ed altri appare, e cossí in sé non può aver altro che opinabilità, e sopra lei non si può formar altro che opinione. Oltre, s'è vero quel che deve essere insegnato e notificato, bisogna che sia insegnato per qualche causa o mezzo: la qual causa e mezzo o bisogna che sia occolta o conosciuta. S'ella è occolta, non può notificar altro. Se la è conosciuta è necessario che sia per causa o mezzo; e cossí, oltre ed oltre procedendo, verremo ad accorgerci che non si gionge al principio de scienza, se ogni scienza è per causa.

Oltre, dicono, essendo che de le cose che sono, altre sieno corpi, altre incorporali, bisogna che de cose, quai vegnono insegnate, altre appartegnano a l'uno, altre a l'altro geno. Or il corpo non può esser insegnato, perciochè non può esser sotto giudicio di senso né d'intelletto. Non certo a giudicio di senso: stante che, secondo tutte le dottrine e sette, il corpo consta de piú dimensioni, raggioni, differenze e circonstanze; e non solamente non è un definito accidente per esser cosa obiettabile a un senso particolare o al commune, ma è una composizione e congregazione de proprietadi ed individui innumerabili. E concesso, se cossí piace, ch' il corpo sia cosa sensibile, non per questo sarà cosa da dottrina o disciplina; perché non bisogna che vi si trove il discepolo ed il maestro per far sapere ch' il bianco è bianco, ed il caldo è caldo. Non può essere anco il corpo sotto il giudicio d'intelligenza, perché è assai conceduto appresso tutti dogmatici ed academici, che l'oggetto de l'intelletto non può esser altro che cosa incorporea. Da qua s'inferisce secondariamente che non può essere chi insegne; né, terzo, chi possa essere insegnato; perché, come è veduto, questo non ha che apprendere o concipere, e quello non ha che insegnare ed imprimere. Giongono un'altra raggione. Se avien che s'insegne, o uno senz'arte insegna un altro senz'arte: e questo non è possibile, perché non men l'uno che l'altro ha bisogno di essere insegnato; o uno artista insegna un altro artista: e ciò verrebe ad essere una baia, perché né l'uno né l'altro ha mestiero del mastro; o quello che non sa insegna colui che sa: e questo verrebe ad essere come se un cieco volesse guidare colui che vede. Se nessuno di questi modi è possibile, rimarrà dunque che quel che sa, insegne colui che non sa: e ciò è più inconveniente che tutto quel che si può imaginare in ciascuno de gli altri tre modi de fingere; perché quello ch'è senz'arte, non può esser fatto artefice quando non ha l'arte, atteso che accaderia che potesse esser artefice quando non è artefice. (Oltre che costui è simile ad un nato sordo e cieco, il qual mai può venire ad aver pensiero de voci e di colori. Lascio quel che si dice nel *Mennone* con l'essempio del servo fugitivo, il qual, fatto presente, non può esser conosciuto che sia lui, se non era noto prima. Onde vogliono per ugual e medesima raggione non posser esser nova scienza o dottrina de specie conoscibili, ma una ricordanza). Né tampoco può esser fatto artefice, quando ha l'arte; perché allora non si può dir che si faccia o possa essere fatto artefice, ma che sia artefice.

Seb. Che pare a voi, Onorio, di queste raggioni?

Onor. Dico che in examinar cotai discorsi non fia mistiero d'intrattenerci. Basta che dico esser buoni, come certe erbe son buone per certi gusti.

Seb. Ma vorrei saper da Saulino (che magnifica tanto l'asinitate, quanto non può esser magnificata la scienza e speculazione, dottrina e disciplina alcuna) se l'asinitade può aver luogo in altri che ne gli asini; come è dire, se alcuno da quel che non era asino, possa doventar asino per dottrina e disciplina. Perché bisogna che di questi quel che insegna o quel che è insegnato, o cossí l'uno come l'altro, o né l'uno né l'altro, siano asini. Dicono se sarà asino quello solo che insegna, o quel solo ch'è insegnato, o né quello né questo, o questo e quello insieme. Perché qua col medesimo ordine si può vedere che in nessun modo si possa inasinire. Dunque dell'asinitade non può essere apprension alcuna, come non è de arti e de scienze.

Onor. Di questo ne raggionaremo a tavola dopo cena. Andiamo dunque, ch'è ora.

Cor. Propere eamus.

Saul. Su!

FINE DEL SECONDO DIALOGO

Dialogo Terzo

Interlocutori: Saulino, Alvaro

Saul. Ho pur gran pezzo spasseggiato aspettando, e m'accorgo esser passata l'ora del cominciamento de' nostri colloquii, e costoro non son venuti. Oh, veggio il servitor di Sebasto.

Alv. Ben trovato Saulino! Vegno per avisarvi da parte del mio padrone, che per una settimana al meno non potrete convenir un'altra volta. A lui è morta la moglie, e sta su l'apparecchi de l'execuzion del testamento, per esser libero di quest'altro pensiero ancora. Coribante è assalito da le podagre, ed Onorio è andato a' bagni. A dio.

Saul. Va in pace. Or credo che passarà l'occasione de far molti altri raggionamenti sopra la cabala del detto cavallo. Perché qualmente veggio, l'ordine de l'universo vuole che, come questo cavallo divino nella celeste regione non si mostra se non sin all'umbilico (dove quella stella che v'è terminante, è messa in lite e questione se appartiene alla testa d'Andromeda o pur al tronco di questo egregio bruto), cossí analogicamente accade che questo cavallo descrittorio non possa venire a perfezione:

> Cossí Fortuna va cangiando stile.

Ma non per ciò noi doviamo desperarci; perché, s'avverrà che questi tornino ad cominciar d'accoppiars' insieme un'altra volta, le rinchiuderò tutti tre dentro del conclave, d'onde non possano uscire sin tanto ch'abbiano spacciata la creazion d'una Cabala magna del cavallo Pegaseo. *Interim,* questi doi dialogi vagliano per una Cabala parva, tironica, isagogica, microcosmica. E per non passar ociosamente il presente tempo che mi supera da spasseggiarmi in questo atrio, voglio leggere questo dialogo che tegno in mano.

FINE DEL TERZO DIALOGO DE LA CABALA PEGASEA

A l'asino cillenico

> Oh beato quel ventr'e le mammelle,
> Che t'ha portato e 'n terra ti lattâro,
> Animalaccio divo, al mondo caro,
> Che qua fai residenza e tra le stelle!
> Mai piú preman tuo dorso basti e selle,
> E contr' il mondo ingrato e ciel avaro
> Ti faccia sort'e natura riparo
> Con sí felice ingegno e buona pelle.
> Mostra la testa tua buon naturale,
> Come le nari quel giudicio sodo,
> L'orecchie lunghe un udito regale,
> Le dense labbra di gran gusto il modo,
> Da far invidia a' dei quel genitale;
> Cervice tal la constanza ch 'io lodo.
> Sol lodandoti godo:
> Ma, lasso, cercan tue condizioni
> Non un sonetto, ma mille sermoni.

L'asino cillenico del nolano

Interlocutori: L'Asino, Micco Pitagorico, Mercurio

l'Asino. Or perché derrò io abusar de l'alto, raro e pelegrino tuo dono, o folgorante Giove? Perché tanto talento, porgiutomi da te, che con sí particular occhio me miraste (*indicante fato*), sotto la nera e tenebrosa terra d'un ingratissimo silenzio terrò sepolto? suffrirò piú a lungo l'esser sollecitato a dire, per non far uscir da la mia bocca quell'estraordinario ribombo, che la largità tua, in questo confusissimo secolo, nell'interno mio spirito (perché si producesse fuora) ha seminato? Aprisi aprisi, dunque, con la chiave de l'occasione l'asinin palato, sciolgasi per l'industria del supposito la lingua, raccolgansi per mano de l'attenzione, drizzata dal braccio de l'intenzione, i frutti de gli arbori e fiori de l'erbe, che sono nel giardino de l'asinina memoria.

Micco. O portento insolito, o prodigio stupendo, o maraviglia incredibile, o miracoloso successo! Avertano gli dii qualche sciagura! Parla l'asino? l'asino parla? O Muse, o Apolline, o Ercule, da cotal testa esceno voci articulate? Taci, Micco, forse t'inganni; forse sotto questa pelle qualch'uomo stassi mascherato, per burlarsi di noi.

Asino. Pensa pur, Micco, ch' io non sia sofistico, ma che son naturalissimo asino che parlo; e cossí mi ricordo aver avuti altre volte umani, come ora mi vedi aver bestiali membri.

Micco. Appresso, o demonio incarnato, dimandarotti chi, quale e come sei. Per ora, e per la prima, vorrei saper che cosa dimandi da qua? che augurio ne ameni? qual ordine porti da gli dei? a che si terminarà questa scena? a qual fine hai messi gli piedi a partitamente mostrarti vocale in questo nostro sottoportico?

Asino. Per la prima voglio che sappi, ch' io cerco d'esser membro e dechiararmi dottore di qualche colleggio o academia, perché la mia sufficienza sia autenticata, a fin che non siano attesi gli miei concetti, e ponderate le mie paroli, e riputata la mia dottrina con minor fede, che—

Micco. O Giove! è possibile che *ab aeterno* abbi giamai registrato un fatto, un successo, un caso simile a questo?

Asino. Lascia le maraviglie per ora; e rispondetemi presto, o tu o uno de questi altri, che attoniti concorreno ad ascoltarmi. O togati, annulati, pileati didascali, archididascali e de la sapienza eroi e semidei: volete, piacevi, evvi a core d'accettar nel vostro consorzio, società, contubernio, e sotto la banda e vessillo de la vostra communione questo asino che vedete ed udite? Perché di voi, altri ridendo si maravigliano, altri maravigliando si ridono, altri attoniti (che son la maggior parte) si mordeno le labbia; e nessun risponde?

Micco. Vedi che per stupore non parlano, e tutti con esser volti a me, mi fan segno ch 'io ti risponda; al qual, come presidente, ancora tocca di donarti risoluzione, e da cui, come da tutti, devi aspettar l'ispedizione.

Asino. Che academia è questa, che tien scritto sopra la porta: *Lineam ne pertransito?*

Micco. La è una scuola de pitagorici.

Asino. Potravis' entrare?

Micco. Per academico non senza difficili e molte condizioni.

Asino. Or quali son queste condizioni?

Micco. Son pur assai.

Asino. Quali, dimandai, non quante.

Micco. Ti risponderò al meglio, riportando le principali. Prima, che offrendosi alcuno per essere ricevuto, avante che sia accettato, debba esser squadrato nella disposizion del corpo, fisionomia ed ingegno, per la gran consequenza relativa che conoscemo aver il corpo da l'anima e con l'anima.

Asino. *Ab Iove principium, Musae*, s'egli si vuol maritare.

Micco. Secondo, ricevuto ch'egli è, se gli dona termine di tempo (che non è men che di doi anni), nel quale deve tacere e non gli è lecito d'ardire in punto alcuno de dimandar, anco di cose non intese, non sol che di disputare ed examinar propositi; ed in quel tempo si chiama *acustico*. Terzo, passato questo tempo, gli è lecito di parlare, dimandare, scrivere le cose udite, ed esplicar le proprie opinioni; ed in questo mentre si appella *matematico o caldeo*. Quarto, informato de cose simili, ed ornato di que' studii, si volta alla considerazion de l'opre del mondo e principii della natura; e qua ferma il passo, chiamandosi *fisico*.

Asino. Non procede oltre?

Micco. Piú che fisico non può essere: perché delle cose sopranaturali non si possono aver raggioni, eccetto in quanto riluceno nelle cose naturali; percioché non accade ad altro intelletto che al purgato e superiore di considerarle in sé.

Asino. Non si trova appo voi metafisica?

Micco. No; e quello che gli altri vantano per metafisica, non è altro che parte di logica. Ma lasciamo questo che non fa al proposito. Tali, in conclusione, son le condizioni e regole di nostra academia.

Asino. Queste?

Micco. Messer sí.

Asino. O scola onorata, studio egregio, setta formosa, collegio venerando, gimnasio clarissimo, ludo invitto ed academia tra le principali principalissima! L'asino errante, come sitibondo cervio, a voi, come a limpidissime e freschissime acqui; l'asino umile e supplicante, a voi, benignissimi ricettatori de peregrini, s'appresenta, bramoso d'essere nel consorzio vostro ascritto.

Micco. Nel consorzio nostro anh?

Asino. Sí, sí, signor sí, nel consorzio vostro.

Micco. Va' per quell'altra porta, messere, perché da questa son banditi gli asini.

Asino. Dimmi, fratello, per qual porta entrasti tu?

Micco. Può far il cielo che gli asini parlino, ma non già che entrino in scola pitagorica.

Asino. Non esser cossí fiero, o Micco, e ricordati ch' il tuo Pitagora insegna di non spreggiar cosa che si trove nel seno della natura. Benché io sono in forma d'asino al presente, posso esser stato e posso esser appresso in forma di grand'uomo; e benché tu sia un uomo, puoi esser stato e potrai esser appresso un grand'asino, secondo che parrà ispediente al dispensator de gli abiti e luoghi e disponitor de l'anime transmigranti.

Micco. Dimmi, fratello, hai intesi gli capitoli e condizioni dell'academia?

Asino. Molto bene.

Micco. Hai discorso sopra l'esser tuo, se per qualche tuo difetto ti possa essere impedita l'entrata?

Asino. Assai a mio giudicio.

Micco. Or fatevi intendere.

Asino. La principal condizione che m' ha fatto dubitare, è stata la prima. È pur vero che non ho quella indole, quelle carni mollecine, quella pelle delicata, tersa e gentile, le quali integnono li fisionotomisti attissime alla recepzion della dottrina; perché la durezza de quelle ripugna a l'agilità de l'intelletto. Ma sopra tal condizione mi par che debba posser dispensar il principe; perché non deve far rimaner fuori uno, quando molte altre parzialitadi suppliscono a tal difetto, come la sincerità de costumi, la prontezza de l'ingegno, l'efficacia de l'intelligenza, ed altre condizioni compagne, sorelle e figlie di queste. Lascio che non si deve aver per universale, che l'anime sieguano la complession del corpo; perché può esser che qualche piú efficace spiritual principio possa vencere e superar l'oltraggio che dalla crassezza o altra indisposizion di quello gli vegna fatto.
[no paragraph break in the original]
A' qual proposito v'apporto l'essempio de Socrate, giudicato dal fisognomico Zopiro per uomo stemprato, stupido, bardo, effeminato, namoraticcio de putti ed inconstante; il che tutto venne conceduto dal filosofo, ma non già che l'atto de tali inclinazioni si

consumasse: stante ch'egli venia temprato dal continuo studio della filosofia, che gli avea pōrto in mano il fermo temone contra l'émpito de l'onde de naturali indisposizioni, essendo che non è cosa che per studio non si vinca. Quanto poi all'altra parte principale fisiognomica, che consiste non nella complession di temperamenti, ma nell'armonica proporzion de membri, vi notifico non esser possibile de ritrovar in me defetto alcuno, quando sarà ben giudicato. Sapete ch' il porco non deve esser bel cavallo, né l'asino bell'uomo; ma l'asino bell'asino, il porco bel porco, l'uomo bell'uomo. Che se, straportando il giudicio, il cavallo non par bello al porco, né il porco par bello al cavallo; se a l'uomo non par bello l'asino, e l'uomo non s'inamora de l'asino; né per opposito a l'asino par bello l'uomo e l'asino non s'innamora de l'uomo.

[no paragraph break in the original]

Sí che quanto a questa legge, allor che le cose sarranno examinate e bilanciate con la raggione, l'uno concederà a l'altro secondo le proprie affezioni, che le bellezze son diverse secondo diverse proporzionabilitadi; e nulla è veramente ed absolutamente bello, se non uno che è l'istessa bellezza, o il per essenza bello e non per participazione. Lascio che nella medesima umana specie quel che si dice de le carni, si deve attendere *respectu habito* a vinticinque circonstanze e glose, che l'accomodino; perché altrimente è falsa quella fisiognomica regola de le carni molle; atteso che gli putti non son piú atti alla scienza che gli adulti, né le donne piú abili che gli uomini: eccetto se attitudine maggiore si chiamasse quella possibilità ch' è piú lontana da l'atto.

Micco. Sin al presente, costui mostra di saper assai assai. Séguita, messer Asino, e fa pur gagliarde le tue raggioni quanto ti piace; perché

> Ne l'onde solchi e ne l'arena semini,
> E 'l vago vento speri in rete accogliere,
> E le speranze fondi in cuor di femine,

se speri che da gli signori academici di questa o altra setta ti possa o debbia esser concessa l'entrata. Ma se sei dotto, contèntati de rimanerti con la tua dottrina solo. *Asino.* O insensati, credete ch' io dica le mie raggioni a voi, acciò che me le facciate valide? credete ch' io abbia fatto questo per altro fine che per accusarvi e rendervi inexcusabili avanti a Giove? Giove con avermi fatto dotto mi fe' dottore. Aspettavo ben io che dal bel giudicio della vostra sufficienza venesse sputata questa sentenza: —Non è convenevole che gli asini entrino in academia insieme con noi altri uomini.— Questo, se studioso di qualsivogli' altra setta lo può dire, non può essere raggionevolmente detto da voi altri pitagorici, che con questo, che negate a me l'entrata, struggete gli principii, fondamenti e corpo della vostra filosofia. Or che differenza trovate voi tra noi asini e voi altri uomini, non giudicando le cose dalla superficie, volto ed apparenza? Oltre di ciò dite, giudici inetti: quanti di voi errano ne l'academia de gli asini? quanti imparano nell'academia de gli asini? quanti fanno profitto nell'academia de gli asini? quanti s'addottorano, marciscono e muoiono ne l'academia de gli asini? quanti son preferiti, inalzati, magnificati, canonizati, glorificati e deificati, nell'academia de gli asini? che se non fussero stati e non fussero asini, non so, non so come la cosa sarrebe passata e passarebbe per essi loro. Non son tanti studii onoratissimi e splendissimi, dove si dona lezione di saper inasinire, per aver non solo il bene della vita temporale, ma e de l'eterna ancora? Dite, a quante e quali facultadi ed onori s'entra per la porta dell'asinitade? Dite, quanti son impediti, exclusi, rigettati e messi in vituperio, per non esser partecipi dell'asinina facultade e perfezione? Or perché non sarà lecito ch'alcuno de gli asini, o pur al meno uno de gli asini entri nell'academia de gli uomini? Perché non debbo esser accettato con aver la maggior parte delle voci e voti in favore in qualsivoglia academia, essendo che, se non tutti, al meno la maggior e massima parte è scritta e scolpita nell'academia tanto universale de noi altri?

Or se siamo sí larghi ed effusi noi asini in ricever tutti, perché dovete voi esser tanto restivi ad accettare un de noi altri al meno?

Micco. Maggior difficultà si fa in cose piú degne e importanti: e non si fa tanto caso e non s'aprono tanto gli occhi in cose di poco momento. Però senza ripugnanza e molto scrupolo di conscienza si ricevon tutti ne l'academia de gli asini, e non deve esser cossí nell'academia de gli uomini.

Asino. Ma, o messere, sappime dire e resolvimi un poco, qual cosa delle due è piú degna, che un uomo inasinisca, o che un asino inumanisca? Ma ecco in veritade il mio Cillenio: il conosco per il caduceo e l'ali. —Ben vegna il vago aligero, nuncio di Giove, fido interprete della voluntà de tutti gli dei, largo donator de le scienze, addirizzator de l'arti, continuo oracolo de matematici, computista mirabile, elegante dicitore, bel volto, leggiadra apparenza, facondo aspetto, personaggio grazioso, uomo tra gli uomini, tra le donne donna, desgraziato tra' desgraziati, tra' beati beato, tra' tutti tutto; che godi con chi gode, con chi piange piangi; però per tutto vai e stai, sei ben visto ed accettato. Che cosa de buono apporti?

Merc. Perché, Asino, fai conto di chiamarti ed essere academico, io, come quel che t' ho donati altri doni e grazie, al presente ancora con plenaria autorità ti ordino, constituisco e confermo academico e dogmatico generale, acciò che possi entrar ed abitar per tutto, senza ch'alcuno ti possa tener porta o dar qualsivoglia sorte d'oltraggio o impedimento, *quibuscumque in oppositum non obstantibus*. Entra, dunque, dove ti pare e piace. Né vogliamo che sii ubligato per il capitolo del silenzio biennale che si trova nell'ordine pitagorico, e qualsivogli' altre leggi ordinarie: perché, *novis intervenientibus causis, novae condendae sunt leges, proque ipsis condita non intelliguntur iura: interimque ad optimi iudicium iudicis referenda est sententia, cuius intersit iuxta necessarium atque commodum providere.* Parla dunque tra gli acustici; considera e contempla tra' matematici; discuti, dimanda, insegna, dechiara e determina tra' fisici; trovati con tutti, discorri con tutti, affratellati, unisciti, identificati con tutti, domina a tutti, sii tutto.

Asino. Avetel' inteso?

Micco. Non siamo sordi.

FINE

The Semiotics of Bruno's Italian
A Linguistic Note

Conrad Sweynheym and Arnold Pannartz established Italy's first printing press in the Benedictine monastery of Subiaco near Rome in 1465, exactly one century before Bruno entered the Dominican order in Naples. But the standardization of Italian spelling and punctuation that such printing presses promoted did not come about until much later, and it did not occur everywhere in the Italian peninsula at the same time or to the same degree. Among the persons who fostered a standardized form of Italian were, first and foremost, Aldus Manutius, the great Venetian printer, and Pietro Bembo, the Venetian editor of Petrarch's vernacular poems for the Aldine press (1501). From that point there was a gradual crescendo throughout the century toward a commonly accepted Italian grammar and lexicon, so that, at least in northernmost Italy, by midcentury the letter *x* was in large part abandoned for either *ss* or *s* and Latinisms in general were eschewed. Although such changes were slower to come to southern Italian writers, the rising acceptance of Tuscan—the language of Dante, Petrarch, and Boccaccio—as the norm for written Italian eventually culminated in the establishment of the Accademia della Crusca in Florence in 1582. The members of this academy published a *Vocabolario* with "correct" spellings intended for all Italian writers, but this seminal and highly influential work did not see the full light of day until 1612, over a decade after Bruno's death and over a quarter century after he produced *The Cabala of Pegasus*.[1]

Although Bruno wrote in a time when Italian was still very much in flux, scholars of the grammar, syntax, spelling, and punctuation of the vernacular works of Bruno continue to debate the reasons for his particularly daunting and perplexing style of written Italian. Questions abound regarding his usage of *la lingua volgare*, but definitive answers to the reasons he chose to write as he did prove to be in short supply. Often we can only speculate as to the author's intentions, for we have few clues as to the production history of his Italian dialogues. In the case of *The Cabala of Pegasus*, for which precious few copies survive, Bruno even attempted to obscure its printing history by listing its place of publication as Paris, though the book was printed in London.

And so we ponder: How carefully did the erstwhile Dominican proofread or edit the proofs of his dialogues for consistency, or did the inconsistencies even trouble him? Was he attempting more than a studied archaism in his plethora of Latinate word choices, spellings, and syntactical complexities? Was his reluctance to adhere to consistent and coherent grammatical and orthographical rules something more than the influence of the free-flowing Neapolitan dialect or the exuberant southern Italian style of speaking in the cinquecento? Was his textual promiscuity, which occurs when he spells the same word in different ways (for example, *cosí / cossí, devoto / divoto, dono / duono, innamora / inamora, istinto / instinto, regione / reggione*), more than printer's errors or an idiosyncratic typesetter? Was it a reflection of the possibly diverse pronunciations of dialogue speakers? Even more important, do such questions relate only to grammarians and scholars of the *ars punctandi*? Might not philosophers, who read Bruno primarily for content, find subtle meaning in the microcosmic elements (from spelling variants to idiosyncratic use of commas) as well as in the macrocosmic format (treatises in the form of dialogues) of his vernacular writings?

Giovanni Gentile, in attempting to explicate Bruno's word formations, refers to the Nolan's "morphological inconstancy" as a possible sign of his refusal to embrace pedantry and pedantic consistency.[2] This notion of grammar as a semiotic field of meaning is appealing, and we would like to suggest that in breaking or ignoring various grammatical and orthographical strictures of his day, Bruno's Italian does reveal his opinion of those whom his characters ridicule as pedants. Indeed, his Italian prose, when viewed as a macaronic whole, echoes and sustains the imagination and daring of his wide-ranging philosophical arguments. Disjunctive and interruptive clauses parallel the clashing and multiple voices that rise from the chorus of competing interlocutors. Our theologian-philosopher did not intend to be a systematic thinker, which for him would have smacked of Aristotelian pedantry. Rather, he sought to oppose Aristotelianism, which emphasized categorization and classification, from as many fronts as possible. One front appears to lie in the general field of grammar, which includes such subfields as morphology, syntax, phonology, semantics, and etymology.

An obvious example of Bruno's syntactical complexity is found in the extended and digressive simile of the potter. This packed comparison constitutes a single compound-complex sentence with multiple dependent clauses in both the vehicle and the tenor, but it forms the entire opening paragraph of the dedicatory epistle to *The Cabala of Pegasus*. Functioning as the opening salvo of the book, this figure of speech is not simply inventive and suggestive of the emergence of the Italian Baroque style, but also aptly illustrative of many of the intricate and meandering arguments that are to come in the dialogues. Syntax, like orthography, can function proleptically in Bruno and thus foreshadow the complexity of the reasoning of the anti-Aristotelian dialogists who are yet to be presented. But the accumulation of dependent clauses in a single sentence can also intermingle and become one with the labyrinthine thought Bruno is trying to articulate. Form and content are inseparably linked.

Despite Bruno's ostensible wish to avoid practices that might hint of pedantic taxonomies, his mélange of spelling peculiarities nevertheless falls into separable and identifiable categories, some of which can be explained by southern Italian speech patterns or dialectal influences and others by Latin etymologies. Several categories of spelling practices, some of which are interconnected, are outlined below.

First, and quickly noticeable, is the author's propensity for doubling consonants not normally doubled in standard or modern Italian. This is the case especially with the letter *g*. Bruno consistently writes *buggia, caggione, pertuggio, priggione, raggione, reggione, spreggiato*. This particular phenomenon clearly reflects the influence of southern Italian pronunciation. Even today in the regions of Latium, Campania, and further south one hears, for example, *reggione* for *regione* in spoken Italian. But Bruno, on occasion, also doubles other consonants, including *s*, *f*, and *d*, and this can be for various reasons. In the case of *cossí* we find an Old Italian form, whereas *diffinizioni* (for *definizioni*) is possibly an affected Latinism. The first-person past remote form of *vedere* found in the *Cabala* is *viddi*, which is an archaic form occurring also in Dante (see, for example, *Inferno* 7.20). Less common and perhaps unprecedented is Bruno's elimination of double consonants in words that invariably have the doubling in ancient, contemporary, and modern Italian, as when he writes *cità* for *città* and *mezo* for *mezzo*.

Second is his substitution, usually after the letter *d* (so as to capture or suggest a Latin subtext), of *e* for *i* (*delettare* [for *dilettare*, from the Latin *delectare*], *dechiarare, dependenza, demostrazione, destrutto*, but also *empiastro* [for *impiastro*, from the Latin *emplastrum*], *fenestra, meglior, recepzion, revelare*, and *vertú*). The preposition *di* appears as *de* throughout the *Cabala*. Occasionally Bruno performs the opposite and replaces an *e* with an *i* (*gittare* [Old Italian] for *gettare*), or an *o* with either an *i* (*dimanda* [Old Italian] for *domanda*) or a *u* (*argumento* [for *argomento*, from the Latin *argumentum*], *difficultà, facultà, particulare, sculpito, suggetto, suspiro*).

Third is his general preference for Latin prefixes over Italian: *ex-* for *es-* (*exaltazione, exercitati, execuzione, examinate, exclusi*); *trans-* for *tras-* (*transformazione*); *ad-* for *a-* (*admirazione*); *ins-* for *is-* (*instituzione, inspirazione*); *ab-* for *a-* (*absolutamente*). This and the preceding practice recall Latin etymologies and confer an academic flavor to the various voices heard in the dialogues.

Fourth is the substitution of *c* for *z*, in words such as *precioso* (for *prezioso*), *giudicio* (for *giudizio*), and *ocioso* (for *ozioso*). This is probably a phonological result of the *c* being pronounced as a surd *z* in certain regions of Italy.

Fifth is Bruno's preservation of the archaic *gli* (from the Latin *illi*) as a masculine plural article for adjectives and nouns that in modern Italian would require *i*. Examples would include *gli poetici figmenti, gli santi rabini, per gli quali, gli discorsi, gli chiamati*. Although this usage is not totally atypical in the cinquecento, his contemporaries Campanella and Tasso prefer *li* and *i* respectively.

Sixth is Bruno's retention of the *a* in -*are* verbs in conjugations of the future tense (*accettarete* [for *accetterete*], *aumentarà* [for *aumenterà*], *costarà, dimandarete, durarà*, etc.). This parallels Latin's retention of the *a* in the first conjugation stem in the future indicative tense.

Finally, we find in the *Cabala* other common Old Italian words as well as various practices involving Latin. Bruno often writes *ei* for *egli*, makes past participles agree with direct objects (*ho volti gli occhi*), uses the enclitic *i* before words beginning with an s-impure (*ispedire* for *spedire*), drops the final *e* on most infinitives (*accader*, *intender, venir*) and some present indicative -*ere* verbs in the third person (*vien*, vuol), flavors his discourse with random Latin words and phrases (*tandem, ministri verbi Dei, vale, vel*), quotes Jerome's Vulgate at length, and has various characters speak sentences in Latin to affect scholarly poses.

This ensemble of practices makes Bruno's vernacular a challenge for the reader accustomed to modern Italian, but the presence of a literal English translation should greatly reduce the effort required to decipher the prose of the *Cabala*.

NOTES

1. See chapter 8 ("Il Cinquecento") in Bruno Migliorini and Ignazio Baldelli, *Breve storia della lingua italiana* (1977), for a much more detailed analysis of spelling (and punctuation) in sixteenth-century Italy.

2. In *Giordano Bruno: Dialoghi italiani* (1958, xlvii), Giovanni Gentile notes how, while editor, he scrupulously maintained "la stessa incostanza morfologica del Bruno" [the same morphological inconstancy of Bruno] because he had no editorial authorization to correct the inconsistencies. Our Italian version of *The Cabala of Pegasus* is based on this standard modern edition of Bruno.

Antipedantry in Bruno's London Dialogues
The Playwright as Dialogist, and the Drama of Dialectic

The cultural transmission of Bruno's vendetta against the Oxford doctors is also assisted by his dramaturgical instincts: drawing upon the same characteristics shaping the ridiculous intellectual Manfurio in his comedy *Il candelaio* (Paris, 1582), he introduces the university doctors and pedants of his dialogues as dolts, buffoons, and boors— and merely elaborates on their given absurdities in the course of dialectical exchanges. These interlocutors are trapped by their creator in the same metalinguistic fashion by which Boethius traps himself in the *Consolation*: "You are playing with me, aren't you," he accuses Fortune, "by weaving a labyrinth of arguments from which I can't find the way out" (112). The philosophical dialogue employs diverse devices of ideological manipulation—whether rhetorically directing reader and interlocutor as Boethius claims, or "recreating" conversation mimetically, creating for the reader the fiction of reporting or reviving arguments previously witnessed. The culturally encoded desire for verisimilitude[1] has also led the theatre traditionally to formulate discourse structures that draw their semantics from the paradigmatic pool of experience. As is true of each of

Bruno's vernacular dialogues composed and published in London, the *Cabala del cavallo pegaseo*'s dramatic effect—an element of the semiological system that communicates a dialogue's drama—derives from the confluence of four factors.

The dialogue writer must first situate discrete listener and speaker roles within a complex interplay of voices. According to Keir Elam, a dramatic character approaches verisimilitude by displaying an epistemological competence that encompasses degrees of communicative mastery and versatility; knowledge of rules governing social milieu; "the ability to 'create' non-actual worlds referred to in the course of the dialogue"; and consciousness of spatio-temporal location (1980, 136–137). The degree to which this multifaceted awareness is manifested determines a character's authority as speaker. Xenophon's Syracusan King Hiero demonstrates himself worthy of the position of instructor to the visiting poet Simonides by defining the goal of interaction between a ruler and his people as mutual happiness—in proof, refuting the common expectation that a king's table must be strewn with exotic condiments. Hiero "earns" the right to lecture Simonides through the signification of wisdom, determined by his competence in a multiplicity of elocutionary acts and by concomitant evidence that he is a practiced listener as well as speaker. Bruno's *Cabala* closes with the triumph of humble scholar over self-proclaimed intellectual: the Ass, having secured entrance to the Pythagorean Academy through the intervention of the god Mercury, underscores his victory with the rhetorical question "Avetel' inteso?" [Have you understood this?], to which the Pythagorean Fool or Ape (a metaphor for all narrow-minded academicians), who had previously blocked his path, replies "Non siamo sordi" [We're not deaf] (923). The dialogist's incorporation of a multiplicity of characters assists narrative pacing, provides the stimulus of variety, and reduces dogmatism by introducing diverse exposition into the discourse. Even in dialogues focused on one spokesperson, the autonomous, conspicuous presence and opinions of other speakers contribute to real or potential conflict, to definition of problems demanding resolution.

Second, the dialogist may cultivate an audience rapport like that available to the dramatist by evoking the familiar, through the fiction of "authentic" action. The comedian who, in order to panic an audience, displays a bucket of water but covertly switches it for a bucket of confetti understands that the relief of not being doused is eminently pleasurable, and that until the rain of paper rather than water drenches the spectators, their conception of reality displaces that of performance. Their immediate expectations make it impossible for them "to be conscious of the fiction-as-fiction and the fiction-as-'real,' within two distinct frames and at two levels, in *exact simultaneity*" (Merrell 1982, 89). In the guise of teacher and prophet, Bruno creates a fiction of authenticity in *De la causa* for his persona, Teofilo, via rhetorical legerdemain:

> Lascio che non senza raggione li necromantici sperano effettuar molte cose per le ossa de' morti; e credeno che quelle ritegnano, se non quel medesmo, un tale però e quale atto di vita, che gli viene a proposito a effetti estraordinarii. Altre occasioni mi faranno piú a lungo discorrere circa la mente, il spirto, l'anima, la vita che penetra tutto, è in tutto e move tutta la materia; empie il gremio di quella, e la sopravanza piú tosto che da quella è sopravanzata, atteso che la sustenza spirituale dalla materiale non può essere superata, ma piú tosto la viene a contenere. (243–244)

> [I leave out the necromancers who—not without reason—hope to accomplish many things through the bones of the dead; and they believe these retain if not the man himself, then his vital principle, which is manipulated to extraordinary effect. On other occasions I will discourse more extensively about the intellect, the spirit, the soul, the life that penetrates everything, is in everything, and moves all matter; it fills the bosom of matter and overflows it rather than being restrained by it, seeing that the spiritual substance of matter cannot be superceded (by it), but rather comes to contain it.]

He includes what he claims to omit, and he promises effects that he may not necessarily deliver (or, at any rate, not immediately deliver), because his promise is sufficient to create an intriguing drama of expectations. The narrative voice(s) of a philosophical dialogue can include significant details contributing to a kinetic atmosphere—stimulating and engaging the reader's imagination—surrounding the development of ideas, parallel to that created in the theatrical mise-en-scène through setting, proxemics, and choreography. The pathos of the scene surrounding Socrates in Plato's *Phaedo* is heightened by Phaidon's descriptions of the actions of friends attending the philosopher. Particularly moving is the characterization of Apollodorus as a man who cannot even pretend to understand Socrates' sublime passivity towards imminent death. Apollodorus weeps wretchedly, uncontrollably. The writer multiplies the dialogue's communicative potential by showing what characters "*do* (active judgments) and *make* (exhibitive judgments), as well as by what they *say* (assertive judgments); the dramatic context pleads for an apprehension of the manner, as well as the content, of what is said and done" (Eckstein 1968, 16). As the reader discovers in the course of the *Cabala*'s "Dedicatory Epistle," wherein the author anticipates the eventual verification of his manuscript's importance, detailing its miraculous properties at length while documenting its rejection by every potential dedicatee to whom it has been offered, Bruno gambles like the dialogists before him that the "dramatic context" of his dialogues will prove an enticement sufficient to ensure reader participation until their didactic content is thoroughly introduced.

The subtext of "authenticity" in the dialogue is reinforced by the third factor, the characterization of individual interlocutors. Some dialogues impress the reader as more effective because "their principals may be more lifelike, more typical, more significant" (Stokes 1986, 29). To guarantee that a character will retain identity "despite the transformations of [narrative] and thematic roles which can affect him/her," it "must be defined empirically by the set of pertinent traits which distinguish its doings and/or being from those of other actors" (Greimas and Courtés 1982, 155). This individuation exists as an extension, or sophistication, of the dramatic system previously established through role discrimination and verisimilitude. In the first book of the *Republic*, Thrasymachus the Cynic feverishly argues the superior profitability of unjust actions over just; even after reluctantly agreeing with every premise Socrates outlines, he perversely clings to his theory, conceding only that Socrates' *elenchos* has served as their mutual entertainment. Thrasymachus's unyielding, unscrupulous character marks him pejoratively as an inferior intellect, while Socrates' condescending good humor confirms his control and authority. To varying degrees, Bruno's London dialogues feature individuated and similarly patterned interlocutor models. In terms of character formulae, they typically include Brunist persona(e); student(s), sympathetic listener(s), or open-minded opponent(s); and opponent(s) resistant to any revision of personal opinions (designated *pedante / pedanti*).

Finally, to avoid subjecting the reader to the lock-step feel of a catechistical determinism, the dialogist must come to recognize what the dramatist learns through experience: conflict is essential. The fiction of dialectical opposition must be realized if the fiction of resolution is to be satisfying. The dramatized dialogue, then, is a subversive enactment regardless of whether the writer argues *in utramque partem* or chooses not to resolve the conflict depicted. As every theatrical performance "of interest will involve a complex dialectic of code-observing, code-making and code-breaking" (Elam 1980, 55), the dialogue can appropriate this complex of responses to capture reader imagination. Bruno employs these tactics extravagantly, frequently foregrounding the fiction of opposition—in effect polarizing the opponents to his personae as psychomachian negatives of the good qualities those personae have. As a result of Bruno's dramatic modifications, these demons, generically designated *gli pedanti* by their creator, become powerfully connotative signifiers. Although the *OED* cites Shakespeare's *Love's Labour's Lost* (3.1.179; though cf. 5.2.406), 1588, as the earliest example of "pedant" denoting "a schoolmaster, teacher, or tutor," the Italian term *pedanteria*, pedantry, appears pejoratively in the opening page of *The Defence of Poesy* (1983, 102) by Sir Philip Sidney (the dedicatee of Bruno's *Spaccio* and *Eroici furori*). Sidney's usage already approaches the *OED's* second definition of pedant (earliest citation, 1596) as "A person who overrates book-learning or technical knowledge, or displays it unduly or unseasonably; one who has mere learning untempered by practical judgment and knowledge of affairs; one who lays excessive stress upon trifling details of knowledge or upon strict adherence to formal rules; sometimes one who is possessed by a theory and insists on applying it in all cases without discrimination, a doctrinaire." This semantic metamorphosis owes much to Bruno's London dialogues, published in 1584–1585. And as a glance at each of them will demonstrate, the ironic effect of this is that whether or not Bruno's philosophy is gleaned from the dialogues, his character type—the pedant, with its curious mixture of ineffectuality and of menace— remains distinctly etched in the memory of the reader.

La cena de le Ceneri (1584)
De la causa, principio e uno
[*On Cause, Principle and the One*] (1584)
De l'infinito, universo e mondi (1584)

La cena de le Ceneri, the first of three dialogues dedicated to Michel de Castelnau, Marquis Mauvissière, ambassador to Elizabeth from Henri III, not only identifies the professors of Oxford as the objects of Bruno's scorn; it also prescribes pejorative reader identification of those individuals through the *pedante* Prudenzio. Joined by Teofilo[2] the philosopher and sympathetic listeners Smitho and Frulla, Prudenzio proposes a tetralogue to discuss the recent encounter between the Nolan and two Oxford doctors, Nundinio and Torquato, on the occasion of a dinner held by Fulke Greville on Ash Wednesday. Frulla asks why their *dia*logue should be called a *tetra*logue, and Prudenzio explains that a tetralogue is *quatuorum sermo*, whereas a dialogue is strictly *duorum sermo;* besides, the "di" in dialogue isn't etymologically derivative of *diversum*, a multiplicity of speakers. Linguistically speaking, his scholastic obsession with minutiae produces a "grammatical structure that is at the same time a signifying structure" (Greimas 1983, 132), connoting Prudenzio's pettiness while directing him to arrive at an absurd conclusion that ignores the obvious. By failing to recognize the suitability of the classical symposium's dialogue form to their topos, he betrays the superficiality of his learning; by insisting that the other interlocutors adopt his epistemology, he dramatizes the intellectual intolerance that the London dialogues repeatedly condemn. Bruno's attack, then, is given its first articulation through Prudenzio as a second-order semiological system[3] created to mythologize the first-order system, which employs Nundinio and Torquato to introduce the "menacing pedant" icon. Careful always to protect his own authority and the integrity of his beliefs, Bruno allows Prudenzio no rebuttal to Teofilo's simple explanation that the four interlocutors will share in the binary processes "di proponere e rispondere, di raggionare e ascoltare" [of proposing and replying, of discussing and listening] (25): "the Ash Wednesday supper" thus is also "the supper of ashes," a humbling repast for those who oppose the Nolan.

Exploiting images familiar to the Elizabethan reader as the demons of schoolboy nightmares, Bruno personifies the intellectual threats of *gli pedanti* as the significantly named Nundinio (*nundine*, the empty nine-day period between markets; *nonnulla*, trifle; the disjunctive / conjunctive *nondimeno*) and Torquato (*torto*, *torcigliato,* twisted; *torchiato,* pressed; Latin *torquatus,* wearing a twisted collar or necklace, a slave to [or master authority of] tradition; Tomás de Torquemada, archetypal Dominican *inquisitore generale*). The menace associated with the pedant icon fuses Nundinio's lack of intellectual substance with Torquato's imperious malice: "Ignoranza ed arroganza son due sorelle individue in un corpo ed in un'amica" [Ignorance and arrogance are two discrete sisters united in body and soul] (127). Nundinio's facade of authority is destroyed in the course of the Copernican debate when, sophistically, he tries to compose and ask the one question which would rhetorically cripple his opponent's argument. After the Nolan declares that the earth and each of the stars have their own individual souls, the learned doctor attacks: "—Credete, disse Nundinio, che sii sensitiva quest'anima?— Non solo sensitiva, rispose il Nolano, ma anco intellettiva; non solo intellettiva, come la nostra, ma forse anco piú.— Qua tacque Nundinio, e non rise" ['Do you believe,' said Nundinio, 'that this soul is sentient?' 'Not only sentient,' responds the Nolan, 'but even intellective; not only intelligent, like our own, but perhaps even more so.' Here Nundinio shuts up, and does not laugh] (109–110). The linguistic patterns in both Bruno's Latin and vernacular works bespeak his love of abstraction when modeling epistemological discourse. Nundinio is method without content,[4] his fluency limited to grammarian strategy. The Nolan stymies his opponent with abstraction, the variable "even more so," and secures his conquest by depriving the doctor of his only weapon—words.

Nundinio is portrayed as no more than an impediment to substantial debate, a joker in the deck; Torquato, however, is the ace of menace. Like Nundinio, Torquato "non è venuto tanto armato di raggioni, quanto di paroli e scommi, che si muoiono di freddo e fame" [hasn't come armed with reason as much as with words and agitations, dying from cold and hunger] (128). Communicating knowledge as impoverished as Nundinio's,[5] this humanist product is

more aggressive, is vindictive by nature, and fights to prevent transmission of any ideology in conflict with his own. When he has
exhausted his argumentative rhetoric, "salta ne' calci de la rab-
bia, acuisce l'unghie de la detrazione, ghigna i denti delle ingiurie,
spalanca la gorgia dei clamori, a fin che non lascie dire le raggioni
contrarie e quelle non pervengano a l'orecchie de' circostanti" [he
leaps into the boots of rage, sharpens the claws of detraction, sneers
showing the teeth of injuries, (and) slashes the throat of dissensions,
in order not to allow contrary reasons to speak, or to reach the ears
of those surrounding] (105). Bruno portrays his Oxford opponents
as mean-spirited villains deserving our contempt; but through a
quasi-Senecan rhetoric of horror, *gli pedanti* are also depicted as
capable of a viscerally tangible malevolence. This, too, has a rhetorical rationale: the dialogist conceives and encodes the fiction of puis-
sant evil in order to facilitate his later metafictional triumph over it.

Bruno constructs the pedant character precisely: he speaks, but
does not listen; though individuated by name, he is constitutionally
resistant to change; his dramatic purpose is to forbid free thought
and to perpetuate error. With this vehicle, the dialogist evokes audience revulsion as surely as the playwright portraying a vicious
antagonist. Readers find the position of the Pelagian heretic Crito-
bulus intolerable in St. Jerome's *Dialogus contra Pelagianos* largely
because Jerome makes him an intolerably unsympathetic character.
Smitho confesses his fear that if he had studied the humanist canon
with doctors such as Nundinio and Torquato, "m'abbi infettata la
mente di perniziose pazzie" [my mind would have been infected
with pernicious lunacies], the effect analogous to a person "mangiar
veleno, la complession de' quali . . . non solamente non ne sente oltraggio, ma ancora se l'ha convertito in nutrimento naturale, di
sorte che l'antidoto istesso gli è dovenuto mortifero" [eating venom,
the body of whom . . . not only feels no abuse, but converts it to
natural nutriment, so that the very antidote has become deadly]

(46–47). Humanist rhetoric—that is, the alleged elevation of style and disciplinary rigidity over substance that rendered Bruno's extravagant syncretism of ideas ineffective during the Oxford debates—is the insidious disease, and Bruno prescribes the Nolan as the cure. In contrast to the heavies Nundinio and Torquato, Prudenzio seems a cipher, merely the comic butt of the *pedante* threat, capable of nothing more than petty semantic quibbles and inappropriate smatterings of Latin. Though this pedagogue poses no threat and is dismissed by Teofilo as simpleminded, he cues the reader to the vulnerability (lack of substantial, empowering knowledge) as well as the danger (rhetorical intimidation and misinformation) of Bruno's primary targets. With the self-righteous justification of a foreigner's objectivity, the author warns all freethinking individuals,

> Questi sono i frutti d'Inghilterra; e cercatene pur quanti volete, che le troverete tutti dottori in grammatica in questi nostri giorni, ne' quali in la felice patria regna una costellazione di pedantesca ostinatissima ignoranza e presunzione mista con una rustica incivilità, che farebbe prevaricar la pazienza di Giobbe. (133)

> [These are the fruits of England; and search for as long as you like, these days you'll find that they're all doctors of grammar, and in that happy nation a constellation of pedantically obstinate ignorance and presumption mixed with provincial incivility reigns, that would undo even the patience of Job.]

Recovered from his encounter with the Oxford duo, the Nolan is advised at the close of *La cena* (by Prudenzio, in the end a convert to the Nolan's philosophy, exemplifying the learned ignorance and "divine asininity" preached so fervently in the *Cabala*) to stick close to the Marquis Mauvissière "(sotto l'auspicii del quale cominci a publicar tanto sollenne filosofia), che forse verrà qualche sufficientissimo mezzo, per cui gli astri e' potentissimi superi ti guidaranno a termine tale, onde da lungi possi riguardar simil brutaglia" [(under whose auspices you commence publication of such solemn philosophy) so perhaps some superabundant means will come by which the stars and most potent celestials guide you to a vantage from which you can simply observe similar brutality] (169). In *De la causa, principio e uno,* the alarm becomes more insistent, calling de Castelnau the "sicuro e tranquillo porto alle vere muse, e ruinosa roccia in cui vegnano a svanirsi le false munizioni de impetuosi dissegni de lor nemiche vele" [sure and peaceful haven for the true Muses, and the rugged crag against which the sham ammunition from the violent schemes of hostile sails peters out and fails (Lindsay 1962, 48)] (177). The first section of Bruno's second London dialogue is devoted to rationalizing and apologizing for his first, and he implies that the public response to *La cena* has been so pronounced that the prior sponsorship of the Marquis has become, of necessity, his protection. Regardless of the size of *La cena*'s readership,[6] the dialogist creates a credible fiction of controversy. Concerning both the substance and the distribution of *De la causa,* Armesso pleads with Teofilo not to let "questi vostri discorsi vegnan formate comedie, tragedie, lamenti, dialogi, o come vogliam dire, simili a quelli che poco tempo fa, per esserno essi usciti in campo a spasso, vi hanno forzato di starvi rinchiusi e retirati in case" [these discourses of yours become comedies, tragedies, laments, dialogues, or whatever we want to call them, like those that not long ago, by being thrust out into the open for amusement, have forced you to be locked up and withdrawn at home] (194). With this self-directed admonition, Filoteo / Bruno takes care to signify the Italian visitor as the injured party, the university savants and those whose judgments they influence as the aggressors. Despite confessing that *La cena* was written in part to secure revenge on these latter (199), the philosopher construes his act as righteous self-affirmation, rationalizing, "Io son stato su la correzione, nell'esercizio della quale ancora siamo simili agli Dei" [I am of the frame of mind concerning correction, that in its exercise we are like unto Gods] (200).

While escalating his emotional fervor in *De la causa,* Bruno drops *La cena*'s dual-level critique and satire of the Oxford doctors, limiting the dialogue's dramatis personae to only one *pedante.* His description of interlocutors, however, is structured to build gradually to the climactic introduction of the perverse anti-intellectual, Poliinnio. When Armesso inquires whether the book of dialogues he sees in Filoteo's possession features a character like *La cena*'s Prudenzio, Filoteo acknowledges that they are, with one exception, "quieti e onestissimi," listing Alessandro Dicsono Aurelio,[7] "che il Nolano ama quanto gli occhi suoi" [whom the Nolan loves as much as his own eyes] and who proposes the subject of their discussion; Teofilo, "che sono io" [who am I], and explicates the topic; and Gervasio, a man "non odora né puzza" [neither perfumed nor putrid], who is not a philosopher like Dicsono and Teofilo, though he enjoys their debates and "prende per comedia gli fatti di Poliinnio" [treats Poliinnio's actions like comedy].[8] Depicted last and with the most elaboration, Poliinnio the "sacrilegio pedante" is said to be

> uno de' rigidi censori di filosofi, onde si afferma Momo, uno affettissimo circa il suo gregge di scholastici, onde si noma nell'amor socratico; uno, perpetuo nemico del femineo sesso, onde, per non esser fisico, si stima Orfeo, Museo, Titiro e Anfione. (215)

> [one of those inflexible censors of philosophers, through whom Momus calls attention to himself, one who is overly excited about his herd of students (whence this love bears the name Socratic); the perpetual nemesis of the female sex, whence in order to avoid acting naturally, fancies himself Orpheus, Musaeus, Tityros, and Amphion.]

Poliinnio's misogyny[9] and imputed homosexuality ("Socratic love") are encoded to establish unambiguously that his responses are unnatural—as, by implication, are those of anyone who persists in opposing Brunist philosophy. Perversity is an essential element of Bruno's pedant figure, yet it is simply the character's heritage received from *gli pedanti* of previous generations. We are reminded, for example, that Poliinnio is a pedagogue when Gervasio derisively refers to him as *magister* at the beginning of the *De la causa*'s "Dialogo Secondo" (225). Hence Prudenzio adjures Nundinio and Torquato, at the end of *La cena*, to return to the

> rustico ed incivile vostro pedagogo che vi di' creanza, e quell'altro archiasino ed ignorante che v' insegnò di disputare; a fin che vi risaldano le male spese e l'interesse del tempo e cervello, che v' han fatto perdere. (170)

> [cloddish and rude pedagogue who created you, and that other master of asininity and ignorance who taught you to dispute; thence they can settle up with you for your bad investments and for the interest on the time and brain that you've lost.]

The locus of intellectual corruption and misinformation is clearly defined as the seat of pedagogy, the university.[10] And by extending the tradition of harmful instruction back a significant but indeterminate distance, Bruno transforms his intellectual opponents at Oxford and elsewhere, along with their predecessors, into members of a mythic army of anti-intellectuals. Consequently, he recodes his embarrassing performance and reception at Oxford as heroic opposition to a formidable threat.

Bruno splits his portrayal of Oxford (itself already a metonym for general pedantry) into two metonymic depictions, one negative (Oxford = Aristotelianism: rule-bound, inflexibly structured and categorized) and one positive (Oxford = freethinking: the Search for Truth), in *De l'infinito*.[11] In the early sections of the dialogue, Bruno continues his castigation of rhetoricians by surrounding his pedagogue Burchio with the vastly more intelligent Fracastorio, an even-tempered truth-seeker; Elpino, an open-minded student; and Teofilo / Filoteo, explicator of Brunist physics and cosmology. As overtly buffoonish as any of his predecessors in the previous two dialogues, Burchio proves incapable of distinguishing between conceptual and visceral operations, confessing in regards to Teofilo's views, "non è possibile che possa esser capito dal mio capo, né digerito dal mio stomaco" [my head can't comprehend them, nor my stomach digest them] (368). On the pretext of maintaining a sense of intellectual integrity he promises Filoteo "se non intenderò li sentimenti, ascoltarò le paroli; se non ascoltarò le paroli, udirò la voce" [If I do not understand your opinions, I will (at least) listen to your words; if I do not listen to your words, I will (at least) hear your voice] (393).

Teofilo asks Fracastorio to take up the anti-Aristotelian gauntlet after he has reasoned with Burchio (as has Elpino) to no avail, explaining that perhaps Burchio is simply weary of their opinions. Rather than waste more ideology on the pedagogue, however, Fracastorio forces Burchio into a reversal of polemical positions—in fact, a university exercise—to make it impossible for the pedant to experience the debate passively:

> Dolce mio Burchio, io per me ti pono in luogo d'Aristotele, ed io voglio essere in luogo di uno idiota e rustico che confessa saper nulla, presuppone di aver inteso niente, e di quello che dice ed intende il Filoteo, e di quello che intende Aristotele e tutto il mondo ancora. (446)

> [My sweet Burchio, I am putting you in the position of Aristotle, and I choose to be in the position of an idiot and rustic who confesses to know nothing either of that which Filoteo says and means, or of that which Aristotle and the entire world besides means.]

By immediately seizing the offensive, Fracastorio deflates his opponent, thwarting Burchio's attempts to cite Aristotelian order as counterproof to the unity of an infinite, universal consciousness. Burchio musters his rhetorical powers, but they fail to extend the debate because they lack the substance of real knowledge. Stymied and impotent, he can only respond with irrational praise for the university grammarians, "dottori profondi, suttili, aurati, magni, inespugnabili, irrefragabili, angelici, serafici, cherubici e divini" [profound, subtle, golden, illustrious, impregnable, indisputable, angelic, seraphic, cherubic, and divine doctors] (466).[12]

To provide serious dramatic conflict in the concluding section of the dialogue, Bruno introduces Albertino, who comes armed with martial rhetoric and images to defend Aristotle: "Molti hanno balestrato e machinato contra Aristotele; ma son cascati i castegli, son spuntate le frecce e gli son rotti gli archi" [Many have taken up weapons and plotted against Aristotle; but their castles are ruined, their arrows blunted and their bows broken] (502). But Albertino argues Aristotelian reputation rather than Aristotelian doctrine, and hence is easily mastered by Filoteo, Fracastorio, and Elpino—since by the dialogue's end, all three are clearly Bruno personae. Again recoding personal history, Bruno has Albertino assert his reputation as an intellectual approved "da mille academie" to quiet his critics, though with as little success as that documented by the author in his epistle to the Oxford doctors. Albertino ultimately accepts Teofilo's advice that he reject Aristotelian dogmatism and instead choose the limitless speculations that can be abstracted in the imagination. This proves that Albertino, though a university product, is not essentially pedantic; although he wields stock grammarian affectations, he has the requisite wisdom to defend his beliefs and to consider seriously the value of others' ideas, particularly those of the Nolan.

Spaccio della bestia trionfante (1584)
*Cabala del cavallo pegaseo con l'aggiunta
dell'Asino Cillenico* (1585)
De gli eroici furori (1585)

The *Spaccio,* typical of the London dialogues in its Brunist intertextuality—and like its two successors, dedicated to Sir Philip Sidney—

includes additional conciliatory gestures germane to the popular reception of *La cena*, as well as allusions to conspiracy surrounding both the text and the events that inspired it. Bruno informs Sidney that he would have accepted (and obviously expected) certain generosities from Fulke Greville "se tra noi non avesse sparso il suo arsenito de vili, maligni ed ignobili interessati l'invidiosa Erinni" [if the envious Erinys of cowardly, malicious, ignoble, and interested parties had not spread her arsenate (Imerti 1964, 70)] (550). He also alludes to the forthcoming publication of the *Cabala del cavallo pegaseo*,[13] and in the *Eroici furori* declares "l'ignoranza è madre della felicità e beatitudine sensuale; e questa medesima è l'orto del paradiso de gli animali; come si far chiaro nelli dialogi de la *Cabala del cavallo pegaseo*" [ignorance is the mother of felicity and sensuous happiness; and this same happiness is the garden of paradise of the animals, as it is made clear in the dialogues of the *Cabala of the Pegasian Horse* (Memmo 1964, 98–99)] (975). The etiology of these intertextual references is rooted psychologically in Bruno's repeated assertions of authority, and they reinforce the intrigue that is Bruno's most dramatic fiction in the dialogues: the paranoiac identification of us and them, the latter characterized as aggressors wielding the blade of superficial or illusory knowledge.

The "menacing pedant" icon becomes more diffuse in the *Spaccio*, moving away from the focus of previous dialogues on the Oxonians and their ilk, yet also becomes more explicitly mythic, as their dangerous influence has spread from university to universe, proportionately raising the stakes of the dialogist's efforts to alert readers to it, and to eradicate it. The explanatory epistle details, at considerable length, the specific traits of cosmic corruption (which have infected the constellations, the gods, even Jove): Cepheus, site of severity, will become wisdom; Perseus's trivial interest will become diligent study; Aquila's tyrannical arrogance, generosity; Pegasus's impatience, divine raptures; on and on throughout the heavens. The vices are those of the university savants who rejected Bruno's hermetic Co-pernicanism; the virtues are those of the Nolan himself. The literary model for the *Spaccio* is Lucian's *Parliament of the Gods,* constructed on accusations by Momus—comedian / satirist of the gods—that Dionysus, already polluted by feminine characteristics, has led a tainted and tainting clan of man-animals into the company of the immortals and must be expelled. Whereas Lucian's Momus is exiled for his audacity, Bruno reinstates him and empowers Momus to censure the gods for their vices; thus Cupid, for example, is in-formed that he must wear clothes (at least from the waist down) when in the presence of other gods. Even Jove acknowledges his sins, and the theme of the dialogue becomes the necessity of change— which, as the dialogist has made patently clear in the previous three works, is anathema to the obstinate *pedante.*

The *Spaccio* is also more precisely employed to direct attention to religious *pedanti,* specifically addressing Calvinism and the doctrine of election. Momus complains to Jove about "quella poltronesca setta di pedanti" [that cowardly sect of pedants] who preach that humans should do good rather than evil, "ma non per ben che si faccia o mal che non si faccia, si viene ad essere degno e grato a' dei; ma per sperare e credere secondo il catechismo loro" [though one comes to be worthy and gratifying to the gods not by the good that is done, or the evil which is not done, but by hoping and believing according to their catechism] (623). This diametrically opposes the emphasis on self-determination that is essential to Brunist meta-physics. Compounding ideological intolerance with hypocrisy and greed, the Calvinists have also profited through the wealth confis-cated from Catholics persecuted in England and forced to desert their goods and land for the sanctuary of exile; a Catholic and a man persecuted for his beliefs, the author identifies with the oppressed.

The *Cabala* has been something of a frustrating puzzle-box— seemingly created to be insoluble—for modern readers who look for doctrinal implications in every Brunist statement. From the testimony of Onorio, for example, is it tempting to construe metempsychosis as one of the author's central philosophical tenets; yet Article 189 of the Italian Inquisition's heresy proceedings against Bruno reads that "Interrogatus negat dixisse, nec tenuisse dari transmigrationem animarum humanarum in corpora brutorum, et in specie negat se dixisse, se alias fuisse in hoc mundo" [Being interrogated he denies that he might have said that he held the transmigration of human souls into beasts to be given, and in particular he denies that he himself had ever existed in another world] (Mercati 1942, 99). When Bruno writes of metempsychosis, he does so not from theological conviction (that is, inspired by the *Corpus Hermeticum* and Pythagorean concepts) but to reinforce figuratively his conception of monadism, of the unity of existence, best represented by an immanent rather than transcendent God. Like a kabbalist, however, Bruno submerges this worthy knowledge (discussed openly in both *De la causa* and *De l'infinito*) beneath the dialogue's discussions of ignorance and asininity.

Assisting him in this effort are three dramatic portraits of asinine pedantry, featuring the characters Coribante, Onorio, and the Pythagorean Fool (or "Ape"). The *Cabala*'s Coribante, like his predecessors Nundinio, Torquato, Prudenzio, and Poliinnio, is a grammarian, who like them speaks in macaronic Latin and interrupts other interlocutors with worthless interjections. He presents rhetorical opposition to many of Brunist persona Saulino's propositions concerning asininity, and just as he is about to accept all of the arguments presented in the "Dialogo Primo," he announces that "è gionta l'ora, in cui debbo licenziar gli miei discepoli" [the hour has arrived when I must dismiss my pupils] (881), reminding the reader that he is in fact a pedagogue and establishing his irresponsibility in that capacity—having abandoned his students for a significant length of time in order to pursue the opportunity to display his Latin facility before adult peers. With the exception of a few additional Latin interruptions in the third portion of the second dialogue, and the *maestro*'s concern with supper at its conclusion (a dialogue convention, but noticeably applied here to mark the superficiality of the *pedante*'s interest in the dialogue's arguments), Bruno has little further use for Coribante, since he has continued the movement begun in the *Spaccio* of condemning intellectual pettiness in a more general fashion. And for private revenge in the short third dialogue, when Sebasto's servant Alvaro delivers apologies to Saulino for the absence of the other three interlocutors, Bruno has him report than Coribante is "assalito da le podagre" [attacked by the gout] (911).

Onorio is a composite character by virtue of his past-life recollections, and Bruno deftly manipulates this internal diversity to affirm his own theories about the nature of the soul and to deny the value of Aristotelian philosophy—by evoking a confession of unworthiness from, as it were, Aristotle himself. When Sebasto inquires about the differences between human and bestial souls, Onorio replies "Quella de l'uomo è medesima in essenza specifica e generica con quella de le mosche, ostreche marine e piante, e di qualsivoglia cosa che si trove animata o abbia anima" [That of the human is the same in specific and generic essence as that of the flies, sea oysters and plants, and of anything whatsoever one finds animated or having a soul] (885). However, this worthy knowledge was subjugated by corruptive, pedantic impulses experienced while he was serving as tutor of Alexander the Great:

> benchè erudito molto bene nelle umanistiche scienze, nelle quali ero piú illustre che tutti li miei predecessori, entrai in presunzione d'esser filosofo naturale, come è ordinario nelli pedanti d'esser sempre temerarii e presuntuosi; e con ciò, per esser estinta la cognizione della filosofia, morto Socrate, bandito Platone, ed altri in altre maniere dispersi, rimasi io solo lusco intra gli ciechi; e facilmente possevi aver riputazion non sol di retorico, politico, logico, ma ancora de filosofo. (893)

[I entered into the presumption (although very learned in the humanist sciences, in which I was more distinguished than all of my predecessors) of being a natural philosopher, as it's ordinary in pedants always to be rash and presumptuous; and with this, the science of philosophy extinct, Socrates dead, Plato banished, and others in various manners dispersed, I alone was one-eyed among the blind and easily gained the reputation not only of rhetorician, politician, logician—but even of philosopher.]

Bruno leads us to the conclusion that Aristotelian philosophy was founded upon asinine (in this case pejorative) ignorance, not least for the reason that Onorio, by contriving not to drink from the waters of Lethe following the death of his ass incarnation, retained his asinine characteristics in all subsequent incarnations. This proves most apparent in his "protosofosso" [protosophist] avatar, Aristotle.

Like other ideologues and pedagogues against whom he declaims, Bruno makes the Fool at the door of the Pythagorean Academy particularly intolerant of knowledge or phenomena that prove incompatible with accepted categories and norms. The presence of a talking Ass requesting entrance to study provokes the Fool spontaneously to welcome him as "O portento insolito, o prodigio stupendo, o maraviglia incredibile" [O uncommon portent, O stupendous prodigy, O incredible marvel] (915), but upon reflection to brand this anomaly "O demonio incarnato" [O demon incarnate] (915). Despite the carefully considered arguments from the Ass defending his preparation and aptitude for study among the Pythagoreans, it is the Fool who exhibits asinine obstinacy and petulantly announces "Può far il cielo che gli asini parlino, ma non già che entrino in scola pitagorica" [Heaven can make asses speak, of course, but not enroll them in the Pythagorean school] (918). The Ass retaliates by firing barbed questions at the Fool and his silent comrades—Bruno makes it clear that the Fool is surrounded by other stubborn pedagogues who share his views, amplifying dramatically the threat posed to the Ass—until the dialogist is obliged to rescue his hero in archetypally theatrical fashion by bringing in Mercury, a *deus ex machina*. In a triumphantly Brunist climax, he confirms the Ass as "academico e dogmatico generale" [universal academician and dogmatician] (923) by the will of the gods, exempts the Ass from the unyieldingly pragmatic four-stage program of the Pythagoreans, and encourages all students to inquire and to teach.

As the emotional impetus giving semantic potency to the "menacing pedant" icon begins to recede somewhat for Bruno, he abandons the overtly dramatic structure of the previous London dialogues in favor of a more conventional, even catechistical design in *De gli eroici furori*. To promote (that is, to endorse through elaboration and repetition) his syncretic, freethinking philosophy as represented in a series of emblematic sonnets, Bruno follows each poem with explication and commentary from one of five more-or-less interchangeable pairs of interlocutors, Tansillo / Cicada, Caesarino / Maricondo, Liberio / Laodinio, Severino / Minutolo, and Laodomia / Giulia.[14] Although he relinquishes his role as dramatist, the Nolan retains the vernacular dialogues' ubiquitous anti-Aristotelianism. Tansillo explains to Cicada that Aristotle's *Poetics* is not a valid tool for judging other poets, inasmuch as it was composed by a writer who was not himself a poet and addresses only the qualities of Homeric epic (957–959). Cicada recognizes that certain "pedantacci" among Italian literary theorists have denigrated many poets' work simply for failing to conform to Aristotle's aesthetic, and he declares these ideologues "non son altro che vermi, che non san far cosa di buono, ma son nati solamente per rodere, insporcare e stercorar gli altrui studi e fatiche" [none other than vermin who don't know how to do anything useful, but are born only to gnaw, foul, and crap on the studies and labors of others] (960).

Replacing the explicit condemnation of intellectual oppression and irresponsibility is the author's insistence on human potential's virtual infinitude:

CICADA. Come l'intelletto nostro finito può seguitar l'oggetto infinito?

TANSILLO. Con l'infinita potenza ch'egli ha. (1062–1063)

[C. How can our finite intellect pursue the infinite object?

T. With its infinite potency.]

Like Onorio in the *Cabala,* human beings retain the memories of all they have been; Neoplatonists and Peripatetics alike believe this can lead them to ascend again to their former union with the creating deity (see *Eroici furori* 1121–1126). In a final analogue to the refusal of the *pedanti* to "see" any epistemologies but their own, however, Severino and Minutolo describe nine blind men who complain of their literal failures in love, but also cling to selfish motives or vices that figuratively cause their blindness. They exhibit self-pity (the first man, blind from birth, wishes like Shakespeare's Gloucester simply to be led to a precipice; the third wonders why "in tante pene / Messo per aver visto il sommo bene" [I am put in such pains for having seen the highest good] [1146]); jealousy (the second man despairs of finding "magico incanto / Né sacra pianta, né virtú de pietra" [magical incantation, nor sacred plant, nor efficacious stone] [1144] to cure his consuming jealousy); fear (the fourth worries about falling into a hole while wandering lovestruck); pride (the fifth man boasts that his endless tears have blinded him); the seventh brags that if anyone draws near his flaming passion, "Crederete che inverno / Sia ritrovars'al fuoco de l'inferno" [You'll believe that the fire of hell feels like winter] [1152] in comparison; the eighth asserts neither heroes or gods have ever suffered torments equal to his); despair (the sixth, who formerly rejoiced only in his tears, has nothing left to live for now that they have dried up); and lust (the ninth man, a mute, is said to be wracked with desire, and ashamed seeks "Di men penosa e piú profonda morte" [A less painful and more profound death] [1153]). Bruno's parting admonition to England, then, is that the premiere enemies of mankind are those who impede others'—and their own—pursuit of truth: that is, *gli pedanti*.

NOTES

1. See Elam (1980, 59). David Marsh cites Lucian's "conscious blend of comedy and dialogue," along with Cicero's Academic methodology of arguing *in utramque partem* (including the "Ciceronian principles of Academic argument and rhetorical freedom which are essential to an unbiased inquiry") (1980, 7, 9, 11), as the structural roots of the quattrocento dialogue. Cf. the discussions of the rhetorical and dramatic structures of the dialogue in Deakins (1980, 5–23); Krentz (1983, 32–47); Levi (1976, 1–20); de Man (1983, 99–107); Pineas (1960, 193–206); and Stokes (1986, 36).

2. Teofilo, as Bruno's persona, reports "the Nolan's" reply when Fulke Greville invites him to debate Copernican theory with some learned Oxford opponents: he relishes the opportunity "di mostrar la imbecilità di contrari pareri per i medesimi principii, co' quali pensano esser confirmati" [of showing the imbecility of their contrary opinions through the same principles by which they think them to be confirmed] (50). In this way Bruno revises history, replaying and avenging his defeat and real or imagined wrongs at the hands of Oxford rhetoricians. The dialogues' personae are transparently employed as means to that end, rather than being developed as characters in the same sense as the nefarious pedant interlocutors; in both *De la causa* and *De l'infinito*, for example, the names Teofilo / Filoteo are used interchangeably, even within the same dialogues, to designate a single interlocutor.

3. See Barthes (1972, 111–127).

4. Teofilo reports the apologies from Greville's other dinner guests for the behavior of the two Oxford "asini," including the complaint that they presumptuously "ne si vendono per oculati, e ne porgeno vessiche per lanterne" [declare themselves seers, and present bladders as lanterns] (142). In Bruno's private semiological system, b(ladders) signify the rhetorical method of intellectual pretenders and frauds like the institutionally insulated doctors of Oxford, for true en(light)enment can only be authentically transmitted through the lanterns of the Nolan's philosophy.

5. For example, Torquato retains nothing more from Copernicus's work than "il nome de l'autore, del libro, del stampatore, del loco ove fu impresso, de l'anno, il numero de' quinterni e de le carte" [the name of the author, the book, the publisher, the place of publication, the year, the number of pages and diagrams] (88). The two doctors are as knowledgeable "di birra" [of beer] as they are "di greco" (21).

6. There are, nonetheless, several reasons to think that there was a

significant readership for Bruno's eccentricity (see Yates [1937–1938, 103–116]).

In *Elizabethan Translations from the Italian* (1916), Mary Augusta Scott lists 394 Elizabethan translations of Italian texts published, as well as thirty-three Italian-language texts published in England (including Bruno's six dialogues). *La cena* draws attention to its author's camaraderie with Matthew Gwinne and John Florio—apparently *not* one of his dialogical fictions—as *Florio's Second Fruites to be Gathered of Twelve Trees* (1591) signals Florio's acquaintance with Bruno's first London dialogue (he appropriates the characters Nundinio and Torquato, the latter "a 'Torquato' who is very fussy over dress" and whose namesake is dressed in splendid doctor's gown and gold chains in *La cena*) and with its author, "a 'Nolano' who wears the same suit every day" (Yates 1982, 252). In his translation, *The Essayes, or Morall and Militarie Discourses of Lo. Michaell de Montaigne*, Florio speaks of "my olde fellow Nolano" who "taught publikely" (Salvestrini 1958, 186). For speculation on Bruno's relationship with Sidney, and related contacts, see Bossy (1991, 98–110), Pellegrini (1943, 128–144), and Warnlof (1973, 55–88).

7. Introduced in *De la causa*'s "Dialogo Secondo" as Alessandro Dicsono, and in "Dialogo Terzo" as Dicsono Aurelio, Alexander Dickson was a Brunist disciple whose debate with a Cambridge Ramist met with much the same success as Bruno's Oxford debacle. For a bibliography of sources discussing Dickson's background and relation to Bruno, see Bossy (1991, 47n55); see also Yates (1966, 266–286).

8. Gervasio elaborates on the nature of Poliinnio's "comedy": "mentre dice che vuol giudicar chi dice bene, chi discorre meglio, chi fa delle incongruità ed errori in filosofia, quando poi è tempo de dir la sua parte, e non sapendo che porgere, viene a sfilzarti da dentro il manico della sua ventosa pedantaria una insalatina di proverbiuzzi, di frase per latino o greco, che non fanno mai a proposito di quel ch'altri dicono" (254) [while he says that he intends to judge who speaks well, who discourses well, who commits incongruities and errors in philosophy, when afterwards the time comes for him to speak his part, not knowing what to suggest, he reaches from inside his bag of bombastic pedantry a little jumble of bulging proverbs, of phrases in Latin or Greek, that are never delivered with respect to what the others are saying].

9. The list of mythic characters Filoteo includes are meant to signify Poliinnio's misogyny: Orpheus was torn apart by Thracian women for choosing, after Eurydice's death, to honor her memory by never loving another woman—selecting boys instead; Musaeus was either son or disciple to Orpheus; Tityrus, a veteran shepherd in Virgil's *Eclogues*, recalls in "Eclogue I" that "while Galatea held me, / There was no hope of liberty nor thought of thrift" (1984, 31); and Amphion joined his brother Zephus in punishing Lycus's wife, Dirce, for wrong their mother had suffered at her hands, by tying her to a wild bull's tail and seeing her dragged through jagged terrain until dead (Lemprière 1984, 46). Misogyny is a convenient straw (wo)man for Bruno: because it is essentially

pejorative, he can employ it as an index for other signifiers he wishes to represent negatively. Poliinnio maintains he is no Orpheus, but lectures that "un uomo senza donna è simile a una de le intelligenze; è, dico, un eroe, un semideo" [a man without a woman is like one of the divine spirits (intelligences); he is, I say, a hero, a demigod], but Gervasio deflates him by adding "Ed è simile ad un'ostreca e ad un fungo ancora, ed è un tartufo" [And he's like an oyster and a mushroom as well, and is a truffle (figuratively, a hypocrite)] (293). Oxford's veneration of Aristotelianism (i.e., from Bruno's perspective, the grammarians become peripatetics, followers of Aristotle) is also associated with misogyny in a continuation of this exchange:

POLIINNIO. In fine, per ritornare al proposito, la donna non è altro che una materia. Se non sapete che cosa è donna, per non saper che cosa è materia, studiate alquanto gli peripatetici che, con insegnarvi che cosa è materia, te insegnaranno che cosa è donna.

GERVASIO. Vedo bene che, per aver voi un cervello peripatetico, apprendeste poco o nulla di quel che ieri disse il Teofilo circa l'essenza e potenza della materia. (296)

[P. After all, returning to our subject, woman is nothing but matter. If you don't know that something is woman, due to not knowing something is matter, study the Peripatetics a good deal, who by teaching you that something is matter, teach you that something is woman.
G. I certainly do see that by having a Peripatetic brain, you understand little or nothing of what Teofilo said here yesterday concerning the essence and potency of matter.]

10. Nevertheless, there is an occasionally prudent, politic side of Bruno that struggles on behalf of objectivity (or self-preservation). Armesso speaks on behalf of all that is non-*pedante* about England: "come molti altri meco, mi dolgo, Teofilo, che voi nella nostra amorevol patria siate incorsi a tali suppositi, che vi hanno porgiuta occasione di lamentarvi con una cinericia cena, che ad altri . . . che si stimano aver le nobilitadi, le scienze, le armi, e civilitadi come da natura" [Teofilo, I and many others regret that in our country you have come up against the sort of persons who provided you with the material for your complaints at an Ash-Supper, rather than the others . . . inclined to all the studies of fine letters, arms, chivalry, humanities, and courtesies" (Lindsay 1962, 66)] (206). At the same time, one recalls Bruno's failure to heed his persona Teofilo's warning to Frulla in *La cena*, as he fears retribution from the university doctors: "keep secret our discourse" lest it "reach the ears of those whom we have bitten" (Jaki 1975, 168).

11. This dual signification can be read as a corollary to Roland Barthes's theory that "every usage is converted into a sign of itself" (1968, 41), as the

Oxford curriculum, which should signify knowledge—in Barthes's terms, to speak of "gaining knowledge" then, should be to speak of Oxford—is variously coded by the author to signify intellectual barbarism or intellectual freedom. Barthes's example of a raincoat (as agent) and the protection it provides (as function), illustrates that the former "cannot be dissociated from the very signs of an atmospheric condition" (1968, 41) unless the viewer acknowledges some disruption in semiotic conventions. Disruption is precisely Bruno's polemical agenda: rather than "the attainment (or presence) of knowledge" immediately being associated with a signifier like "Oxford," for the author it is associated with "someplace other than Oxford"; he thereby reinforces his own image as disseminator of knowledge by dissociating himself from the institution.

12. Demonstrating once again the paradoxes of Brunist semiotics, Burchio, intellectually insufficient to advance the cause of Aristotle, instead directs curses (e.g., "figol de Momo, postiglion de le puttane" [son of Momus, post-boy of whores], 469) at Fracastorio and the others, signifying thereby both menace and ineffectuality.

13. During Jove's "state of the heavens" speech: "Circa l'intemerata maestà di que' doi Asini che luceno nel spacio di Cancro, non oso dire, perché di questi massimamente per dritto e per raggione è il regno del cielo: come con molte efficacissime raggioni altre volte mi propono di mostrarvi" ['Concerning the upright majesty of those two Asses, who sparkle in the space of Cancer, I do not dare speak, because to these, especially belongs the Kingdom of Heaven, by right and by reason, as on other occasions, with many most efficacious arguments, I propose to show you' (Imerti 1964, 109)] (602–603).

14. For analysis of the *Eroici furori*'s interlocutor structure, see Nelson (1958, 163–166). There is also a dialogue-within-the-dialogue between Fileno ("Reason") and Pastore the lover, printed in a descending stair-step pattern (981–982).

References

EDITIONS OF BRUNO'S WORKS

Angrisani, Isa Guerrini, ed. *Candelaio*. Milano: Rizzoli Editore, 1976.

Aquilecchia, Giovanni. "Lezioni inedite di Giordano Bruno in un codice della Biblioteca universitaria di Jena." *Atti della Accademia Nazionale dei Lincei* 17 (1962): 464–485.

Gentile, Giovanni, ed. [1st–2d editions and notes]. *Giordano Bruno: Dialoghi italiani*. Ed. Giovanni Aquilecchia [3d edition]. Firenze: Sansoni, 1958; 2d printing, 1985.

Greenberg, Sidney. *The Infinite in Giordano Bruno: With a Translation of His Dialogue Concerning the Cause, Principle, and One*. New York: King's Crown Press, 1950.

Guzzo, Augusto, and Romano Amerio, eds. *Opere di Giordano Bruno e di Tommaso Campanella*. Milano: Riccardo Ricciardi Editore, 1956.

Imerti, Arthur D., trans. and ed. *The Expulsion of the Triumphant Beast*. New Brunswick, N.J.: Rutgers University Press, 1964.

Jaki, Stanley L., trans. *The Ash Wednesday Supper: La cena de le Ceneri*. Paris: Mouton, 1975.

Lindsay, Jack, trans. *Cause, Principle, and Unity: Five Dialogues by Giordano Bruno*. Castle Hedingham, Essex: Daimon Press, 1962.

Memmo, Paul Eugene. *Giordano Bruno's "The Heroic Frenzies": A Translation with Introduction and Notes*. Chapel Hill: University of North Carolina Press, 1964.

Singer, Dorothea Waley. *Giordano Bruno: His Life and Thought, with*

Annotated Translation of His Work, On the Infinite Universe and Worlds. New York: Henry Schuman, 1950.

Tocco, F., and H. Vitelli. *Iordani Brvni Nolani: Opera Latine Conscripta*. Florentiae: Typis Svccessorvm Le Monnier, 1891. 3 vols. Rpt. Stuttgart-Bad Cannstatt: Friedrich Frommann Verlag Gunther Holzboog, 1962.

BRUNO STUDIES AND ADDITIONAL WORKS CITED

Abbot, George. *The Reasons VVhich Doctovr Hill Hath Brovght, For The vpholding of Papistry, which is falselie termed the Catholike Religion: Vnmasked, and Shewed to be very weake, and vpon examination most insufficient for That Purpose*. Oxford: Joseph Barnes, 1604.

Aelian. *On the Characteristics of Animals*. Trans. A. F. Scholfield. Loeb Classical Library. 3 vols. Cambridge, Mass.: Harvard University Press, 1958.

Agrippa von Nettesheim, Cornelius. *Of the Vanitie and Vncertaintie of Artes and Sciences*. Trans. James Sanford. Ed. Catherine M. Dunn. Northridge: California State University, 1974.

Alighieri, Dante. *Dante's "Vita Nuova": A Translation and an Essay*. Trans. and ed. Mark Musa. Bloomington: Indiana University Press, 1973.

Apollodorus. *The Library*. Trans. James George Frazier. 2 vols. New York: G. P. Putnam's Sons, 1921.

Aquilecchia, Giovanni. "Lo stampatore londinese di Giordano Bruno e altre note per il edizione della *Cena*." *Studi di filologia italiana* 18 (1960): 101–162.

———. "Ancora su Giordano Bruno ad Oxford (in margine ad uno recente segnalazione)." *Studi secenteschi* 4 (1963): 3–13.

Aretino, Pietro. *The Letters of Pietro Aretino*. Trans. and ed. Thomas Caldecot Chubb. North Haven, Conn.: Archon Books, 1967.

Ariosto, Ludovico. *The Satires of Ludovico Ariosto: A Renaissance Autobiography*. Trans. Peter DeSa Wiggins. Athens: Ohio University Press, 1976.

———. *Orlando furioso*. Trans. Guido Waldman. Oxford: Oxford University Press, 1983.

Aristotle. *On Generation and Corruption*. Trans. H. H. Joachim. In *The Works of Aristotle*, vol. I. Ed. W. D. Ross. Chicago: Encyclopaedia Britannica, 1952.

——. *Metaphysics*. Trans. W. D. Ross. In *The Works of Aristotle*, vol. I. Ed. W. D. Ross. Chicago: Encyclopaedia Britannica, 1952.

——. *Meteorologica*. Trans. H. D. P. Lee. Loeb Classical Library. Cambridge, Mass.: Harvard University Press, 1952.

——. *Select Fragments*. In *The Works of Aristotle*, vol. XII. Trans. and ed. W. D. Ross. Oxford: Clarendon Press, 1952.

——. *The Physics*. Trans. Philip H. Wicksteed and Francis M. Cornford. Loeb Classical Library. 2 vols. Cambridge, Mass.: Harvard University Press, 1957.

——. *Problems. Rhetorica ad Alexandrum*. Trans. H. Rackham. Loeb Classical Library. 2 vols. Cambridge, Mass.: Harvard University Press, 1957.

——. *Nichomachean Ethics*. Trans. Martin Ostwald. Indianapolis: Bobbs-Merrill, 1962.

——. *On the Soul. Parva Naturalia. On Breath*. Trans. W. S. Hett. Loeb Classical Library. Cambridge, Mass.: Harvard University Press, 1964.

Augustine of Hippo. *The Soliloquies of Saint Augustine*. Trans. Rose Elizabeth Cleveland. Boston: Little, Brown, 1910.

Badaloni, Nicola. *La filosofia di Giordano Bruno*. Firenze: Parenti Editore, 1955.

Barber, Richard. *The Knight and Chivalry*. Ipswich: Boydell Press, 1974.

Barbera, M. L. "La Brunomania." *Giornale critico della filosofia italiana* 59 (1980): 103–140.

Barnes, Alexander McKinney. "La lingua in giova: The Heresy of Giordano Bruno." Ph.D. diss., University of California, Los Angeles, 1992.

Barr, Alan. "Passion, Extension, and Excision: Imagistic and Structural Patterns in Giordano Bruno's *Il Candelaio*." *Texas Studies in Literature and Language* 13 (1971): 351–363.

Barthes, Roland. *Elements of Semiology*. Trans. Annette Lavers and Colin Smith. New York: Hill and Wang, 1968.

——. *Mythologies*. Trans. Annette Lavers. New York: Hill and Wang, 1972.

Battaglia, Salvatore. *Grande dizionario della lingua italiana*, vol. X. Torino: Unione Tipografico-Editrice Torinese, 1978.

Berry, Lloyd E., ed. *The Geneva Bible: A Facsimile of the 1560 Edition*. Madison: University of Wisconsin Press, 1969.

Bertazzi, Giambattista Grassi. "G. Bruno letterato, antipetrarchista ed antiaccademico." *Prometeo* n. v. (1911): 35–41.

Blau, Joseph Leon. *The Christian Interpretation of the Cabala in the Renaissance*. New York: Columbia University Press, 1944.

Blum, Paul Richard. *Aristoteles bei Giordano Bruno*. München: W. Fink, 1980.

———. "D'ogni legge nemico e d'ogni fede: Giordano Brunos Verhaltnis zu den Religionen." *Renaissance-Reformation: Gegensatze und Gemeinsamkeiten*, pp. 65–75. Ed. August Buck. Wiesbaden: Harrassowitz, 1984.

Bossy, John. *Giordano Bruno and the Embassy Affair*. New Haven and London: Yale University Press, 1991.

Boulting, William. *Giordano Bruno: His Life, Thought, and Martyrdom*. 1914; rpt. Freeport, N.Y.: Books for Libraries Press, 1972.

Braudel, Fernand. *The Mediterranean and the Mediterranean World in the Age of Philip II*. Trans. Siân Reynolds. 2 vols. New York: Harper and Row, 1973.

Breiner, Laurence A. "Analogical Argument in Bruno's *De l'infinito*." *Modern Language Notes* 93 (1978): 22–35.

Bumke, Joachim. *The Concept of Knighthood in the Middle Ages*. Trans. W. T. H. Jackson and Erika Jackson. New York: AMS Press, 1982.

Caldwell, Richard. *The Origin of the Gods: A Psychoanalytic Study of Greek Theogonic Myth*. Oxford: Oxford University Press, 1989.

Calogero, Guido, and Giorgio Radetti. "La professione di fede di Giordano Bruno." *Cultura* 1 (1963): 64–77.

Campanella, Tommaso. *La città del sole e altri scritti*. Ed. Franco Mollia. Milano: Arnoldo Mondadori, 1991.

Campanini, Massimo. "L'infinito e la filosofia naturale di Giordano Bruno." *Acme: Annali della facoltà di lettere e filosofia dell'università degli studi di Milano* 33 (1980): 339–369.

Cassirer, Ernst. *The Individual and the Cosmos in Renaissance Philosophy*. Trans. Mario Domandi. Philadelphia: University of Pennsylvania Press, 1963.

Castiglione, Baldesar. *The Book of the Courtier*. Trans. Charles S. Singleton. Garden City, N.Y.: Anchor Books, 1959.

Ciardo, Manlio. *Giordano Bruno tra l'umanesmo e lo storicismo*. Bologna: Patron, 1961.

Cicero. *Tusculan Disputations*. Trans. J. E. King. Loeb Classical Library. Cambridge, Mass.: Harvard University Press, 1960.

———. *The Letters to His Friends*. Trans. J. E. King. Loeb Classical Library. Cambridge, Mass.: Harvard University Press, 1979.

Ciliberto, Michele. "Filosofia e lingua nelle opere volgari di Bruno." *Rinascimento* 18 (1978): 151–179.

———. "Asini e pedanti: Ricerche su Giordano Bruno." *Rinascimento* 24 (1984): 81–121.

———. *La ruota del tempo: Interpretazione di Giordano Bruno*. Roma: Editori Riuniti, 1986.

Corsano, Antonio. "Un ventennio di studi italiani su G. Bruno." *Cultura e Scuola* 27 (1968): 94–113.

Couliano, Ioan P. *Eros and Magic in the Renaissance*. Trans. Margaret Cook. Chicago: University of Chicago Press, 1987.

Dagron, Tristan. *Unité de l'être et dialectique: L'idée de philosophie naturelle chez Giordano Bruno*. Paris: Vrin, 1999.

Dan, Joseph, ed. *The Early Kabbalah*. Trans. Ronald C. Kiener. New York: Paulist Press, 1986.

Daniel, Samuel. *The Complete Works in Verse and Prose of Samuel Daniel*. Ed. Alexander B. Grosart. 5 vols. London: Hazell, Watson & Viney, 1896.

Davidson, Gustav. *A Dictionary of Angels Including the Fallen Angels*. New York: Free Press, 1967.

Deakins, Roger. "The Tudor Prose Dialogue: Genre and Anti-Genre." *Studies in English Literature, 1500–1900* 20 (1980): 5–23.

de Bernart, Luciana. *Immaginazione e scienza in Giordano Bruno: L'infinito nelle forme dell'esperienza*. Pisa: ETS Editrice, 1986.

Dee, John. *A True & Faithful Relation of What passed for many Yeers Between Dr. John Dee (a Mathematician of Great Fame in Q. Eliz. and King James their Reignes) and Some Spirits: Tending (had it Succeeded) To a General Alteration of most States and Kingdomes in the World*. London: D. Maxwell, 1659.

Delaney, John J., and James Edward Tobin. *Dictionary of Catholic Biography*. Garden City, N.Y.: Doubleday, 1961.

De León-Jones, Karen. *Giordano Bruno and the Kaballah: Prophets, Magicians, and Rabbis*. New Haven and London: Yale University Press, 1997.

de Man, Paul. "Dialogue and Dialogism." *Poetics Today* 4 (1983): 99–107.

Dollimore, Jonathan. *Radical Tragedy: Religion, Ideology and Power in the Drama of Shakespeare and His Contemporaries.* Chicago: University of Chicago Press, 1984.

Durling, Robert M. *The Figure of the Poet in Renaissance Epic.* Cambridge, Mass.: Harvard University Press, 1965.

Eckstein, Jerome. *The Platonic Method: An Interpretation of the Dramatic-Philosophic Aspects of the Meno.* New York: Greenwood, 1968.

Elam, Keir. *The Semiotics of Theatre and Drama.* London: Methuen, 1980.

Elton, O. "Giordano Bruno in England." *Quarterly Review* 196 (1902): 483–508.

Epicurus. *The Extant Remains.* Trans. Cyril Bailey. Oxford: Clarendon Press, 1926.

Erasmus, Desiderius. *The Praise of Folly and Other Writings.* Trans. and ed. Robert M. Adams. New York: W. W. Norton, 1989.

Falcini, Fiorenzo. "A Proposito di un'epistola dedicatoria di Giordano Bruno." *Rivista di filosofia neo-scolastica* 55 (1963): 217–218.

Farley-Hills, David. "The 'argomento' of Bruno's *De gli eroici furori* and Sidney's *Astrophil and Stella.*" *Modern Language Review* 87 (1992): 1–17.

Fellmann, Ferdinand. "Giordano Bruno und die Anfänge des modernen Denkens." *Die Pluralität der Welten: Aspekte der Renaissance in der Romania,* pp. 449–488. Ed. Wolf-Dieter Stempel and Karlheinz Stierle. München: Fink, 1987.

Firpo, Luigi, ed. *Scritti scelti di Giordano Bruno e di Tommaso Campanella.* Torino: UTET, 1965.

Florio, John. *A Worlde of Wordes, Or Most copious, and exact Dictionarie in Italian and English.* London: Arnold Hatfield for Edw. Blount, 1598.

———. *Qveen Anna's New World of Words, Or Dictionarie of the Italian and English tongues.* London: Melch. Bradwood for Edw. Blount and William Barret, 1611.

Fowden, Garth. *The Egyptian Hermes: A Historical Approach to the Late Pagan Mind.* New York: Cambridge University Press, 1986.

Franchini, Raffaello. "Giordano Bruno e l'ideale del filosofo." *Settanta* 16–17 (1971): 37–48.

Gager, William. *William Gager: Oedipus (acted 1577–1592), Dido (acted 1583).* Ed. J. W. Binns. New York: Georg Olms Verlag, 1981.

Galli, Gallo. *La vita e il pensiero di Giordano Bruno.* Milano: Marzorati, 1973.

Gatti, Hilary. *The Renaissance Drama of Knowledge: Giordano Bruno in England.* New York: Routledge, 1989.

———. *Giordano Bruno and Renaissance Science.* Ithaca, N.Y.: Cornell University Press, 1999.

———. "The State of Giordano Bruno Studies at the End of the Four-Hundredth Centenary of the Philosopher's Death." *Renaissance Quarterly* 54 (2001): 252–261.

Gellius, Aulus. *The Attic Nights of Aulus Gellius.* Trans. John C. Rolfe. Loeb Classical Library. 3 vols. New York: G. P. Putnam's Sons, 1927.

Gettings, Fred. *Dictionary of Demons: A Guide to Demons and Demonologists in Occult Lore.* North Pomfret, Vt.: Trafalgar Square, 1988.

Gibbon, Edward. *The Decline and Fall of the Roman Empire. Volume III: 1185 A.D.–1543 A.D.* New York: Modern Library, 1932.

Gosselin, Edward A. "Fra Giordano Bruno's Catholic Passion." *Studies in Honor of Paul Oskar Kristeller*, pp. 537–561. Binghamton: Center for Medieval and Early Renaissance Studies, State University of New York, 1987.

Greimas, A. J. *Structural Semantics: An Attempt at a Method.* Trans. Daniele McDowell et al. Lincoln: University of Nebraska Press, 1983.

———, and J. Courtés. *Semiotics and Language: An Analytical Dictionary.* Trans. L. Crist. Bloomington: Indiana University Press, 1982.

Groce, A. *Giordano Bruno. Der Ketzer von Nola: Versuch einer Deutung. Erster Teil: Werdegang und Untergang.* Wien: Europäischer Verlag, 1970.

Hart, Thomas R. *Cervantes and Ariosto: Renewing Fiction.* Princeton, N.J.: Princeton University Press, 1989.

Hata, Gohei. "The Story of Moses Interpreted within the Context of Anti-Semitism." *Josephus, Judaism, and Christianity*, pp. 180–197. Ed. Louis H. Feldman and Gohei Hata. Detroit: Wayne State University Press, 1987.

Haydn, Hiram. *The Counter-Renaissance.* 1950. Rpt. Gloucester, Mass.: Peter Smith, 1966.

Heninger, S. K., Jr. *Touches of Sweet Harmony: Pythagorean Cosmology and Renaissance Poetics*. San Marino, Calif.: Huntington Library, 1974.

Hiley, David R. *Philosophy in Question: Essays on a Pyrrhonian Theme*. Chicago: University of Chicago Press, 1988.

Hirzel, Rudolf. *Der Dialog: Ein literar-historischer Versuch*. 1895; rpt., Hildesheim: Georg Olms, 1963.

Hodgart, Amelia Buono. "*Love's Labour's Lost* di William Shakespeare e *il Candelaio* di Giordano Bruno." *Studi secenteschi* 19 (1978): 3–21.

Horace. *Satires, Epistles and Ars Poetica*. Trans. H. Rushton Fairclough. Loeb Classical Library. Cambridge, Mass.: Harvard University Press, 1947.

Horowitz, Irving Louis. *The Renaissance Philosophy of Giordano Bruno*. New York: Coleman-Ross, 1952.

Howe, James Robinson. *Marlowe, Tamburlaine and Magic*. Athens: Ohio University Press, 1976.

Idel, Moshe. *Kabbalah: New Perspectives*. New Haven and London: Yale University Press, 1988.

Ingegno, Alfonso. "Ermetismo e oroscopo della religione nello *Spaccio* bruniana." *Rinascimento* 7 (1967): 157–174.

———. *Cosmologia e filosofia nel pensiero di Giordano Bruno*. Firenze: La Nuova Italia, 1978.

———. *La sommersa nave della religione: Studio sulla polemica anticristiana del Bruno*. Napoli: Bibliopolis, 1985.

Janson, H. W. "The 'Image Made by Chance' in Renaissance Thought.'" *Sixteen Studies*, pp. 55–74. New York: Harry N. Abrams, 1974.

Julius Caesar. *The Gallic War*. Trans. H. J. Edwards. Loeb Classical Library. Cambridge, Mass.: Harvard University Press, 1970.

Kahn, Charles H. *Plato and the Socratic Dialogue: The Philosophical Use of a Literary Form*. Cambridge: Cambridge University Press, 1996.

Kaufmann, Thomas DaCosta. *Variations on the Imperial Theme in the Age of Maximilian II and Rudolf II*. New York: Garland, 1978.

———. "'Ancients and Moderns' in Prague: Arcimboldo's Drawings for Silk Manufacture." *Leids Kunsthistorisch Jaarboek 1984*, pp. 179–207. Delft: Delftsche Uitgevers Maatschappij Bv, 1984.

Knight, Gareth. *A Practical Guide to Qabalistic Symbolism*. York Beach, Me.: Samuel Weiser, 1978.

Kogan, Barry S. *Averroes and the Metaphysics of Causation*. Albany: State University of New York Press, 1985.

Krentz, Arthur A. "Dramatic Form and Philosophical Content in Plato's Dialogues." *Philosophy and Literature* 7 (1983): 32–47.

Kuhlenbeck, Ludwig. *Bruno: Der Martyrer der neuen Weltanshauung: Sein Leben, seine Lehren und sein Tod auf dem Scheiterhaufen*. Leipzig: Rauert and Rocco, 1980.

Lakin, Barbara Holbeach. "The Magus and the Poet: Bruno and Chapman's 'The Shadow of Night.'" *Sixteenth Century Journal* 10 (1979): 1–14.

Leaman, Oliver. *Averroes and His Philosophy*. Oxford: Clarendon Press, 1988.

Lemprière, J. *Lemprière's Classical Dictionary: Proper Names Cited by the Ancient Authors*. Ed. F. A. Wright. London: Bracken Books, 1984.

Levergeois, Bertrand. *Giordano Bruno*. Paris: Librairie Arthème Fayard, 1995.

Levi, Albert William. "Philosophy as Literature: The Dialogue." *Philosophy and Rhetoric* 9 (1976): 1–20.

Limentani, Ludovico. "La lettera di Giordano Bruno al Vicecancelliere della Università di Oxford." *Sophia* 1 (1933): 317–354.

Lord, Carnes. "The Argument of Tasso's *Nifo*." *Italica* 56 (1979): 22–45.

Lotman, Juri M., et al. "Theses on the Semiotic Study of Cultures (as Applied to Slavic Texts)." *The Tell-Tale Sign: A Survey of Semiotics*, pp. 57–83. Ed. Thomas A. Sebeok. Lisse, The Netherlands: Peter de Ridder Press, 1975.

Lucian. *Lucian*. Trans. A. M. Harmon. Loeb Classical Library. 8 vols. Cambridge, Mass.: Harvard University Press, 1968.

Maiorino, Giancarlo. "The Breaking of the Circle: Giordano Bruno and the Poetics of Immeasurable Abundance." *Journal of the History of Ideas* 38 (1977): 317–327.

Manca, Franco. "*Il candelaio:* Vis comica et lectio etica." *Italianistica* 11 (1982): 277–282.

Mancini, Sandro. *La sfera infinita: Identità e differenza nel pensiero di Giordano Bruno*. Milano: Mimesis, 2000.

Marsh, David. *The Quattrocento Dialogue: Classical Tradition and Humanist Innovation*. Cambridge, Mass.: Harvard University Press, 1980.

Marziani, Adriano. "La negazione bruniana dell'estetica." *Rinascimento* 23 (1983): 303–327.

Massa, Daniel. "Giordano Bruno's Ideas in Seventeenth-Century England." *Journal of the History of Ideas* 38 (1977): 227–242.

May, Rollo. *Psychology and the Human Dilemma*. Princeton, N.J.: D. Van Nostrand, 1967.

McIntyre, J. Lewis. *Giordano Bruno*. New York: Macmillan, 1903.

McKnight, Stephen A. *Sacralizing the Secular: The Renaissance Origins of Modernity*. Baton Rouge: Louisiana State University Press, 1989.

McMullen, Ernan. "Giordano Bruno at Oxford." *ISIS* 77 (1986): 85–95.

McNulty, Robert. "Bruno at Oxford." *Renaissance News* 13 (1960): 302–303.

Memmo, Paul E., Jr. "Giordano Bruno's *De gli eroici furori* and the Emblematic Tradition." *Romantic Review* 55 (1964): 1–15.

Mendoza, Ramon G. *The Acentric Labyrinth: Giordano Bruno's Prelude to Contemporary Cosmology*. Shaftesbury: Element, 1995.

Mercati, Angelo, ed. *Il sommario del processo di Giordano Bruno*. Città del Vaticano: Biblioteca Apostolica Vaticana, 1942.

Merrell, Floyd. *Semiotic Foundations: Steps toward an Epistemology of Written Texts*. Bloomington: Indiana University Press, 1982.

Michel, Otto. "*onos, onarion*." *Theological Dictionary of the New Testament*, vol. V, pp. 283–287. Ed. Gerhard Friedrich. Trans. and ed. Geoffrey W. Bromiley. Grand Rapids, Mich.: Wm. B. Eerdmans, 1967.

Michel, Paul-Henri. *The Cosmology of Giordano Bruno*. Trans. R. E. W. Middleton. Ithaca, N.Y.: Cornell University Press, 1973.

Migliorini, Bruno, and Ignazio Baldelli. *Breve storia della lingua italiana*. Firenze: Sansoni, 1977.

Montaigne, Michel de. *Essais*. Ed. Alexandre Micha. 3 vols. Paris: Garnier-Flammarion, 1969.

Moore Smith, G. C., ed. *Marginalia*. Stratford-upon-Avon: Shakespeare Head Press, 1913.

Murphy, Stephen. "Bovelles. Sceve. Bruno. Antiperistasis." *Allegorica* 14 (1993): 39–52.

Nelson, John Charles. *Renaissance Theory of Love: The Context of Giordano Bruno's "Eroici furori."* New York: Columbia University Press, 1958.

Nicholas of Cusa. *Unity and Reform: Selected Writings of Nicholas de Cusa.* Ed. John Patrick Dolan. South Bend, Ind.: Notre Dame University Press, 1962.

Nowicki, Andrzej. "Giordano Bruno nella cultura contemporanea." *Atti dell'Accademia di scienze morali e politiche* 83 (1972): 391–450.

Onions, C. T., ed. *The Oxford Dictionary of English Etymology.* Oxford: Clarendon Press, 1966.

Ordine, Nuccio. "Simbologia dell'asino: A proposito di due recenti edizioni." *Giornale storico della letteratura italiana* 161 (1984): 116–130.

———. "Giordano Bruno et l'âne: Une satire philosophique a double face." *La Satire du temps de la Renaissance,* pp. 203–221. Ed. M. T. Jones-Davies. Paris: Jean Touzot Libraire-Editeur, 1986.

———. *La cabala dell'asino: Asinità e conoscenza in Giordano Bruno.* Napoli: Liguori, 1987.

———. *Giordano Bruno and the Philosophy of the Ass.* Trans. Henryk Baranski and Arielle Saiber. New Haven and London: Yale University Press, 1996.

Origen. *Origen: An Exhortation to Martyrdom, [On] Prayer, First Principles: Book IV, Prologue to the Commentary on the Song of Songs, Homily XXVII on Numbers.* Trans. Rowan A. Greer. New York: Paulist Press, 1979.

———. *Origen, Spirit and Fire: A Thematic Anthology of His Writings.* Trans. Robert J. Daly. Ed. Hans Urs von Balthasar. Washington, D.C.: Catholic University of America Press, 1984.

Ossola, Carlo. "Dei legami di senso e dell'analogia in Giordano Bruno: Studi recenti." *Lettere italiane* 43 (1991): 244–249.

Ovid. *Metamorphoses.* Trans. Frank Justus Miller. Loeb Classical Library. 2 vols. Cambridge, Mass.: Harvard University Press, 1976.

Papi, Fulvio. *Antropologia e civiltà nel pensiero di Giordano Bruno.* Firenze: Nuova Italia, 1968.

Pellegrini, Angelo [Mario]. "Giordano Bruno and Oxford." *Huntington Library Quarterly* 5 (1941–1942): 303–316.

———. "Bruno, Sidney, and Spenser." *Studies in Philology* 40 (1943): 128–144.

Petrarch. *Letters from Petrarch.* Trans. and ed. Morris Bishop. Bloomington: Indiana University Press, 1966.

———. *The Triumphs of Petrarch.* Trans. Ernest Hatch Wilkins. Chicago: University of Chicago Press, 1962.

Pico della Mirandola, Giovanni. *Heptaplus, or Discourse on the Seven Days of Creation*. Trans. Jessie Brewer McGaw. New York: Philosophical Library, 1977.

Pindar. *The Odes of Pindar*. Trans. Richmond Lattimore. Chicago: University of Chicago Press, 1947.

Pineas, Rainer. "Thomas More's Use of the Dialogue Form as a Weapon of Religious Controversy." *Studies in the Renaissance* 7 (1960): 193–206.

Plato. *The Collected Dialogues of Plato, Including the Letters*. Ed. Edith Hamilton and Huntington Cairns. Princeton, N.J.: Princeton University Press, 1961.

Plotinus. *Plotinos: Complete Works*. Trans. Kenneth Sylvan Guthrie. London: George Bell and Sons, 1918.

Plutarch. *Lives*. Trans. Bernadotte Perrin. Loeb Classical Library. 11 vols. Cambridge, Mass.: Harvard University Press, 1958.

———. *Moralia*. Trans. Frank Cole Babbitt. Loeb Classical Library. 15 vols. Cambridge, Mass.: Harvard University Press, 1969.

Popkin, Richard H. *The History of Scepticism from Erasmus to Spinoza*. Berkeley: University of California Press, 1979.

Puglisi, Filippo. "Del linguaggio antiaccademico del Bruno." *Cultura e scuola* 22 (1983): 17–22.

Pulci, Luigi. *Il Morgante*. Ed. Giuseppe Fatini. 2 vols. Torino: Unione Tipografico-Editrice, 1948.

Raab, Felix. *The English Face of Machiavelli: A Changing Interpretation, 1500–1700*. London: Routledge and Kegan Paul, 1964.

Ricci, Saverio. *La fortuna del pensiero di Giordano Bruno, 1600–1750*. Firenze: Le Lettere, 1991.

———. *Giordano Bruno nell'Europa del cinquecento*. Roma: Salerno Editrice, 2000.

Roensch, Frederick J. *Early Thomistic School*. Dubuque, Iowa: Priory Press, 1964.

Russell, Jeffrey Burton. *The Devil: Perceptions of Evil from Antiquity to Primitive Christianity*. Ithaca, N.Y.: Cornell University Press, 1977.

Salvestrini, Virgilio. *Bibliografia di Giordano Bruno, 1582–1950*. Firenze: Sansoni, 1958.

Sannazaro, Jacopo. *Arcadia and Piscatorial Eclogues*. Trans. Ralph Nash. Detroit: Wayne State University Press, 1966.

Santonastaso, Giuseppe. "Il cavallo pegaséo di Bruno." *Nuova antologia* 516 (1973): 496–502.

Schmidt, Charles B. *John Case and Aristotelianism in Renaissance England.* Kingston: McGill-Queen's University Press, 1983.

Schmidt, Heinz-Ulrich. *Zum Problem des Heros bei Giordano Bruno.* Bonn: Bouvier, 1968.

Scholem, Gershom. *Origins of the Kabbalah.* Trans. Allan Arkush. Ed. R. J. Zwi Werblowsky. Princeton, N.J.: Princeton University Press, 1987.

Scott, Mary Augusta. *Elizabethan Translations from the Italian.* Boston: Houghton Mifflin, 1916.

Sedley, David. "The Motivation of Greek Skepticism." *The Skeptical Tradition,* pp. 9–29. Ed. Myles Burnyeat. Berkeley: University of California Press, 1984.

Sextus Empiricus. *Against the Professors.* Trans. R. G. Bury. Loeb Classical Library. 4 vols. Cambridge, Mass.: Harvard University Press, 1949.

———. *Outlines of Pyrrhonism.* Trans. R. G. Bury. Loeb Classical Library. 4 vols. Cambridge, Mass.: Harvard University Press, 1955.

Sheinkin, David. *Path of the Kabbalah.* Ed. Edward Hoffman. New York: Paragon House, 1986.

Shumaker, Wayne. *The Occult Sciences in the Renaissance: A Study in Intellectual Patterns.* Berkeley: University of California Press, 1972.

———. *Natural Magic and Modern Science: Four Treatises, 1590–1657.* Binghamton, N.Y.: Medieval and Renaissance Texts and Studies, 1989.

Sidney, Sir Philip. *Selected Prose and Poetry.* Ed. Robert Kimbrough. 2d ed. Madison: University of Wisconsin Press, 1983.

Smart, J. S. *The Sonnets of Milton.* Oxford: Clarendon Press, 1966.

Snyder, Jon R. "The Last Laugh: Literary Theory and the Academy in Late Renaissance Florence." *Annals of Scholarship* 6 (1989): 37–55.

Sondergard, Sid[ney L.]. "Bruno's Dialogue War on Pedantry: An Elizabethan Dramatic Motif." Ph.D. diss., University of Southern California, 1986.

———. " 'To scape the rod': Resistance to Humanist Pedagogy and the Sign of the Pedant in Tudor England." *Studies in Philology* 91 (1994): 270–282.

Sowell, Madison U. "Observations on Pulci's Reworking of the Anonymous *Orlando.*" *Journal of the Rocky Mountain Medieval and Renaissance Association* 3 (1982): 65–74.

Spampanato, Vincenzo. *Giordano Bruno e la letteratura dell'Asino.* Portici: Premiato Stab. Tip. Vesuviano di E. della Torre, 1904.

———. *Documenti della vita di Giordano Bruno.* Firenze: Leo S. Olschki, 1933.

Spruit, Leen. *Il problema della conoscenza in Giordano Bruno.* Napoli: Bibliopolis, 1988.

Stokes, Michael C. *Plato's Socratic Conversations: Drama and Dialectic in Three Dialogues.* Baltimore: Johns Hopkins University Press, 1986.

Sturlese, Rita. *Bibliografia, censimento e storia della antiche stampe di Giordano Bruno.* Firenze: Olschki, 1987.

Suetonius. *The Twelve Caesars.* Trans. Robert Graves. Rev. Michael Grant. New York: Penguin Books, 1979.

Symonds, John Addington. *The Renaissance in Italy, Part II: The Catholic Reaction.* New York: Henry Holt, 1887.

Tacitus. *The Histories. The Annals.* Trans. Clifford H. Moore [*Histories*] and John Jackson [*Annals*]. Loeb Classical Library. 3 vols. New York: G. P. Putnam's Sons, 1931.

Tasso, Torquato. *Tasso's Dialogues: A Selection, with the "Discourse on the Art of the Dialogue."* Trans. Carnes Lord and Dain A. Trafton. Berkeley: University of California Press, 1982.

Thorndike, Lynn. *A History of Magic and Experimental Science.* 8 vols. New York: Columbia University Press, 1923–1958.

Tillyard, E. M. W. *The Elizabethan World Picture.* 1943; rpt. New York: Random House, 1960.

Tomarken, Annette. "Flea Encomia and Other Mock Eulogies of Animals." *Fifteenth-Century Studies* 11 (1985): 137–148.

Topsell, Edward. *Topsell's Histories of Beasts.* Ed. Malcolm South. Chicago: Nelson-Hall, 1981.

Traister, Barbara Howard. *Heavenly Necromancers: The Magician in English Renaissance Drama.* Columbia: University of Missouri Press, 1984.

Virgil. *The Aeneid.* Trans. W. F. Jackson Knight. New York: Penguin Books, 1956.

———. *The Eclogues.* Trans. Guy Lee. New York: Penguin Books, 1984.

Waller, G. F. "Transition in Renaissance Ideas of Time and the Place of Giordano Bruno." *Neophilologus* 55 (1971): 3–15.

Warnlof, Jessica J. "The Influence of Giordano Bruno on the Writings of Sir Philip Sidney." Ph.D. diss., Texas A&M University, 1973.

Weinapple, Fiorenza. "Ideologia e prassi linguistica in Aretino e Bruno." *Lettere italiane* 36 (1984): 591–600.

Weiner, A. D. "Expelling the Beast: Bruno's Adventures in England." *Modern Philology* 78 (1980): 1–13.

Westman, Robert S. "Magical Reform and Astronomical Reform: The Yates Thesis Reconsidered." *Hermeticism and the Scientific Revolution*, pp. 3–91. Los Angeles: William Andrews Clark Memorial Library, 1977.

Whiston, William, trans. *The Life and Works of Flavius Josephus*. London: Chatto and Windus, 1875.

White, Laura Sanguinetti. " 'In tristitia hilaris in hilaritate tristis': armonia nei contrasti." *Quaderni d'italianistica* 5 (1984): 190–203.

Whittaker, Thomas. "Giordano Bruno." *Mind* 9 (1884): 236–264.

Wood, Anthony à. *The History and Antiquities of the College and Halls in the University of Oxford*. Trans. and ed. John Gutch. Oxford: Clarendon Press, 1786.

Woodhouse, H. F. *Language and Style in a Renaissance Epic: Berni's Corrections to Boiardo's 'Orlando Innamorato.'* London: Modern Humanities Research Association, 1982.

Yalouris, Nikolas. *Pegasus: The Art of the Legend*. Trans. Helen Zigada. Ed. Derek Birdsall. Edenbridge, Kent: Westerham Press, 1975.

Yates, Frances A. "Italian Teachers in Elizabethan England." *Journal of the Warburg Institute* 1 (1937–1938): 103–116.

———. *Giordano Bruno and the Hermetic Tradition*. Chicago: University of Chicago Press, 1964.

———. *The Art of Memory*. Chicago: University of Chicago Press, 1966.

———. *Lull and Bruno*. Boston: Routledge and Kegan Paul, 1982.

———. *Renaissance and Reform: The Italian Contribution*. Boston: Routledge and Kegan Paul, 1983.

Zingarelli, Nicola. *Il nuovo Zingarelli: Vocabolario della lingua italiana*. Ed. Miro Dogliotti and Luigi Rosiello. Bologna: Zanichelli, 1984.

Index